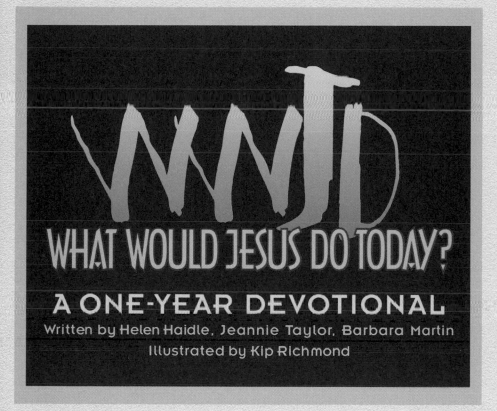

WWJD
WHAT WOULD JESUS DO TODAY?
A ONE-YEAR DEVOTIONAL

Written by Helen Haidle, Jeannie Taylor, Barbara Martin

Illustrated by Kip Richmond

Zonderkidz

The Children's Group of ZondervanPublishingHouse

WHAT WOULD JESUS DO TODAY?

ISBN: 0-31070-042-6

What Would Jesus Do Today? was previously published by
Gold and Honey, a division of Multnomah Publishers

 Zonder**kidz**™

The Children's Group of ZondervanPublishingHouse

Grand Rapids, Michigan 49530
www.zonderkidz.com

Zonderkidz is a trademark of the Zondervan Corporation

Printed in the United States of America

99 00 01 02 03 / RRD-C / 8 7 6 5 4 3 2

This book is dedicated to all of you who shared your experiences and gave permission to use them: Linda Price, Karen Law, Carolyn Hopkins, Martha Spencer, Michele Dollar, Judy Wallitner, Mary Jo Carnahan, Christi Carnahan, Cari Carnahan, Sara Martin, Rebekah Martin, Sam Martin, Marla Cutrer, Tori Taylor, Ty Taylor, Tevin Taylor, Shirley Johnson, John Ellingson, Jonathan Haidle, Paul Haidle, Elizabeth Haidle, Lincoln Biletscher, Lee Smith, Dorothea Fix, Tiffany Hickman, Joal Kinzinger, Jeff Knutsen, Janell Martinez, Amy McKelvy, Matt Pouttu, Adam Rothrock, Julliam Shaw, Clare St. John, Jennifer Kociemba, Kim Loeffler, Jane Loeffler, Caressa Gay, Michael Gay, Ella Beckman, Luke Upton, Karen Cecilia Johnson, Linda Champagne, Linda Alexander, John Bennett, Jennifer Counts, Martin, Annie Rueda, Art Lutz, the Keith Reetz family, the Kris Wolverton family, the Rob Anthony family, the John Molen family, Kara Wigowsky, Jennifer Fagaragan, Kristin Zimmel, Katie Nicklas, Becky Neumann, Blayne Sweeney, Bethany Taft, Sam Paulsen, Michael Jienken, Matthew Roberts, Osiris Wilson, Shane Moore, Irena Koch, Andy Larsen, Melodie Stockwell, Philip Robinson, Lauren McNabb, Chemi Wamhalaha, Anna Budden, Sean Lavelle, Royce Williams, Kelsey Niehuser, Nick Owen, Nicole Jones, Becky Dugan, Gladys St. John, Karl St. John, Elsie Taylor, Harold Taylor, Darren Wiedman, Whitney Utter, Kendall Utter, Laurel Upton, Sharon Rueda, Linda Sattgast, Daniel Connor in New Guinea, Pepe Callasi in Pisac, Peru, Maropeng in South Africa, Beulah Faraday in Nigeria, Thembi in Mamelodi, South Africa, Igor, Oksana, and Olesya in Kazakhstan, Chinomnso Iwuchukwu in Nigeria, and Amanda Malangeni in Willowvale, South Africa.

With special thanks to Roseanne Croft for the following devotions that she wrote: The Pink Ruler, String of Fish, The Flying Horse, and The Burning Bush.

Weekly Themes

1. Trust Jesus as Your Savior
2. Don't Be Afraid—Trust God
3. God Keeps Every Promise
4. Serving One Another
5. Praying for One Another
6. Show Jesus' Love to One Another
7. Choosing What Jesus Wants
8. Heaven Is Your Home!
9. God's Good Rewards
10. Answered Prayer
11. Loving One Another
12. Forgiving Others
13. Secret Prayer
14. Doing What's Right
15. Good Samaritans
16. Attitude Alert!
17. You Are the Light of the World
18. All Things Work for Good
19. Hearts Full of Love
20. Following Jesus
21. Hang-in-There Prayer
22. Giving Hearts
23. Getting Along
24. How Do You See Yourself?
25. Choosing to Do Right
26. God's Direction

Weekly Themes

27.   Showing Your Faith

28.   Sharing the Love of Jesus

29.   Attitude toward Others

30.   Prayers of Faith

31.   Love in Action

32.   Forgiveness

33.   The Family God Gave You

34.   To Tell the Truth

35.   Care for God's Creatures

36.   God Cares for You

37.   Facing Temptation

38.   Following Jesus' Example

39.   Showing Kindness

40.   Praying for Others

41.   Attitudes toward Others

42.   Making Decisions to Do Right

43.   Show That You Care

44.   Obedience

45.   Do unto Others

46.   Honest and Fair

47.   A Thankful Heart

48.   Choosing between Right and Wrong

49.   Honoring Older Folks

50.   Christmas Blessings

51.   Heritage of Faith

52.   Remembering Our Heritage

*W*e three writers pray that your lives will be touched and blessed by these devotional stories. These amazing experiences are based on true events from the lives of God's precious children. Names and personal details were sometimes changed to protect privacy.

To use this devotional, let family members take turns reading the Scripture, the story, and the memory verse. Then discuss the questions together. The weekend activities are written to involve children. Let them help find and set out the various objects needed. Encourage them to lead other family members in the activity, discussion, Bible reading, and prayer.

You may want to read the weeks in the order they're written or choose a week by its theme.

Writing this book has deeply moved us to a closer walk with Jesus and more sensitivity to live for him. Our prayer is that the love of Jesus will fill your hearts and your homes. And we pray that each of you will do what Jesus would do today.

Helen Haidle, Jeannie Taylor, and Barbara Martin

How to Ask Jesus to Be Your Savior

God made you. And God loves you!
"For God so loved the world that he gave his only Son, so that
everyone who believes in him will not perish but have eternal life."
(John 3:16)

No one lives a perfect life or does everything they
should. Everyone needs forgiveness.
For all have sinned; all fall short of God's glorious standard.
(Romans 3:23)

Everyone deserves to be punished. We've all failed to
love God and others. We need God's gift of Jesus.
For the wages of sin is death, but the free gift of God is
eternal life through Christ Jesus our Lord.
(Romans 6:23)

God sent Jesus to take our punishment and die for us.
But God showed his great love for us by sending
Christ to die for us while we were still sinners.
(Romans 5:8)

Jesus came alive and rose from the dead.
Jesus said, "Look! Here I stand at the door and knock.
If you hear me calling and open the door, I will
come in, and we will share a meal as friends."
(Revelation 3:20)

Open the door of your heart to Jesus.
You can pray a prayer similar to this one:

Thank you, Jesus, for dying on the cross
for me. Please forgive all I've done wrong.
Come into my life and be my Savior. Thank you for loving
me and giving me eternal life. Fill me with your Holy Spirit
and help me live for you. Amen.

As soon as you ask Jesus for his forgiveness, you can be sure
he forgives you. Trust God's promise that Jesus is your Savior and
that you have a home in heaven.
For if you confess with your mouth that Jesus is Lord and believe
in your heart that God raised him from the dead, you will be saved.
(Romans 10:9)

CB

Now that Jesus is your Savior, you are ready to read this book.
The stories from other children will help you learn how to
follow Jesus. And Jesus will help you do what he would do.
Jesus said, "I have given you an example to follow.
Do as I have done to you.... Just as I have
loved you, you should love each other."
(John 13:15, 34)

God's Gift

Get Set Choose a small gift for each person in your family. Think of fun little items such as cookies, sticks of gum, or coupons for back rubs or special times together. Wrap the gifts in bright napkins or newspaper comic pages. Add name tags. Place the gifts in a basket. Don't open the gifts yet.

Go! *When do you usually give and receive gifts?*
What makes you decide you'd like to give a gift to someone?

Tell about a special gift you've received.

Read Romans 6:23.

What gift does God offer us?
How can we receive God's gift of eternal life?
How is hearing about God's gift, but not asking Jesus to be our Savior,
like looking at a gift but not opening it?

Hand out everyone's gifts.

Open the gifts.

Thank one another.

Pray, thanking God for his gift of Jesus.

Close by saying John 3:16 together. Put your own name into the verse. ("For God so loved [your name]....")

Early Morning Rescue

Kenny hurried to the barn as soon as it was light enough to see. Bessie, the black Angus, had mooed all night. Something must be wrong.

When Bessie saw Kenny, she dropped her head and nosed the ground. Kenny looked closely. There was a newborn calf! Kenny realized that the calf's small body was trapped in manure. Bessie must have dropped the calf there when she gave birth. It would die if Kenny didn't help it.

The helpless calf looked at Kenny with pleading brown eyes. Kenny loved it instantly. He plunged his hands into the muck and drew his arms around the calf. Leaning backward, he pulled with all his might. The calf didn't budge.

He hollered for his sister. "Emily!"

Kenny strained backward again. With a *plop!* he fell onto his back. The calf landed on top of him. It was free! He could see its breath in the morning air.

His sister appeared at the fence in her nightgown.

"Get rags and warm water!" Kenny barked instructions at Emily while he grabbed some hay to pile around the shivering animal.

When Emily brought the water and rags, Kenny began scrubbing the calf.

"You're covered with yucky stuff!" said Emily.

Kenny ignored her and rubbed the calf to warm it. Three hours later, the calf was finally out of danger. Kenny took time to wash the dried manure from his own face and arms. As he hosed off his clothes, he noticed admiration in Emily's eyes.

"Do you think our sins felt yucky like that to Jesus when he was on the cross?" she asked.

"I didn't mind the manure because I loved saving the calf," Kenny said.

"And Jesus loves us even more than that," Emily added.

"He was wounded and crushed for our sins.... He was whipped, and we were healed!" *(Isaiah 53:5)*

 *How can you show that you appreciate what Jesus did for you?*

Looking to Heaven

The chocolate chip cookie Robyn was eating stuck in her throat as she stared at the TV. Moments ago she'd watched the space shuttle *Challenger* blast off the launch pad and soar into the bright blue sky. Then it exploded in a glowing ball of fire.

A reporter talked about the astronauts on the space shuttle, including Christa McAuliffe, the first schoolteacher chosen to ride into space. He showed pictures of her husband and children. He interviewed shocked fellow teachers who told what a wonderful person she had been.

Feeling troubled, Robyn turned to her mother. "Did Christa McAuliffe go to heaven?"

"I hope so, honey. If she was a Christian, she's with Jesus right now."

"But, Mom, she didn't know that she was going to die."

"None of us know when we'll die, Robyn."

"That's scary."

"You don't have to be afraid to die if Jesus is your Savior."

Robyn reached for her mother's hand. "I'm not sure I'm a Christian. I want to go to heaven when I die. Can I pray right now?"

"Let's do," said her mother.

Robyn prayed, "Dear Jesus, forgive my sins and make me your child. Be my Savior. Amen."

Peace flooded Robyn's heart. She said to her mother, "Now I'm not afraid to die. I know Jesus forgives me and will take me to heaven."

"Today is the day of salvation." *(2 Corinthians 6:2)*

Are you sure you'll go to heaven when you die? Have you accepted Jesus as your Savior?

Janie's Shoes

One afternoon Janie burst into the kitchen. "Oh, Mama! Annabelle let me try on her clogs today. I want a pair more than anything else in the world!"

Janie made a bank out of a small box and started saving her change. Her mother added change each time she bought groceries. Every afternoon Janie opened her box, counted the coins, and dreamed of the day she could slip the wooden shoes onto her feet.

After many weeks of saving, Janie and her mother went to the store and bought the shoes. Arriving home, Janie sat on the porch steps, took off her old shoes, and wiggled her feet into the wooden clogs. Standing up with a radiant smile, she posed in front of her mother.

"Aren't they wonderful? I can hardly believe they're mine! They're the most—" Suddenly Janie's eyes opened wide. She gasped and stared at her mother.

"What's wrong?" Mother asked.

"Oh, Mama!" Tears filled Janie's eyes. She couldn't believe what she felt deep inside. "I...Now I want a new coat!" she wailed.

Mother said softly, "You thought you would be the happiest girl in the world once you got your new shoes, didn't you?"

Janie buried her head in her mother's lap. "Yes," she sobbed.

"Dear girl," said Mother. "You have learned something many adults haven't. Things never satisfy your heart. Nothing in life brings complete happiness except Jesus."

"Pray with me," begged Janie. "I don't want to be greedy. I want Jesus to be more important to me than anything else."

Jesus said, "Your heavenly Father...will give you all you need from day to day if you live for him and make the Kingdom of God your primary concern." *(Matthew 6:32–33)*

Have you ever wished for something, only to find it didn't make you happy for very long? What happens if we love "things" more than we love Jesus?

Boy's Best Friend

Ben's pencil froze above his homework as he listened to the news report.

"A speeding car careened down the alley and headed straight for five-year-old Jason."

Ben's dad looked up from his paper as the reporter continued. "The boy's father was too far away to reach him, so he screamed Jason's name. When the family dog heard the father, he ran to the little boy and knocked him out of the path of the car. Unfortunately, the dog couldn't escape being hit. He died instantly, but the boy's life was spared."

"Wow!" said Ben. "Is that a 'What would Jesus do?' story, Dad?"

"We can't really compare a dog to Jesus, but that dog certainly gave his life to save someone he loved."

"I'm glad the dog didn't suffer," said Ben, feeling sad. "Jesus suffered for us on the cross, didn't he? I've never thought about that. I wonder if I really appreciate what Jesus did for me."

"I know what you mean," Dad agreed. "We often take Jesus' suffering and death for granted."

Ben got up from his schoolwork. "Jesus saved my life. I want to read my Bible and thank him."

"I'll join you," said Dad.

"We know what real love is because Christ gave up his life for us."
(1 John 3:16)

Take a minute to thank Jesus for what he did.
Do you believe Jesus would have died just for you?

Jesus, Do You Love Me?

Colleen watched her best friend Lacey get weaker every day. Lacey didn't play at recess anymore; she just sat in the classroom. Today her skin looked gray as she breathed oxygen through a plastic tube in her nose. Lacey was cheerful, but she knew she was dying. So did everyone else.

After school, Colleen asked her mother, "Why is Jesus letting Lacey die? I know he could make her well."

Her mother held her and cried along with her. "God doesn't always tell us why he allows his children to suffer."

"I don't think God really loves us!" Colleen burst out. "If God cared about Lacy, he wouldn't let her die!"

"How do you know I love you?" asked her mother, pouring some juice in a glass for Colleen.

"Well, you shop for groceries, make my breakfast, wash my clothes, take me to school, give me presents, and say 'I love you.'"

"I also take away privileges when you disobey, make you clean up your room when you don't want to, and sometimes let you experience the painful consequences of your actions. Do you always agree with me or understand why I do certain things?"

"No," admitted Colleen.

"But I love you so much I would give my life for you. Do you know anyone else who does things like that?"

Understanding flooded Colleen's mind and heart. "Jesus! And he died for me!"

"Yes, he did," said her mom. "You know, sometimes when I experience pain or troubles, I ask, 'Jesus, don't you care?' Then I remember he loved me enough to die for me. And he promises to be with me, no matter what happens."

Colleen said thoughtfully, "I think I'll make Lacey an early Valentine card and write down all the ways Jesus and I love her."

"Nothing in all creation will ever be able to separate us from the love of God." *(Romans 8:39)*

 *How has Jesus shown his love for you?*

Strength Test

Get Set Collect blindfolds and ten large paper clips for each person.

Go!

Sit around a table. **Give** each person a blindfold and ten paper clips.

Put on the blindfolds.

"Go!" See who can be the first to link all his or her paper clips together without peeking.

Remove the blindfolds and **link** everyone's paper clip chains together into one long chain.

Slip pencils into the last paper clip at each end of the long chain.

Take turns trying to pull the paper clips apart.

Read Romans 8:35–39.

How hard was it to separate the paper clips?
How much stronger is God's love than paper clips?
How does the strength of God's love help you trust him?

Keep your paper clip chain as a reminder of God's strong love for you.

To Trust or Not to Trust

Get Set   In the middle of a room, set out a chair, an empty cardboard box, a balloon, and a large stack of newspapers.

Go!   *Which of these things would you sit on? Which would you not? Why?*

Sit   on one of the items.

How does sitting on something show trust?
What kinds of things do we put our trust in every day?

Read   Deuteronomy 33:27.

How do we know it's safe to trust in God?

Stand   up, facing each other.

Parent, *tell* your child, "Please trust me. I won't let you fall."

Child, *tell* your parent, "I trust you." Then turn around, stiffen your body, and fall back into your parent's arms.

Was it easy or hard to fall back? Explain.
How can we show our trust in God?

Pray   and ask God to help your trust in him grow each day.

God's Promises

Kyle woke up crying from another nightmare. He shivered in the darkness, imagining a dozen terrible things that could happen.

Our house might catch on fire, or a robber could break in, he thought. He pulled his quilt up under his chin and shook with fear, unable to close his eyes.

The bedroom door opened and Dad peeked in. "Another nightmare, son?"

"Yes," he whispered. "Pray with me, Daddy. I'm thinking scary thoughts."

Dad prayed with Kyle, then went back to bed.

The next day at breakfast Kyle's father said, "I have an idea that might help you at night: Get your mind on what *God* says, not on what you're afraid might happen. Try memorizing Bible promises. When you've learned fifty promises, I'll get you that backpack you've wanted for our summer trip in the mountains."

"*Fifty* verses?" asked Kyle. It was hard to learn one!

"Pick the verses you think would help you the most."

At first Kyle only learned two or three verses a week. Then one day he had an idea. He recorded all fifty verses on a small tape recorder. Every morning when he got up, he punched the Play button and listened while he dressed. He carried the tape recorder into the kitchen and listened during breakfast.

Before long, Kyle was memorizing thirteen verses a week! And he hardly ever woke up with nightmares. If he did, he would begin speaking God's promises aloud. That took away his fear and helped him relax so he could fall asleep again.

Kyle was excited when Dad gave him the sturdy leather backpack. He said, "Thank you for the backpack. It's great! But I've learned to trust God more than ever. And that's more important to me than any backpack."

"I rejoice in your word like one who finds a great treasure." *(Psalm 119:162)*

 *When do you have the most trouble trusting God? What will you do to learn and memorize God's promises?*

Jump In!

Salina stood all alone at the end of the dock and shivered. Everyone else was having fun splashing and swimming in the lake. She wanted to jump in and join in the fun, but she felt afraid. She couldn't swim very well, and the water looked dark and scary.

"Come on in and play with us," Salina's father called.

Salina shook her head. "No, I can't!" she said through chattering teeth.

"Jump off the dock and I will catch you," said her father, coming closer.

Salina hesitated. She couldn't see under the water. "I'm scared…I can't do it!" she cried.

"Trust me, Salina! I promise to catch you. Jump in!"

The six-year-old took a deep breath, said a quick prayer, and closed her eyes. Then she jumped off the dock—and landed in her father's strong arms.

"Salina, I'm glad that you trusted me enough to jump in," he said. "But most of all I hope you will trust Jesus to care for you. Jesus doesn't want you to be full of fear."

"Oh, Daddy," said Salina. "You take such good care of me. I know Jesus loves me even more than you do, so I shouldn't be afraid. I just have to remember to think about him and not about the problem."

Jesus said, "I am here! Don't be afraid." *(John 6:20)*

What does Jesus want you to do in times of fear? What's one new way you can trust in Jesus?

The Invisible Army

Aaron jumped under the quilt as his grandfather climbed up the creaky stairs to the attic bedroom. The wind howled. Rain pelted the roof. Aaron had felt excited about spending an extra week with Grandpa, but now he missed his dad.

"I'll leave the hall light on downstairs," said Grandpa, "so you can see."

Suddenly thunder cracked outside. Aaron's heart raced, but he didn't say anything.

Grandpa sat down on the edge of Aaron's bed. "Once Elisha faced a big problem. Elisha's servant opened his window one morning and saw a mighty army with horses and chariots. The king of Syria had sent his army to capture Elisha. When the servant realized the danger, he felt terrified."

Grandpa continued, "Elisha told him not to be afraid. He asked God to open his servant's eyes. So God let the servant see what Elisha saw. Behind the enemy army stood a much bigger army of God's mighty troops! All of the mountains were covered with horses and chariots of fire, sent by God to protect Elisha."

Grandpa smiled. "I'm praying that you can close your eyes and picture God's chariots of fire surrounding and guarding you." Grandpa gave Aaron a hug, then walked back down the stairs.

Aaron didn't even notice the storm or the creaking stairs. He already imagined God's heavenly army standing guard over him.

The next thing Aaron heard was a rooster crowing in the morning. He dressed quickly and ran to help Grandpa collect eggs for breakfast. Aaron couldn't wait to tell Grandpa how much it helped to think about God's mighty power instead of his own fears!

Elisha told his servant: "Don't be afraid!...For there are more on our side than on theirs!" *(2 Kings 6:16)*

 *What does Jesus want you to do instead of be afraid?*

Making a Champion

Caleb walked over to his little sister, who stood holding Mom's hand at the sidelines of the soccer field. He needed Brooke's help, but he could already imagine her reaction.

"Are you giving me a chance to help Brooke overcome her fears?" Caleb asked Jesus.

"Brooke," Caleb said, kneeling beside her, "we don't have enough players to start the game. We need you to stand on the field. We'll have to forfeit the game if you don't."

Brooke's eyes grew big and her face paled. "I'm just in kindergarten," she said. "I can't."

"All you have to do is stand on the field."

Brooke looked terrified.

"Jesus will help you, Brooke. Without your help, we'll lose this game without even getting to play it!"

Brooke hesitated, then nodded. Hand in hand they walked onto the field.

The whistle blew. Caleb pulled Brooke along with him as he trapped a pass and dribbled toward the goal. "You can do anything with Jesus' help," he said as they ran.

For the next hour they ran together, holding hands, kicking the ball, and scoring six goals. Caleb kept encouraging Brooke. Before long, Brooke was smiling.

By the time Brooke graduated from high school, she had played on six state championship soccer teams and was ranked one of the best soccer players in the state of Oregon.

"I will declare the wonder of your name to my brothers and sisters." *(Psalm 22:22)*

 *How can you show Jesus' love to your brother or sister?*

The Operation

Hannah lay on the sofa holding back her tears. "Aunt Janice," she said, "my stomach really hurts." This was the first time she had been away from home for a whole week and she missed her parents.

Her aunt quickly stopped washing dishes and went over to the sofa. "What's the matter? Where does it hurt?" she asked Hannah.

"Here." Hannah placed a hand below her stomach and tried hard not to cry.

"I'll make you some warm ginger tea with honey," Aunt Janice offered. "That will help your stomach ache."

Hannah's stomachache worsened. Finally Aunt Janice, who was a nurse, insisted on taking Hannah to the hospital.

The doctor examined Hannah and announced that she needed immediate surgery to remove her appendix.

An operation! Hannah thought. *And Mom and Dad are more than a day's drive away! What will I do?*

As they wheeled her to the X-ray room, Hannah began to pray. She asked Jesus to be with her, hold her hand, and help her be brave. While the nurses prepared her for surgery, Hannah prayed for each one of them and for Aunt Janice, too. When they wheeled her down the hall to the operating room, she prayed for Jesus to guide the doctor during the surgery.

At the operating room door, Aunt Janice gently squeezed her hand and said, "Don't be afraid. I'm praying for you."

"Oh, Aunt Janice," exclaimed Hannah with a big smile. "I've been so busy praying, I forgot to be afraid!"

Jesus said, "Don't be afraid. Just trust me." *(Mark 5:36)*

When have you felt lonely?
How could praying for others help you?

Fearless in the Fort

Get Set Gather a Bible, flashlights, and several blankets.

Go!

Build a tent fort by draping several blankets over a table or a group of chairs.

Darken the room, then **crawl** inside the tent.

Is darkness something we need to fear? Why or why not?

Turn on a flashlight and **read** John 8:12.

Why does Jesus call himself the light of the world?
How does Jesus' light shine in our lives?
Is Jesus' light with us even when it's dark? Explain.

Pass the flashlight around and **take turns** finishing this sentence:
Jesus, thank you for being my light when...

Pray: Dear Jesus, thank you for being our light. Help us to look to you instead of thinking of things that scare us or worry us. Help us to walk in your light. Amen.

Week
3

God's Rainbow Promises

Get Set Work together to make Rainbow Dessert: Layer different-colored fresh or canned fruit into clear glasses— one for each person. Use your choice of blueberries, kiwi, bananas, strawberries, peaches, grapes, or mandarin oranges. Spoon whipped topping in between the layers of fruit.

Go!

As you **enjoy** Rainbow Dessert, **tell** what you remember about Noah and the flood (Genesis 6–8).

After the flood, when Noah left the ark, what did God promise?

Read Genesis 8:15–22.

Has God kept these two promises?
What are some other promises God has kept?
When has our family seen God keep his promises in our lives?
What promises of God are we still waiting to see happen?
Why do you think God can be trusted to keep every promise?

Pray, each person thanking God for one of his promises.

Fishing for Promises

Nuk Shugak grabbed his sister's arm as she reached to snatch a fish from Old Charlie's fish wheel. His netted baskets had more fish in them than any of the other fish wheels on the river. Obviously Old Charlie hadn't checked his baskets that morning.

Nina looked at her older brother in surprise. She glanced around. "No one is watching!"

"We aren't going to take fish from Old Charlie's fish wheel anymore," said Nuk.

"Why not? He'll never know."

"Remember what the missionary said in church last Sunday?"

Nina wrinkled her brow. "About God keeping his promises?"

"Yes. He said God takes care of those who trust him."

"But we *need* the fish! There are seven mouths to feed in our family. Old Charlie only has himself to feed."

Nuk thought ahead to the winter months when the river would freeze. If his family didn't harvest enough fish now, they would go hungry.

Nina continued to argue. "Everyone in the village takes fish from other fish wheels."

Nuk shook his head. "Now that I'm a Christian, I want to live for Jesus. I'm going to do what's right. And I'll trust God's promise to take care of us."

Throughout the autumn months, Nuk and Nina checked their family's fish wheel three times a day. Each time the baskets were full. This had never happened before! At the end of the season, Nuk's family had more than enough dried fish to last all through the long winter.

When neighbors ran out of food, Nuk even shared his fish with them. He also shared the story of how God was faithful and kept his promise to care for them.

"God...will supply all your needs from his glorious riches, which have been given to us in Christ Jesus." *(Philippians 4:19)*

What promises of God does Jesus want you to trust today?
How can you give God the glory when he keeps his promises to you?

For God's Glory

Tori stared straight ahead and followed her basketball team into the gym. She pretended not to notice the boys with crossed arms lining the hall. Tonight her team was competing for the sixth-grade city championship and since Tori was the only girl in the entire league, everyone was watching her. Tori had an important job to do: she wanted to shine for Jesus.

"That's her!" A hoarse whisper came from somewhere behind her. Another voice hissed a filthy name at her back. She ignored them. She knew Jesus ignored it when they called him names.

The game started and Tori jumped for the tip-off, but Number 18 from the opposing team yanked her long braid. Instead of getting angry, Tori threw herself into the game.

The game got even rougher. Boys elbowed her and pushed her down. Parents yelled, "Ref! Where's the foul?" Number 18 swore at her. Tori ignored it all and played harder, determined to do her job.

Then, for no reason, Number 18 threw an elbow at her forehead. Tori's teammate grabbed him. "I'll rip your face off!" he snarled.

"Let it go," Tori said. "Jesus said nothing when Roman soldiers hurt him."

Tori's team lost by one point, but Tori had done her job well. She'd played exactly the way Jesus wanted her to.

"Not to us, O Lord, but to you goes all the glory." *(Psalm 115:1)*

How did Tori shine for Jesus?
What does it mean to give God the glory?

False God

"Lian," Mary told the Chinese exchange student who had come to live with them for a few weeks, "I love your little doll."

Mary sat on the blue bedspread in what used to be the spare bedroom playing with the brown statue Lian had brought with her from China. It was a funny-looking little man with a fat tummy and a jewel in his forehead. He made Mary want to laugh.

"It's not a doll." Lian sat down beside Mary. "He's a god."

Mary jumped up and dropped the statue. *I said I loved her false god!* she thought. *Oh Jesus, please forgive me!* She couldn't breathe.

Lian laughed. "You don't like my little god?"

Mary didn't know what to say. She didn't want to hurt Lian's feelings. "No. I'm a Christian." Mary wanted to run away. "I have to help Mom set the table," she mumbled. She didn't want Lian to see how upset she was.

Her whole body trembled when she told her mom what happened.

Mary's mom put both arms around her and pulled her close. "Honey, Jesus understood. Did you know it was a god when you said you loved it? Or did you just think it was a cute little doll?"

"I thought it was a cute little doll."

"Jesus knows that. It's only a piece of wood. It can't help Lian and it can't hurt you."

Mary started to feel better. "Should we tell Lian to put the little god away?"

"Let's pray about that. Maybe we won't say anything yet. But we will look for an opportunity to tell her about Jesus. And let's trust that Jesus will save her."

"Their god...cannot speak, and it needs to be carried because it cannot walk. Do not be afraid of such gods, for they can neither harm you nor do you any good." *(Jeremiah 10:5)*

Who could you tell about Jesus?
How would you share Jesus with someone
who believed in another god?

The Wave

Ty skipped a stone across the water and asked without looking at his friend, "You are a Christian, aren't you, Justin?"

Justin sounded offended. "Going to church doesn't make you a Christian."

"Attending a church service doesn't make you a Christian," Ty agreed. "But don't Christians go to church to worship God?"

"Church is boring." Justin plopped on the grass.

Jesus, help me explain this, Ty prayed.

"Justin, did you ever see a wave at a professional baseball game?"

"See one!?" Justin tossed a rock into the creek. "Last summer I was smack in the middle of one. It started at one end of the stadium and swept all the way around. Man, it was cool!"

"I've only seen them on television," said Ty. "But I think church on Sunday is like a giant wave for God." He paused. "You've seen videos taken from space that show the sun coming up as the earth turns, haven't you? Well, as the sun rises around the earth on Sunday, people who go to church raise their voices and hands to God. As their worship circles the whole earth, it forms a huge praise wave for God."

"God must love it," said Justin. He looked thoughtful. "Maybe I'll be part of God's wave next Sunday."

"And let us not neglect our meeting together." *(Hebrews 10:25)*

Why do you go to church?
Why do you think Jesus wants us to go to church?

What Color Is Your Heart?

Shelli glanced at the clock. In twenty minutes Mrs. Cramer would return and Shelli would successfully finish her first baby-sitting job. She watched five-year-old Bonnie and her twin brother Peter busily coloring at the kitchen table.

Suddenly Bonnie grabbed a crayon from Peter's hand. "I need the green crayon!" she insisted.

"That's mine!" Peter yelled, and pulled her braid. Bonnie screamed and kicked him.

Shelli didn't know what to do. *Dear Jesus, help me calm them down,* she prayed. The package of construction paper on the table gave her an idea. "Do you want to hear a story about hearts?" she asked them.

They stopped fighting, and Peter asked, "Like operations?"

"No! Like boyfriends, silly," said Bonnie.

"Wait and see," said Shelli, pulling out gray, red, white, green, and light blue sheets of paper. The children watched closely as she made a heart-shaped pattern, then cut a heart of each color and stapled the hearts together.

Holding up the hearts, she said, "This is my 'heart book.' If you listen carefully, I'll sing you the story." Bonnie and Peter watched Shelli turn each "heart page" so the color would match the words of her song:

Though my heart was dark within, Jesus saved me from my sin.
When he shed his blood, I know he washed me as white as snow.
If I follow Jesus' way, I'll grow more like him each day.
He has promised when I die, I will live in heaven on high.

Bonnie pointed to the dark gray heart. "My heart is like that. I took Peter's crayon and kicked him. How can I have a white heart, Shelli?"

Shelli smiled. Getting to tell Bonnie about Jesus was the best part of this baby-sitting job!

"The blood of Jesus...cleanses us from every sin." *(1 John 1:7)*

Have you told someone about Jesus?
What could you say?

The Heart Book

Get Set   Gather scissors, a stapler, and five colors of construction paper: gray, red, white, green, and blue.

Go!

Cut   out a heart pattern (about six inches high)

Use the pattern to   *cut*   five identical hearts out of the colored paper.

> Gray—for sin
> Red—for Jesus' blood
> White—for a clean heart/forgiven sins
> Green—for growth
> Blue—for heaven

Staple   the hearts together in the upper left corner.

Sing   this song to the tune of "Jesus Loves Me" as you   *turn*   the pages of the book.

> (Gray) —————— Though my heart was dark within,
> Jesus saved me from my sin.
> (Red) —————— When he shed his blood, I know
> (White) ——— He washed me as white as snow.
> (Green) ——— If I follow Jesus' way
> I'll grow more like him each day.
> (Blue) —————— He has promised when I die
> I will live in heaven on high.

Take turns reading   the Heart Book. Share it with others.

Week
4

What's Missing?

Get Set   Slice rounds of refrigerated sugar cookie dough. Fold a chocolate mint or a teaspoon of jam inside each slice of dough and seal it shut. Bake according to directions.

Gather three or four battery-powered items such as toys, a flashlight, or a CD player. Secretly remove the batteries.

Go!

Invite   everyone to turn on the items you've collected.

Why won't they work?
What's wrong?

Open   the empty battery slots and   *show*   the missing "power source."

Read   Galatians 5:13–14.

What does God want us to do for each other?
Why is it important for us to love and serve other people?

Read   Galatians 5:16, 22.

How will other people know that you love Jesus?
What will give you the power to love and serve like Jesus (verse 22)?
Who would Jesus want you to serve this week?

Pray,   and ask Jesus to help you serve and love one special person this week.

Eat   your snack and   *talk*   about how we need God's power on the inside so we can do what God made us to do.

Christopher at Camp

"Head for home base!" yelled Christopher, racing through the woods. "We found the last item on our list! We've won the treasure hunt!" His teammates joined him in a sprint to the main cabin, where a plate of peanut butter cookies awaited the winning team.

While they ate their treats in the dining room, the cook banged on her pot with a wooden spoon. "Attention!" she said. "One of our servers injured her ankle. We need help to get lunch ready. Any volunteers?"

Nobody volunteered. Some campers headed for the creek while others ran to the treehouse. Everyone wanted to be outdoors in the Oregon woods.

"Let's swing on the big rope, Christopher," said Bethany, holding the door open.

Christopher looked back at the cook. *It's no fun when you need help and can't find any,* he thought. "Go ahead. I'll try to come later," he answered.

Pushing open the kitchen door, Christopher smelled the rolls that had just come out of the oven.

"These need to be pulled apart and set out in baskets," explained the cook.

Christopher washed his hands, spread checkered napkins in all the straw baskets, then filled them up with warm rolls. They looked good! Next Christopher set out 125 small dessert bowls and dished up the plum cobbler. *Thank you for letting me serve you this way, Jesus,* he prayed. He hurriedly set the dining room tables and filled all the water glasses. By the time lunch was served, Christopher was exhausted. But inside, he felt joy and satisfaction.

"You missed out on a lot of fun," commented Bethany when she came to lunch.

"But I had a great chance to serve!" said Christopher with a broad smile.

Jesus said, "I...came here not to be served but to serve others, and to give my life as a ransom for many." *(Matthew 20:28)*

Where would Jesus want you to serve today?
What kind of attitude do you have toward serving?

Pepe from Peru

Feeling a warm hand on his shoulder, Pepe stopped painting and looked up.

"What a wonderful job you have done painting these ceramic crosses, my son," said Pepe's father. "Your mother and I appreciate your working every day. I know a lot of your friends are playing soccer."

Pepe smiled. "I'm glad the shops want to sell the jewelry we make. If I can help you pay for food and send all six of us kids to school, I am happy." He didn't tell his father that he had been asked to play in the grade-school soccer tournament. Practice after school and on weekends would mean an end to this work which Pepe knew Jesus wanted him to do.

"Your older brother will fire more ceramics tonight in the kiln. A new batch of jewelry will be ready to paint tomorrow." Father bent down and examined the cross Pepe was painting. "Where do you get your ideas for these beautiful designs?" he asked.

Pepe smiled broadly. "I'm not sure. I don't plan what I will do. I just pick up the paintbrush and try out different lines and colors. Do you think Jesus is helping me?"

"I know Jesus is blessing you because of your willing heart to help here at home. We thank God for you," said his father.

"Never be lazy in your work, but serve the Lord enthusiastically."
(Romans 12:11)

In what ways does Jesus want you to serve your family with a good attitude?

Thembi, the Dish Washer

Thembi skipped home from school as fast as she could in the South African heat. She could hardly wait to see the little children in the Mamelodi Nursery School next door to her house. The busy place opened at 5:30 in the morning and didn't close until 8:00 at night. How Thembi loved Mama Florah and the boys and girls—all eighty-five of them!

"Mama Florah!" she called out, walking into her neighbor's courtyard, "I'm here to help. What do you need me to do today?"

Mama Florah gave Thembi a warm hug. "Here's my little Good Samaritan! Well, what do you think needs to be done today? Dishes always wait to be washed. And lots of little children want you to play with them."

Smiling broadly, Thembi said, "You know that I want to be a Good Samaritan, like Jesus said we should be. I try to find people who need help—like *you*, Mama Florah!"

The good-natured seven-year-old went straight to the kitchen. When the water was hot, she washed a huge pile of bowls. Then she carefully rinsed, dried, and stacked all of them.

"Thembi!" exclaimed one of the kitchen helpers, "how you scrub those dishes! They get so clean when you wash them. But I don't understand it. Why do you work here? You never get paid for it. And you don't even complain about all the work!"

Thembi just smiled and said softly, "I'm a Good Samaritan, and I want to do my best for Jesus."

Could you remember Thembi in your prayers? She is a small child who is doing a big job working for Jesus in South Africa.

Jesus ended the story of the Good Samaritan by telling his followers, "Now go and do the same." *(Luke 10:37)*

When have you helped someone in need who could not pay you?
Has anyone ever been a Good Samaritan to you? When?

A Servant's Heart

Maropeng frowned as she swept the floor of her family's house in South Africa. She loved serving her family. She willingly carried her younger sister on her back, fixed meals, and took hand-washing bowls around at mealtimes. But she was troubled. She wondered if there was a god she could serve.

One day a missionary came to her door and invited her to a meeting the next Sunday. Curious, Maropeng visited the worship service held in a small whitewashed building.

The missionary told everyone about Jesus Christ, God's Son, who came to earth as a baby. He told them Jesus came to serve others. He explained that we serve God by serving the people around us.

Maropeng's heart filled with joy. She had her answer! There was a god she could serve if she invited Jesus into her heart. She wanted to serve Jesus by helping others.

Every Sunday morning Maropeng returned to the meeting place. She arrived early to straighten chairs and dust the room for worship services. During the week she brought the neighbor children to Bible classes and she helped the missionaries by translating their Bible lessons into her Sotho language.

Now Maropeng smiled when she performed her daily tasks. Her heart was filled with joy because she knew she was serving God and others.

God honored Maropeng's service. The little group of believers in her village became a strong church that still exists thirty years later!

"Live to please Christ, who died and was raised…" *(2 Corinthians 5:15)*

 *How can you be a servant today?*

Antonio and the Flu

Antonio's little brother woke up from his nap and started screaming at the exact moment when Antonio's mom rang her bell for help. Antonio hurried to his mom's bedside first.

"Ice chips, please," his mom whispered.

Mom had gotten the flu yesterday and Dad was away on business.

"Here's your ice." Antonio set the glass on Mom's nightstand and ran to his brother's crib to see why he was crying. What could he fix for dinner? Hot dogs? Soup? He had never cooked before.

Antonio went in and picked up his baby brother. "Yuck! How can anything smell this bad?" He wanted to hold his nose but didn't have an extra hand. *I hate changing diapers,* he thought.

The doorbell rang and Antonio raced to answer it with his brother in his arms.

Nadia, their neighbor, stood at the door holding a casserole. "I thought you might need dinner," she said, setting the dish on the kitchen table.

"Thanks!" said Antonio.

"Pfew!" Nadia took Antonio's little brother from him. "I'll change his diaper for you. You look like you need a break."

"You're doing what Jesus would do," said Antonio. Nadia gave him a funny look.

After Mom felt better, Antonio told her how Nadia had helped. "Nadia is a wonderful Christian," Antonio said.

"Why do you say that?" asked Mom.

"She did everything Jesus would do."

"Nadia is wonderful," said Mom, "and we love her. But doing nice things doesn't make you a Christian. You have to trust Jesus and ask him to forgive your sins. I don't think Nadia has done that."

"Then we should pray for her, shouldn't we?" Antonio asked. "Nadia served us by helping when you had the flu. Now I'll serve her by praying she'll accept Jesus."

"He saved us, not because of the good things we did, but because of his mercy." *(Titus 3:5)*

 *Why won't doing good deeds get you to heaven? How can you get to heaven?*

Open Hands

Get Set Set out one pencil for each person. Hide a small package of peanuts under a napkin. Hide a package of chocolate kisses somewhere else in the room.

Go!

Ask everyone to hold a pencil in one hand and make a fist with the other.

Try to *give* someone the package of peanuts. (You can't because their hands are closed.)

Have everyone *open* their hands and *offer* their pencils to you.

Give one person the bag of peanuts and *take* that person's pencil.

Read 2 Corinthians 9:7.

God is a giving God. What does God want us to do with the things he gives us? What should be our attitude when we give to others?

Tell the person with the peanuts to *give* them away.

Surprise that person by giving him or her the bag of chocolate kisses.

Why can't we ever out-give God?
What can we learn today about giving to each other?

Open the bags of peanuts and chocolates.

Who is willing to share?

Eat the snacks and *discuss* how your family will give to someone else this week.

Pray that Jesus will help you be giving servants.

Calling God?

Get Set   Unplug a telephone and put it on a table.

Go!

What's nice about having a telephone?
How would our lives be different without one?
How is prayer like a telephone?
In what ways is prayer better than a telephone?
Does God ever put on an answering machine, give you a busy signal,
charge you for a call, or disconnect you? Explain.

Start dialing   the phone and *ask:*

What is God's telephone number?

Read   John 14:6.

How can you "dial" directly to God?
How can you be sure God hears your prayers?
Do you ever treat God like a 911 emergency call? Explain.
In your prayers, how can you remember who God is, not just what he
can do for you?

Thank   God for the privilege of prayer. Take time to *pray* for your
fellow Christians in a faraway country.

Rip Tide!

Tina and her mother ran barefoot across the ocean beach in Mexico. "This sand is so-o-o sparkly and white!" squealed Tina. "I'm glad we came."

Mother laughed. "I am, too," she said. "It's the first time you and I have gone on a vacation together."

"Let's play catch with our beach ball out in the waves," said Tina.

"The hotel manager said this area is known for its strong undertow," warned Mother. "Let's not go too far." She and Tina played in the water for an hour, bobbing up and down with the ocean tide. Suddenly Tina heard her mother gasp.

"Mom! What's wrong?" she asked.

"Look at the shoreline!" cried Mother. "We're moving farther away. Even when I walk toward shore, I'm being pulled deeper— out to sea."

Tina stood still. Her heart sank as she felt the ocean current shift the sand under her feet. She—and the sand—were sliding out a little farther with each wave.

Tina let go of the ball as Mother yelled, "Swim for shore!" She and her mother swam as hard as they could toward the beach, but they couldn't fight the undercurrent.

"Swim parallel to the shore!" hollered Mother.

Neither of them said another word. Silently they prayed for strength. Kicking as hard as they could, they swam sideways. When the relentless undertow paused with an incoming wave, they turned and headed for the shore until the undertow began again. Then they switched and swam sideways. Slowly they inched toward shore. When they finally reached the shore, Tina and her mother collapsed, totally exhausted.

Later Tina told her mother, "Remember the disciples in the storm? They were scared to death, but Jesus saved them anyway. Jesus saved us when I didn't believe we'd reach the shore alive!"

Jesus said, "Why are you afraid? You have so little faith!" *(Matthew 8:26)*

When were you afraid and Jesus helped you?
Why does Jesus want you to have more faith?

The Tick

Kia awakened with her brother B. J. on her mind. She wondered if she had been dreaming about him. *What time is it?* she wondered as she rolled over to look at her clock. It was midnight.

Kia remembered her mother saying, "When someone keeps coming to your mind, God is telling you to pray for that person." Kia sleepily said a quick prayer for B. J., who was away at church camp.

Turning over, Kia couldn't get B. J. off her mind. Finally she dragged herself out of bed and knelt down. She wondered how she should pray for him.

"Dear Jesus," she began, "please protect B. J." Feeling she should pray more specifically, she added, "Protect his body and his mind."

Kia crawled back into bed but couldn't sleep. She kept praying until she finally drifted off to sleep at four o'clock in the morning.

Mom woke Kia at 8:30 A.M. after the camp director called.

"B. J.'s counselor found a tick that carries Rocky Mountain spotted fever in B. J.'s hair this morning," she said.

Kia gasped and sat up in bed. "Is B. J. going to die?"

"No," said Mother. "They rushed him to the hospital and cut out the tick. But the counselor had no idea why he checked B. J.'s scalp." Mother looked at Kia. "What do you think?"

Kia smiled sleepily. "I think Jesus protected B. J."

Jesus said, "Ask anything in my name, and I will do it!" *(John 14:14)*

 *Who would Jesus want you to pray for right now?*

Caitlin's Quick Prayer

"Everybody get in the car," called Mrs. Everett. "We'll grab some hamburgers before we take Caitlin home."

Caitlin slipped on her coat and followed her best friends, Frances and Chelsey, out the door. The girls sat together in the backseat, laughing and giggling on the way to the restaurant.

Glancing out the side window, Caitlin caught her breath at the sight of a big car approaching like a bolt of lightning. It careened around a corner at high speed and headed straight toward a man riding his bicycle across the intersection.

Her heart pounding, Caitlin could hardly speak. "Watch out!" she called to Mrs. Everett, who saw the car and put on her brakes.

The speeding car struck the bicycle rider. His body flew up high in the air and came back down on the street, landing with a thud. As Caitlin watched, she prayed a quick prayer, "Dear Jesus, please help that man. Let him be all right. Bring someone along to help."

Every car stopped. Mrs. Everett, along with several other people, ran over to the bike rider. In seconds, Caitlin saw a doctor in a white coat running to the scene of the accident. He opened his black bag and bent down to examine the man who had been hit.

A policeman came around to talk with people who saw the accident. When he reached the car where the girls were waiting, Caitlin asked, "How did the doctor get here so fast?"

"He was across the street! He says the biker seems to be fine. It's amazing!"

"Thank you, Jesus," whispered Caitlin. "You sure answered my prayer quickly! You do marvelous things!"

"Don't worry about anything; instead, pray about everything. Tell God what you need, and thank him for all he has done." *(Philippians 4:6)*

When have you prayed for others in trouble? Who needs your prayers right now?

Bobby's Prayer Time

Now that Trisha was in third grade, having a mentally challenged twelve-year-old brother had become a big problem. Her new friends didn't like Bobby standing around with his mouth open, staring at everything they did.

"Bobby, my friends are coming today," said Trisha with a stern voice. "Stay away from us. We want to play by ourselves."

"But sis…" Bobby stumbled excitedly over his words. "Jesus tell me…happy day…be all fine."

"Mom! Make Bobby leave the room before my friends come."

Mother came and explained, "When Bobby came out from his prayer time today, he insisted that Jesus spoke to him. He said Jesus told him that someday, in heaven, he would be just like the rest of us."

Trisha felt bad about her attitude. She hugged her brother. "I'm sorry for fussing at you. Please forgive me. Someday you *will* be just fine."

Several months later, Trisha told her pastor, "Every day for a whole hour, my brother goes in his bedroom, kneels down, and prays for everyone he knows. He knows that Jesus loves him and died for him, yet he can't write his own name, read, or talk very well. I used to think I was smarter than Bobby. But my brother is teaching me to pray."

Jesus said, "O Father…thank you for hiding the truth from those who think themselves so wise and clever, and for revealing it to the childlike." *(Luke 10:21)*

What attitude does Jesus want you to have toward those who are different?

Week
5

Delcy Is Missing

Jesus, please help us find my sister, Todd prayed desperately. Two-year-old Delcy had been missing for five hours. Todd's flashlight swept the hillside behind their new house. He called, "Del-cy!" Then he stopped to listen. He could see the beams from dozens of flash-lights moving through the trees. He heard the voices of his father and neighbors calling Delcy's name.

Jesus, he prayed, *please help me hear her voice.* His ears hurt from straining to hear. As if in answer to his prayer, Todd thought he heard a faint cry. His heart thumped.

He called, "Delcy!" again, then stood still, listening. Had it been his imagination? "Dear Jesus!" Todd sobbed aloud, "Please help me find her!"

Todd heard a whimper.

"Delcy! Where are you?" Todd dropped to his knees. He groped through moss and dead leaves, creeping toward the sound of faint crying. His hand felt a hole and he shined his flashlight in the partially filled-in old well. Crumpled at the bottom of the six-foot hole was his little sister.

"I'll help you, Delcy," he assured his sister.

Her dirt-streaked face smiled up at him and she held out her arms.

"Wait just a little longer," he said. Todd jumped up and waved his flashlight in the air, mixing screams for help with shouts of, "Thank you, Jesus!"

Todd again knelt by the hole to comfort Delcy while he waited for the rescuers. *The hole isn't big enough for an adult,* he realized. *I'll climb down and lift Delcy to them.*

When his dad and neighbors arrived, they tied a rope around Todd's waist and lowered him to his sister. She clung to him, fright-ened but unhurt. Todd had never felt happier. Jesus had answered his prayer and saved Delcy.

"Have mercy on me and hear my prayer." *(Psalm 4:1)*

When has Jesus answered your prayers in an amazing way?
Why can you be certain Jesus hears your prayers?

Pretzel Prayers

Get Set Buy a box of mini pretzels (curved, not straight ones) or bake a batch of frozen pretzels.

Go!

Hold up a pretzel.

Explain: Because of its unique shape, the pretzel is a symbol of prayer. Christians long ago prayed with their arms across their chests and their hands on the opposite shoulders. The crossing of their arms reminded them of Jesus' dying for them on the cross.

Read Jesus' words in John 14:14.

Make this simple pretzel prayer reminder:

Place five "prayer pretzels" in a vertical line and glue them together. Glue another pretzel on each side between the second and third pretzels to make a cross shape.
Hang your pretzel cross by a string on your bulletin board or above your bed.

Pass a bowl of pretzels. Take a pretzel, pray aloud for a specific person, then eat the pretzel. *Continue* your pretzel prayers until each person has prayed for two or three people.

Week
6

Givers or Takers?

Get Set   Prepare instant pudding in a large bowl and keep it in the refrigerator. Place a small bowl and spoon for each person on a tray out of sight.

Set out an empty serving bowl, a small measuring spoon, a measuring cup, and a canister or bag of rice.

Go!

Read   Luke 6:38.

Is Jesus a giver or a taker? Explain. Which are you?

Spoon   rice into the serving bowl.

What did Jesus say would happen if we give only a little?

Using the cup,   **pour**   rice into the empty bowl.

What happens if we give a lot?
How do you want God to give to you?
How are you giving to God right now?

Bring   out the pudding and the tray of bowls and spoons.   **Serve** two spoonfuls of pudding into each small bowl. Then set the spoon aside and   **dip**   generous servings with the measuring cup.

Read   Jesus' words in Luke 6:38 once again.

How can you be generous today?

Enjoy   your pudding and   **discuss**   how your family can give of your time, friendship, money, etc., to show Jesus' love to others.

The Graduation Gift

Joel listened to the principal talk to the auditorium full of sixth-graders. "As you all know, Patrick Morgan has been in and out of the hospital for many years because of his damaged heart." Joel held his breath. Had Patrick died?

"We have good news." The principal smiled. "Patrick is now at the top of the heart transplant list! With a new heart, Patrick will be able to attend school regularly and even play soccer."

The students clapped and whistled.

The principal raised her hands to quiet them. "However, heart transplants are expensive. Patrick's parents don't have enough money to pay for his operation. Any ideas on how we could help?"

"A bake sale," yelled one student.

"A jog-a-thon," shouted another.

An idea popped into Joel's mind. He wondered if the other kids would go along with it. He knew it was something Jesus would do. Slowly he stood up. "We could give Patrick the two thousand dollars we raised for our graduation trip to Washington, D.C."

One girl called out, "We can't give up our trip! It's a tradition."

"Yeah. And what about the day of school we miss?" said the boy next to her. The students laughed.

After lots of discussion, the class voted to give the two thousand dollars to Patrick's family and have a graduation party in the school cafeteria. Joel felt good and bad. He would miss the graduation trip, but he had helped bless Patrick and his family.

This story was broadcast by radio. Many other people and businesses donated money to the Morgans and to the class graduation fund. Joel's class went to a nearby amusement park for their graduation trip and Patrick received a new heart.

"Let us stop just saying we love each other; let us really show it by our actions." *(1 John 3:18)*

Who would Jesus want you to help today?
What could you give someone in need?

Emergency on the Train

Martin prayed as he pressed his face against the cold glass of the train window. He listened to his mom pray with the lady across the aisle.

Mrs. Vogel first started labor shortly after the train left Klamath Falls. The conductor asked if there was a doctor on board, but there wasn't. He asked if anyone knew how to deliver a baby. No one did. Then he announced, "The train won't stop until we cross the mountains into Junction City."

Martin heard Mrs. Vogel moaning. Her husband looked worried. Martin asked his mother, "Is the baby in danger? How can I help?"

"Keep praying," said Mother. "She needs an ambulance at the next city, but their insurance won't pay for it."

Martin took his ski hat and started down the aisle, whispering to the other passengers. All the while he prayed silently. An hour later, he returned to his seat.

"The conductor called ahead for an ambulance," said Mother.

Fifteen minutes later paramedics rushed onto the train with a stretcher. Ambulance lights flashed while the other passengers gathered to say good-bye to the Vogels. They cheered as Martin turned over his hat and emptied its contents onto Mrs. Vogel's stretcher.

Out poured nearly four hundred dollars…almost enough to pay for the ambulance!

"Make the most of every opportunity for doing good in these evil days…. Try to understand what the Lord wants you to do." *(Ephesians 5:16–17)*

What opportunities has Jesus given you to be generous today?

Moving Day

"I hate moving!" Jeannie sobbed, looking out the car window. Through her tears, she waved to her best friend, Joy, who stood crying in front of the empty house.

"This is the worst day of my life!" Jeannie said gloomily.

"It's not the end of the world," retorted her brother, Chip.

"I'll never have another best friend like Joy," wailed Jeannie. The girls had been in the same class at school for five years. They'd stayed over at each other's houses on weekends. They loved to roller-skate and play house. They even attended Sunday school together.

Driving north, Jeannie's dad described their new house to the family. Jeannie knew she would hate it. She worried about starting school the following Monday. Jeannie was shy and didn't make friends easily.

Then she remembered that Joy had promised to pray for her. Jeannie knew she could pray, too. "Dear Jesus," she prayed silently, "help me not to be so shy. And please give me some friends."

"We're almost there," announced her dad.

The car turned into a neighborhood with lots of houses. Children of all ages were playing outside in their yards. When Jeannie and her brother piled out of the car, neighbor children ran to greet them. Within half an hour, Jeannie and three new friends were roller-skating down the sidewalk.

"Thank you, Jesus, for answering Joy's prayer and mine!" she murmured.

"Always be joyful. Keep on praying." *(1 Thessalonians 5:16–17)*

 *Do you know someone who is worried? Will you take time to pray for them?*

A Giving Friend

Kyle heard Heather yell, "Hey!" He looked up from his spelling book and saw Bobby holding a bright, rainbow-colored pencil.

"Bobby took my pencil!" Heather squealed. Bobby wasn't using the pencil. Kyle knew Bobby never did any schoolwork.

The teacher wearily walked over, took the pencil from Bobby, and handed it to Heather. Scowling, Bobby hit his fist on the desk and glared at Heather.

The bell rang for recess and Kyle followed Bobby outside. Kyle's mom had helped him figure out why Bobby was the worst-behaved kid in third grade. It was because he couldn't read and everyone made fun of him.

For the last week, Kyle had tried to make friends with Bobby. Kyle knew Jesus could help Bobby. *Please, Jesus,* Kyle prayed, *show me what you want me to do for Bobby.*

Kyle walked over to where Bobby was standing alone, leaning against the fencepost. Using a long stick, Kyle formed the letter "B" in the dirt by the fence.

"Hey, Bobby," he said. "Do you know what sound that letter makes?"

"Why ask me? I'm the dumb kid, remember?"

"It's the sound your name starts with," said Kyle. "B makes the sound of 'buh.' Want to learn some more?"

Bobby dropped his eyes. "I'm too stupid. I can't."

"You can if we ask Jesus to help," said Kyle.

"I'm not a Christian," said Bobby.

"I am," said Kyle. "Jesus answers my prayers."

"Okay. If you can get Jesus to help, I'll try," Bobby said.

During the next months, Kyle taught Bobby during recess. First he helped Bobby sound out letters. Then he helped Bobby make letters into words. In a few months, Bobby could read. No one made fun of him anymore. And Bobby stopped acting up.

Now Kyle prays every day for Bobby to know Jesus.

"God has commanded us…to love one another." *(2 John 6)*

How could you show Jesus' love to someone who's always in trouble?
How could you be a friend to someone who's lonely?

Two Ways to Win

Seven-year-old Jonathan couldn't help smiling as he followed his little brother, Paul, into the house.

"Mommy! I won, I won!" hollered Paul, bounding into the kitchen. "I won the big race. I really did!" He gave Mother a big hug.

Jonathan looked into Mother's eyes and wondered, Did she see our race from the kitchen window? Grinning at his little brother's excitement, Jonathan wasn't sure why he felt such a warm glow inside.

"Paul ran a terrific race, Mom," said Jonathan. "He is fast as lightning and he never fell down once. I didn't know he was so good! He beat me, I must admit."

Jonathan watched his four-year-old brother twirl around the kitchen, then race back outside, exclaiming, "I'm going to practice running some more! I'll be even faster!"

"Mmm," Mother said with a grin. "So your little brother beat you in a race, did he? What happened? Did you fall down?"

Grabbing a freshly baked cookie, Jonathan sat down at the counter. "Mom, I had so much fun letting Paul win. It was better than winning myself."

He thoughtfully ate his cookie, then helped himself to another. "Is that why Jesus said that it is more blessed to give than to receive?" he asked.

Mother smiled. "I think so."

"Mom, you should watch Paul play with me. His little face gets all hot and red. And his short legs try so hard to keep up with me. I just can't win all the time...I don't want to." Jonathan's eyes sparkled. "I'm not sure why, but it makes me feel so good when I make Paul happy. I think it makes Jesus happy, too."

"You should remember the words of the Lord Jesus: 'It is more blessed to give than to receive.'" *(Acts 20:35)*

Do you always have to win? When have you found joy in giving to others?
How could you bring happiness to others in your family?

What Will You Give Jesus?

Get Set Gather gift wrap, ribbon, scissors, note cards, pencils, a candle, and a fancy dish.

Go! On the blank side of the wrapping paper, *trace* around note cards and *cut out* the rectangles. You'll need one or two rectangles for each person.

Read 1 John 4:10.

Why do we love Jesus?
How do you show Jesus that you love him?

Think about what you could give Jesus. Remember that whatever you do for someone else, you do for him.

On the blank side of your rectangle, *write* or *draw* what you will do for Jesus today.

When you've finished, *roll* your rectangle like a scroll and *tie* a ribbon around the middle.

Place the scrolls in a fancy dish and set the dish in the center of the table by a candle.

Light the candle and *pray* together, thanking Jesus for his love.

Give him the gift of your scrolls.

Pathfinders

Get Set Set out a road map and the largest Bible you have. Use yarn, string, or masking tape to mark a path on the floor of your house. Put lots of curves and twists in the first part of the path. Use straight lines for the second part of the path.

Go!

Take turns walking the pathway.

Which section of the pathway was easiest to follow?

With the road map, *find* the way to a favorite destination.

Where can you find God's directions for your life?

Read Proverbs 3:5–6.

What does God's Word tell you about your path?

Read Proverbs 4:10–19, 25–27.

*Is it hard or easy to follow the path God has for your life? Explain.
What will help you keep on the right path?
Who is the only one who never stepped off God's right path?
Why is that important?*

Pray, asking Jesus' forgiveness for the times you go off the path God has planned. Pray for God's help in choosing the right path each day.

The Pink Ruler

"Juanita stole my pink ruler; I know she did," Emily said to her friend Jeri as the third-graders sat munching tacos in the lunchroom. Juanita, a girl with dark curls and olive skin, sat at the next table with her friends, laughing and talking.

"Are you sure it's not in your desk?" asked Jeri.

"Yes. Everyone knows people like Juanita steal. She borrowed it from me yesterday. I don't think she returned it."

"Why don't you ask her to give it back?" said Jeri.

"She'll probably lie," Emily replied. "See them laughing over there? They're laughing at me."

What would Jesus want me to say? Jeri wondered.

After lunch, Mrs. Shaw told the class, "Please take out your pencils and rulers."

Emily glanced over at Jeri, who shook her head sympathetically. They watched Juanita take something out of her desk. But it was a plain white ruler, not Emily's fancy pink one.

Emily sighed. Reaching all the way to the back of her desk for a pencil, she felt a familiar object. When she pulled it out, she discovered…her ruler! Jeri saw the ruler. Emily shrugged innocently, but Jeri frowned.

After school, Emily hurried across the playground to catch up with Jeri. After apologizing, Emily said, "I was wrong about Juanita."

"You can't accuse people just because they look different than you do," said Jeri. "Jesus looks at the inside of people, not at the outside. I've already invited you to my sleepover, but I've decided to invite Juanita, too."

"I feel awful about saying those things about her," said Emily. "Let's get to know her better so we can all be friends."

"Be done with hypocrisy and jealousy and backstabbing." *(1 Peter 2:1)*

What do you think Jesus would have wanted Jeri to say to Emily?
What happens when we judge others before we know them?

Finders Keepers

"That looks like a wallet!" John's bike slid sideways as he braked beside the red Buick. John dropped his bike in the gravel and raced ahead of his two friends to retrieve the black lump he had spotted under the car.

"It is a wallet," he said triumphantly, "and there's money inside! A bunch of money!"

"Let us see, too!" Andrew tried to grab the wallet.

"I'll count it." John tugged bills from the wallet. Rosa and Andrew counted with him. "Five...fifty...one hundred..."

"Three hundred dollars!" John said, amazed.

The three friends stared at each other, wide-eyed. John thought about all the things he could buy with three hundred dollars.

"Finders keepers," said Andrew.

"You can keep it if there's no identification," said Rosa.

John's fingers trembled as he checked the cellophane windows. "Nuts, the guy's name and phone number are in here. It's even got his picture!"

John threw down the wallet. Andrew quickly picked it up. "I bet the owner doesn't know exactly how much money is here. We could keep twenty bucks. Like a reward."

For a moment John considered Andrew's idea. "It wouldn't be right," he said. "Jesus would give it all back. We'll feel better if we do what Jesus wants us to do." They all headed home to call the owner.

"You are to live clean, innocent lives as children of God in a dark world." *(Philippians 2:15)*

What would you do if you found money?
What would Jesus say about Andrew's attitude?

Sarah and the Club

Chelsea and her friends turned their backs, but Sarah still heard them laughing at her. This school was smaller than her old one, but Sarah found it was harder to make friends.

Chelsea called loudly, "You can't join our club! You don't wear designer jeans!"

Sarah looked down at the shirt and jeans that had seemed so nice when she put them on that morning. The ache in her chest grew.

That night at bedtime, Sarah said, "Mommy, I need some new pants and tops."

"But we just bought you school clothes," said Mother.

"They aren't what the other girls wear," Sarah insisted.

Her mother was quiet for a moment. "Did something happen at school today, honey?"

Sarah burst out sobbing. "Chelsea said I can't join her club. My clothes are all wrong. All the other fourth-grade girls are in the club."

Her mother frowned. "This is a problem. Let's ask Jesus what to do." After they prayed together, Sarah's mother sang softly while Sarah fell asleep.

At breakfast the next morning, Mother asked, "Sarah, would you like to surprise Chelsea? Every time she says something mean or tries to leave you out, you could do the opposite. Say something nice. She won't expect that."

"That *would* surprise her," Sarah agreed.

"After a while, she may change her attitude toward you," Mother said. "And, well…I think it's what Jesus would do. Remember how he treated those who nailed him on the cross?"

"Yes. He asked God to forgive them," said Sarah. "Let's pray, Mommy. I want to forgive all the girls for being mean. Let's ask Jesus to give me kind words for Chelsea."

Jesus said, "Love your enemies! Pray for those who persecute you! In that way, you will be acting as true children of your Father in heaven." *(Matthew 5:44–45)*

When has someone treated you badly? What did you do?
What would Jesus want you to do when others are mean to you?

The Burning Bush

Tara's bedroom door crashed open and her younger brother burst into the room. "Hurry! Call the fire department!" he cried.

Tara quickly took off her headphones. "What's the matter?" she asked.

"There's a big fire by our garage!" Bobby said, looking scared. "It could burn down our house!"

Tara quickly called 911 and gave the firefighters their address. Then she and Bobby ran outside. Next to the garage, a bush crackled with flames. It threatened to ignite the house.

"Pray!" Tara screamed, feeling panicky. She quickly attached the garden hose to the outside faucet and turned on the water.

"Jesus, we need your help!" she prayed out loud as she squirted a gushing stream of water on the bush. "And fast!" The flames began to die down and were replaced by a thick column of smoke. One side of the house was black with soot.

Firefighters arrived moments later. They poured more water on the bush to make sure the fire wouldn't restart. Then Tara heard a car door slam.

"What happened?" Mom asked as she ran up to them.

"Bobby played with matches and started the fire," said Tara.

"Tara, I put you in charge. It was your responsibility to watch your little brother while I went grocery shopping. I was depending on you."

"Mom, it's my fault, too," explained Bobby. "I found some matches in our camping stuff in the garage. I thought they were wet. I know I'm not supposed to play with matches, but I did. I'm sorry."

On Saturday, Bobby and Tara helped Mom sand and paint the charred side of the house. They planted a new bush, too. They knew that was what Jesus wanted them to do.

"I want you to see clearly what is right and to stay innocent of any wrong." *(Romans 16:19)*

When have you caused a problem by failing to be responsible?
What does Jesus want us to do when we have been irresponsible?

Sarah's Victory

Sarah ran into the kitchen, grabbed a cookie, and danced around her mother.

"I've been doing what you said, Mom. I'm trying to be as nice as I can when Chelsea and her mean friends laugh and make fun of me. It's hard! But I'm praying every day and Jesus is helping me be kind to Chelsea and the other girls."

Mother waved her dish towel like a flag. "Hurrah!" she said. "How has Chelsea treated you lately?"

"Well, she still won't let me join their club. And she won't let me play wall ball during recess. But it doesn't bother me anymore." Sarah hugged her mother. "You gave me a good idea, Mom, when you suggested I say something nice to Chelsea whenever she is mean. I know it always surprises her. The other day she said my shirt looked ugly. I just smiled back and told her the truth about what she was wearing. I said, 'You certainly have a beautiful skirt and top, Chelsea. Those colors look terrific with your red hair.'"

"Have any of the other girls noticed what you're doing?" asked Mother.

"Oh, yes! Some of them smile at me in the hall. And today one girl asked me to play basketball! I really think someday we'll all be friends."

"Don't let evil get the best of you, but conquer evil by doing good."
(Romans 12:21)

When has someone been mean to you?
How would Jesus want you to respond?

Are Little Things Important?

Get Set Place the following items in a small paper bag: a straight pin, a match, an acorn (or other nut), a package of flower seeds, and a little water in a jar.

Go!

Lift the pin out of the paper bag.

What could a dirty pin do if it pricked you?

Hold up the match. *What could one small match do?*

Show the acorn. *What can one small acorn do?*

Open and pass the packet of flower seeds.

How big will these seeds grow?

Pass the jar of water. A few drops of water won't quench our thirst, but a lot of water can... (cause a flood, make a lake for swimming, etc.).

Read James 3:3–6.

What little things are big in God's sight?

Think and *share:*

What are some little things you've done that turned out to be important?
What little but important things would Jesus want you to do today?

A New You

Get Set   In the kitchen, set out carrot sticks, pineapple slices, celery, and cherries. Fold a sheet of paper in half and cut out the shape of butterfly wings. Color the wings if you wish. Tape the wings to a straw to form a body.

Go!

Read   John 11:25–26.

What did Jesus call himself?

Fly   your butterfly by waving the straw up and down.

How does a butterfly remind us of Jesus' resurrection?

Tell   about the various stages a butterfly goes through in its development.

Where else in nature do we see "resurrection" and new life?

Read   Luke 24:35–49.

How was Jesus different after his resurrection?
What do you think our bodies will be like in heaven?

Make   Butterfly Resurrection Salad:

> Place a carrot stick on a plate for the body. Cut a pineapple slice in half and turn the halves outward to form wings. Add a cherry for the head. tiny strips of celery for antennae.

Pray   together, thanking God for the promise of resurrection and a new you in heaven. Enjoy the salad!

Brave Barney

"Are you afraid?" whispered Blake to his twelve-year-old twin in the next hospital bed.

"No, are you?" Barney whispered back in the dark.

"A little bit. I'm worried that we might die. The doctors don't know if your body will reject my kidney." He choked back a sob. "And I hope my other kidney will work all right."

"God made your kidney a perfect match for mine," said Barney softly. "I'm trusting God will heal both of us."

He paused. "But I don't think we should be afraid to die. Remember when we went to Seattle to see Grandma and Grandpa last Christmas? We fell asleep on the way and didn't even wake up when we got to their place."

"Right!" agreed Blake. "I never felt Dad carry me from the car to Grandpa's house."

"Neither did I! In the morning we woke up in that king-sized water bed and wondered where we were. We had never been in our grandparents' new apartment."

Blake laughed. "Bouncing around in that bed was neat!"

"That's why we don't have to worry about dying," said Barney. "We'll just fall asleep down here and Jesus will carry us to heaven. We'll wake up healthy in God's wonderful home. We don't need to be afraid. Jesus will help us when it's time to die."

"How we thank God, who gives us victory over…death through Jesus Christ our Lord!" *(1 Corinthians 15:57)*

 *Why does Jesus not want us to be afraid to die?*

Someday We Will See

Mary Beth prayed as she hurried home from grade school. *Jesus, I know Grandma won't live much longer. I would like to be there and hold her hand when you take her to heaven.*

Every day Mary Beth used to come home from school to afternoon tea parties with Grandma. The house would smell of peppermint tea, Scottish shortbread cookies, and flowers from the garden. But now Grandma was blind and paralyzed. She spent all day in bed.

Opening the door to Grandma's room, Mary Beth found both of her parents standing by the bed. Grandma seemed to be sleeping.

Father spoke softly, "The doctor was just here. He says Grandma's heart is very weak."

Taking her grandmother's frail hand, Mary Beth said, "It's me, Grandma. I love you and I'm praying for you. You're going to be with Jesus soon. That's good for you, but hard for me. I'll miss you. But I know…you'll be waiting for me in heaven."

Mary Beth wiped her tears, bent down, and kissed Grandma's cheek. Then she and her parents quietly sang "Amazing Grace" together.

When they finished singing, Grandma suddenly opened her eyes very wide and looked toward the foot of her bed. Her wrinkled face broke into a broad smile and she exclaimed in a clear voice, "There's Jesus! And, oh, he is so beautiful!" Then Grandma closed her eyes and breathed her last breath.

"Oh!" said Mary Beth. "Grandma could see when she died!"

Mary Beth and her parents prayed and thanked God for the blessing of Grandma's life. "And thank you, Jesus," added Mary Beth, "for letting me be with Grandma when she saw you. I can't wait to see you, too!"

"In my body I will see God!…I will see him with my own eyes."
(Job 19:26, 27)

What would Jesus want you to tell someone who didn't have long to live?
What does Jesus want you to remember when a Christian dies?

The Cocoon

Eric saw tears in his mother's eyes when she sat down on the front porch steps. "I need to talk to you," she said.

She must have bad news, thought Eric, sitting down and leaning against her arm.

"I know you'll feel sad when you hear this," his mother said softly. "Grandma just phoned to tell us Uncle Ben died this morning." She hugged her son tightly. "Remember how he loved you and taught you to play chess? He's been sick with cancer a long time, but now Jesus is giving him a new life in—"

Suddenly Mother stopped. She reached down in the grass by the porch. "Look, Eric!" she said. "A cocoon! This is strange. Cocoons are usually found in trees or bushes. I wonder if Jesus sent it to us."

She held up the brown cocoon for Eric to see. "A caterpillar has a difficult life. It crawls very slowly and must spend all day eating and trying to keep from being eaten. Then it spins a cocoon and looks like it's dead. Would Jesus want us to be sad that the caterpillar is gone? Or should we remember the new and wonderful life—"

"Oh, Mom!" interrupted Eric. "It's coming out!"

They held still as the butterfly crawled out, sat in Mother's palm, and dried its wings. Eric quietly watched the beautiful blue and green wings gain strength and lift the butterfly up in the air. It circled above his head before flying off.

"Jesus came out of the grave with a new body, too," said Eric. "If Jesus turns an ugly caterpillar into a beautiful butterfly, I know he will give Uncle Ben a new body in heaven. I wonder what our new bodies will look like!"

"Our bodies now disappoint us, but when they are raised, they will be full of glory...full of power." *(1 Corinthians 15:43)*

What would Jesus want you to remember if someone you loved died?
Why is Jesus' resurrection important?

A Welcoming Home

"How much longer until Yuki gets here?" Belinda looked at the photograph of a smiling Asian girl. She hoped Yuki, their Japanese exchange student, would like living with them for the next year.

Her mother smoothed the bedspread and rearranged the flowers on the dressing table. "We'll head for the airport in about a half hour."

"Do you think she'll like the candy I bought her?" Belinda asked, carefully placing a chocolate bar and a red rose on the pillow.

Her mom hugged her. "In Yuki's letters she said she loves chocolate."

"I hope she'll like it here," Belinda said, looking at the freshly ironed curtains.

"I think she will. We've spent lots of time preparing this room just for her. And she already has a place in my heart, even though I don't know her yet."

"Mine, too," said Belinda.

"Did you know that someone far away is preparing a home for you?" her mom asked.

Belinda was surprised. "I'm not an exchange student."

"Jesus is preparing a home for us in heaven, where we'll live forever. And he's doing it with even more love than we have for Yuki."

Belinda glanced out the window and saw an airplane soaring in the sky. She smiled. Someday she'd take a trip to heaven. "Thank you, Jesus, for preparing a special place just for me," she whispered.

Jesus said, "I am going to prepare a place for you." *(John 14:2)*

 *Are you sure Jesus is preparing a place for you?*

No More Tears

Brittany closed her eyes and raised her hands while she sang, "God is so good…he's so good to me. I'll praise his name…he's so good to me."

At the end of the song, her father said quietly, "Let's pray for Mommy."

Brittany closed her eyes and said, "Dear Jesus, please take care of Mommy. And help me and Daddy not to be too sad." She opened her eyes to look at her mother sleeping on the hospital bed in their living room. Her mother's face was thin and pale. The doctors had tried many treatments, but none of them worked. Now she only woke up and talked to Brittany for a few minutes each day.

"Mommy will only live here on earth another day or two," said her father.

Brittany didn't quite understand what happened when someone died. The six-year-old asked, "What's heaven like? Is it fun?" Remembering the cake and ice cream at her friend's birthday party, Brittany added, "Does the food taste good?"

"Mommy will be so glad to see Jesus when she gets to heaven. She won't hurt or feel any more pain. There are no more tears in heaven," Brittany's father explained. "Heaven is more beautiful than anything we've seen. And I'm sure the food tastes yummy good."

He tickled his daughter under her chin. "In heaven you'll laugh and sing and giggle more than you ever have before! Just think—you'll never have to go to bed!"

Smiling, but with tears in his eyes, he added, "It's hard to tell Mommy good-bye. But we don't have to worry. Jesus will take good care of her."

"Mommy told me she'd be waiting for me at heaven's gate," said Brittany, hugging her daddy. "She said Jesus would take care of me till then."

"God will wipe away all their tears." *(Revelation 7:17)*

Are you looking forward to being with Jesus in heaven?
Who is waiting for you in heaven? (Jesus is!)

Are You Ready?

Get Set Set out a small suitcase or overnight bag. Stack up items to be packed, such as clothes, a toothbrush and toothpaste, and books. On the bottom of the pile, put photos of your family and friends.

Go!

Open up your suitcase and begin packing.

What would you pack for a trip?
What's the biggest trip you've taken? the best? What is the <u>last</u> trip we will all take?

Read John 14:1–3.

What did Jesus promise to do?
Can we take anything with us to heaven?

Hold up photos.

Who will be waiting for us in heaven?
How do you get ready for your trip to heaven?

Read Revelation 22:1–5, 14.

How do we "wash our robes" so we're ready to enter God's home?
Have you asked Jesus to forgive and "wash" you?

Join pinkie fingers and *pray:* Dear Jesus, thank you for dying for all the wrong things we've done. Forgive us and wash us clean. Keep us close to you and to each other so we are ready to see you face to face. Amen.

Rewards in Heaven

Get Set Set out several pieces of jewelry, straw or dried weeds, and a few scraps of wood or twigs. On slips of paper write simple household jobs that can be completed quickly, such as dusting the living room, cleaning the kitchen sink, sweeping the kitchen floor, or emptying wastebaskets. Put the slips and a timer in a paper bag. Have a CD of favorite Christian music and a board game ready.

Go!

Read 1 Corinthians 3:5–15.

What is the foundation we build our life on? (verse 11)

Explain: Jesus gives us the gift of forgiveness and eternal life. Now our job is to build on this new life we have in Jesus.

What do we do that is like building with gold? With wood or straw?

Read verse 8 again.

What will God reward us for?
How does it make you feel to know that someday you'll be rewarded in heaven?
Does God view the simple jobs we do each day as part of our life's work? Explain.

Have everyone **pull** a job out of the bag.

Give everyone three minutes to complete their job. **Play** music as you work and encourage everyone to sing along. When the jobs are complete, **gather** for prayer. Ask God to help you do his work faithfully and well.

Reward yourselves for your work by playing a favorite game together.

Connor's Trophies

Connor silently watched his brother step onto the winners' platform. The crowd chanted. "Tra-vis, Tra-vis, Tra-vis…" Travis held up the golden trophy while the band played and applause shook the bleachers. Connor knew he should be happy for his older brother, but he felt discouraged. *It's no fair,* he thought. *I had polio.*

When the family returned home from the wrestling tournament, Connor hurriedly jumped in bed and turned off the light just as his father stepped into the room. His father came in and sat down on the bed. "Your brother keeps winning awards," he said. "Do you wonder if you'll ever win any?"

Tears filling his eyes, Connor nodded. "I'm a big failure," he said quietly. "People will never cheer for me like they do for Travis."

"You may never wrestle or run like Travis, but you're no failure! I remember how you patiently helped your baby brother learn to walk. Tonight you cleared the table before the game. You have been a servant…like Jesus." Father paused. "Oh, Connor, you can't imagine the award ceremony Jesus is going to have for you someday."

Connor opened his eyes wide. "For me?"

"Yes! We don't get to heaven because of anything we've done—Jesus is the only way. But Jesus never forgets our *serving.* He has promised to reward everything good we do. Don't you think God's rewards will be a lot more exciting than a roomful of trophies?"

Father hugged Connor and they knelt together to pray.

"Jesus," Connor whispered, "help me do a good job of loving and serving my family. I want to live for you. And thanks for having Dad tell me that I'm not a failure."

Jesus said, "Whoever wants to be a leader among you must be your servant." *(Matthew 20:26)*

Have you ever felt like a failure?
What would Jesus say to you?

Befriending Matt

Andrew rushed toward the gang of boys surrounding Matt on the playground.

"Hey!" Andrew yelled. "Get away from him!" Then he thought, *Why am I helping Matt? I don't even like him.*

Pushing his way through the crowd, Andrew yelled, "What do you think you're doing?" He tried to sound tough.

The boy twisting Matt's arm let go and faced Andrew. "Do you want to fight?" he asked Andrew. Matt took off running.

Andrew had never fought before. *How am I going to fight six guys all at once?* he wondered. He felt sick as he said quietly, "Not really."

To his surprise, the boy said, "Forget it. I'll get that little punk another time."

When Andrew got back to the classroom, Matt was in the reading corner with a book. Matt looked up and asked, "Why did you help me?"

"I didn't want to," Andrew said, "but in Proverbs God says if you see anyone being dragged off to slaughter you should help. And it looked like those boys were going to slaughter you!"

Matt agreed. Andrew waited for him to say thanks, but he said nothing and went back to reading.

Oh well, thought Andrew. *I know Jesus will reward me someday.*

"Don't get discouraged and give up, for we will reap a harvest of blessing." *(Galatians 6:9)*

What does Jesus' promise mean to you?
Do you think Andrew will be rewarded on earth?
Why or why not?

Kevin's Messy Kitchen

"Kevin!" a voice called from the kitchen.

Kevin sat down at his desk and pretended to study. He knew Mother wasn't happy about the mess in the kitchen, but he didn't care. When his bedroom door opened, he didn't look up from his book.

"Okay," said Mother. "Tell me—why can't you clean up after yourself? You've made a mess in the kitchen every day this week. I know you're hungry after school, but you don't have to spill cereal, leave the milk out, and scatter dirty dishes all over the counter. Why are you acting like this?"

Kevin thought for a minute. He looked up at his mother and admitted, "I guess I've been feeling mad."

"Mad about what?" asked Mother.

"I feel like it doesn't matter what I do. Someone always complains. When I do something right, nobody notices anyway, so why bother?"

Mother put her arm around his shoulder. "I'm glad you told me how you feel. I guess I take it for granted that you empty wastebaskets and unload the dishwasher. And I do forget to thank you for cleaning up after supper. Will you please forgive me?"

Kevin hugged his mother. "I forgive you, Mom. Will you forgive me, too?"

"Of course," said Mother. "Aren't you glad we can forgive, like Jesus does?"

"Yes," said Kevin. He realized how much better he felt inside. He hadn't enjoyed being mean and hurtful. "It's hard to help when it seems like nobody appreciates it," he explained. "But I'm going to pray about having a good attitude—for Jesus' sake."

"Don't forget, Kevin, someday Jesus will thank you...even when no one else does."

Jesus said, "See, I am coming soon, and my reward is with me, to repay all according to their deeds." *(Revelation 22:12)*

How does Jesus' promise make you feel?
What will you do for Jesus today?

Tim's Thoughtful Gift

Tim held the chair for his grandmother when she came to eat dinner. As the rest of the family sat down at the table, Tim's father asked, "What do you want for Christmas, Mom?"

Each Christmas, the family tried to figure out what to get their seventy-five-year-old widowed grandmother who lived alone.

Grandma doesn't need anything, thought Tim. *Her clothes from last Christmas still look nice.*

Grandma Laurel smiled. "Well," she said slowly, "I can't think of anything I need. But there is one thing I would like. The older I get, the more I want to love others like Jesus loves me. If I had extra money, I'd give it to the widows and orphans fund of the Good Samaritan charity. For only ten dollars they can buy enough rice and beans to feed fifty people."

The next Saturday when Tim's family went Christmas shopping, his parents picked out a flowered tablecloth for Grandma's kitchen table. Tim's sister bought her a coffee mug and some napkins. Tim kept wondering what to give his grandmother. When he prayed about it, an idea came to him.

On Christmas morning after Grandma opened all her gifts, Tim handed her a special card he'd made on his computer. Tim watched tears fill Grandma's eyes as she read: *Grandma, I love you! This is my gift to give to your favorite charity. Love from Tim.* Inside was a new ten-dollar bill!

She smiled at Tim. "Thank you! This will help feed fifty widows and orphans! It makes me very happy to be able to send it from both of us! This Christmas gift will show God's love to many people."

Tim hugged Grandma and felt the same joy inside his own heart.

"Remember that the Lord will reward each of us for the good we do."
(Ephesians 6:8)

What would Jesus want you to give to others in need?
What is God's promise for those who give?

First to See Jesus

"Daddy, why did God let me get cystic fibrosis?" asked David.

Dad turned on David's football lamp and said, "I'm not sure he did."

David sat up while his dad thumped his back to help him breathe more easily. "Is God trying to punish me?"

"No," said Dad, "God sees and understands things differently than we do."

David leaned forward so his dad could reach lower on his back. "God knows heaven is better than here, right?"

"That's right," said Dad.

David slid between his jungle sheets.

"You are very special, David," said Dad. He tucked David's wool blanket around him and sat down on the edge of David's bed. "You will get to see God sooner than most of us."

"I'll see Jesus before I even grow up," said David. "I feel sort of good about that and sort of bad."

Dad nodded.

"Dad." David felt a lump in his throat. "Will you miss me?"

"Oh, David!" Dad's voice was a hoarse whisper. "You can't imagine how much." David felt Dad's arms around him. "But Mom and I love Jesus, too. We'll see you again in heaven."

"I will take you on a tour around heaven when you get there," said David. He smiled sleepily, closed his eyes, and snuggled against his dad.

Jesus said, "I am leaving you with a gift—peace of mind and heart." *(John 14:27)*

What would Jesus tell someone who didn't have long to live?
Are you looking forward to heaven?

Goodies to Give

Get Set   Set out crisp rice cereal, miniature marshmallows, butter, plastic wrap, and ribbon. You'll also need art supplies for making greeting cards.

Go!

Read   Jesus' words in Matthew 25:31–40.

What does Jesus say is important?
How can we do kind things for Jesus?

Decide   on two or three people who will receive an act of kindness from you today.

Work   together to make crispy rice treats:
>   Place 3 tablespoons butter and 4 cups miniature marshmallows in a large glass bowl.
>   Melt the mixture on very low heat in a microwave oven (or in a large saucepan over low heat).
>   Stir in 6 cups of crisp rice cereal and mix well.
>   Pour into a large buttered cake pan.

While the treats are cooling, **make** simple greeting cards. Have some people **draw** colorful designs on the front of folded paper as others **write** encouraging Bible verses inside.

Cut the treats into squares and **wrap** them with plastic wrap.

Tie the cards to the treats with ribbon and **pray** for the people who will receive them.

Deliver the treats with lots of smiles.

Pizza Faith

Get Set   Secretly prepare a tray of veggies and dip and place it inside an old pizza box. Place the pizza box on a table along with a cordless phone. Write down the number of your favorite pizza delivery restaurant.

Go!

If you phoned out for pizza, would you believe it was going to be delivered?

Call   and order a pizza.

If we truly believe that the pizza is coming, what will we do?

Work together   to set the table and prepare beverages of everyone's choice.

Is anyone doubting whether the delivery man will show up?
Why or why not?
Do you ever doubt that God will answer your prayers?
Why do some people trust pizza delivery men more than they trust God?
Does God promise to give us everything we ask for?

Open   your old pizza box with the vegetables inside.

Does God ever give us something different than what we asked for? Why?
Are the things God gives us sometimes better than the things we ask for?
Explain.

When the pizza arrives, **thank** God for his faithfulness in answering prayer.

Scruffy's Operation

"Scruffy won't die," Tevin said confidently on the way home from the vet's office with his mom. He looked out the car window and added, "I asked Jesus to heal her."

Tevin knew his dog was badly hurt. He had seen the car run over her leg, but he prayed for her right away. "Jesus always answers prayer," he told his mom.

"Jesus always answers," Mom quietly agreed. "But sometimes the answer is no. We can't afford to pay for surgery on Scruffy's leg. I signed the papers for the doctor to put her to sleep. She's in too much pain." Mom's shoulders shook as she started to cry. "He's probably put her to sleep already."

That evening at dinner the whole family looked sad. Tevin tried to comfort them. "Scruffy will be fine. Jesus will save Scruffy."

Dad pulled Tevin onto his lap. "Jesus has the power to do anything," he told Tevin. "But sometimes Jesus chooses not to answer the way we think he should."

Tevin just smiled. Dad looked at Mom, who cleared her throat and said, "Tevin, it is impossible for Scruffy to come home. The vet has put her to sleep by now."

"She'll be fine," Tevin insisted. His parents sighed.

All day Saturday and Sunday Tevin kept asking, "When can we go and get Scruffy?" Mom and Dad silently shook their heads.

Early Monday morning the phone rang. Tevin listened on the extension as Mom talked to the vet.

"I couldn't put Scruffy to sleep," the vet told Mom. "I know she's a special dog. I've kept her on pain medication all weekend. If you would pay for the supplies, I'll operate on her leg at no extra charge."

"Thank you," Mom said, softly crying. "We can afford that."

Tevin ran and hugged his mom. "I knew Jesus would save her."

"For nothing is impossible with God." *(Luke 1:37)*

 *What impossible thing would Jesus want you to pray for?*

Red Shoes

Cecile closed the door to her bedroom, sat on the bottom bunk, and took off her shoes. She briskly rubbed her cold feet to warm them.

She looked at her shoes—her only shoes. Holes as big as quarters stared back at her. This morning she had stuffed cardboard inside them to keep out the snow on her walk to school. But the cardboard quickly fell apart. Soaking wet socks kept her shivering all day.

Cecile didn't know what to do. She couldn't show her mother the shoes. There was no money for anything. Dad hadn't sent child support for three months.

She knelt by her bed and asked, "Jesus, what would you do?" She knew Jesus prayed all night long to his Father. "Were you asking your Father for help, Jesus?"

Cecile knew she couldn't ask her dad for anything.

I can ask my heavenly Father, she thought. *I can ask in Jesus' name.*

"Dear heavenly Father," she prayed. "I need a pair of shoes. May I please have some red ones? I love red...." The doorbell rang and Cecile went to answer it.

Her grade-school teacher stood outside. "Cecile, would you mind if I bought you a pair of shoes? I saw some red ones at the store that look like your style."

"Oh, thank you," said Cecile. *And thank you, Lord!* she added.

Jesus said, "The Father will give you whatever you ask for, using my name." *(John 15:16)*

 *Why doesn't God answer every prayer right away?*

85

The Black Widow Scare

Kent slowly unpacked his toys and books. He didn't like this house where they'd had to move after Dad left. He felt lonely.

"Are you finished unpacking in here?" Mother looked in Kent's bedroom. "I need your help—"

Kent looked at her white face and followed her eyes to the bedroom window. A big black spider sat in the middle of the striped curtain! Kent and his mother were scared to death of spiders.

"Lord, help me," Mother prayed. Grabbing one of Kent's magazines, she whacked the spider and it fell to the floor. Kent cautiously edged his magazine under the spider and turned it over.

"Oh, Mom! See the red mark on its belly? It's a poisonous black widow! What are we going to do? If there is one, there are probably others."

"Let's pray!" urged Mother. They knelt by Kent's bed and prayed, "Dear Jesus, protect us from getting bit. Make these spiders come out where we can see them and get rid of them. Give us courage and take away our fear."

During the next month, Kent and his mother found seven spiders.

"Jesus answered our prayers," Kent told his mother later. "He helped find the spiders and gave us courage to kill them. Now we haven't seen any spiders for months and we're not afraid anymore."

Jesus asked, "Why are you so afraid? Do you still not have faith in me?" *(Mark 4:40)*

When has Jesus helped you to be brave?
Where in your life do you need more courage?

Danger on the Lake

"Paddle harder on the left!" Austin screamed at his little brother. "We're going in circles!"

Seven-year-old Matthew hit the flat of his canoe paddle on the water. "I'm trying to!" he yelled. Matthew started crying. He looked as terrified as Austin felt. Even Dad, in the other canoe with four-year-old Julie, looked scared.

Austin remembered how Mom and Dad had argued earlier.

"You can't take three kids out on a lake in canoes," she had said. "Storms come up suddenly here in Minnesota."

"Don't worry. We'll be fine." Dad had laughed and kissed her.

Austin knew Mom tended to worry a lot, so he hadn't thought too much of her objections. But this time her worries were right on target.

Another wave smashed against their canoe and pushed them further from shore. *We'll never make it back,* thought Austin. *Matthew and I aren't strong enough to battle two-foot waves. The next wave will topple our canoe.*

Dad yelled, "Stick together!" But the powerful waves pushed them apart. Austin could see Dad frantically paddling to reach them. Julie's little face looked white. Her lips were moving. Austin knew she was praying.

"Pray!" Austin screamed at Matthew over the roar of the wind and waves.

Jesus, save us! Austin prayed, pulling against the water.

Austin felt a jerk as Dad's strong hand grabbed the side of his canoe. Dad wrapped a rope around Austin's seat, then around the seat in his own canoe. Now they could join forces.

"Paddle and trust God!" Dad shouted.

For the next hour they fought against the wind and waves. The shore gradually moved closer. Finally they heard the scraping of stones against the bottoms of their canoes. They all tumbled out and leaped around on the beach shouting, "Thank you, Jesus!"

Jesus said, "I am here! Don't be afraid." *(Matthew 14:27)*

When has Jesus helped you in time of trouble? What are you trusting him for today?

Mountain Rescue

"Are we lost?" asked Dana's little sister anxiously. Dana stroked Angie's hair and tried to keep from crying. She wondered how they'd gotten lost. She and her family had hiked on Lazy Mountain for years.

Glaring at her older brother Luke, Dana fussed, "You and your shortcuts!" Her legs stung from wading through the scrubby bitterbrush that grew all over the mountain.

"Poor Angie." Dana squeezed her sister's hand. "Your legs and hands are scratched, too."

Angie sighed and brushed back the dark curls hanging in tangles around her dirty face. "Will we be home before bedtime?" she asked. "I'm cold."

Dana stared at the snow-covered mountains in the distance. Alaska could be cold at night, even in the summer.

"You can see our house right down there," Luke said impatiently. "We just have to keep hiking toward the house."

Dana retorted, "You mean that tiny dot way down there? We should have stayed on the path, Luke!"

Angie looked from one to the other. Then she bowed her head, folded her hands, and prayed. "Jesus, we're lost. Please come get us. And please come soon. Amen."

Dana said, "Dad must be looking for us by now. Put my jacket on a stick. Hold it up while we climb down. Maybe the red color will stand out against all the bushes."

Luke held up the stick with Dana's jacket on it and they continued to half walk and half slide down the mountain slope.

Then they heard a shout. Off to their right they saw a figure waving both hands above his head.

"It's Tom Eagle!" cried Angie, recognizing their Native American friend. She smiled at Luke and Dana. "Jesus answered my prayer. He sent Tom to rescue us!"

"When they call on me, I will answer; I will be with them in trouble. I will rescue them." *(Psalm 91:15)*

Take a minute to thank Jesus for what he did.
Do you believe Jesus would have died just for you?

Prayer and Praise Tree

Get Set   Set out a loaf of bread, a large stone, a fish (plastic or canned), and a rubber snake or a picture of a snake. You'll also need tape, green and brown construction paper, and markers.

Go!

Read   Matthew 7:7–11.

Ask   someone to use the bread, stone, fish, and snake to **explain** this Scripture in their own words.

Have each person **tell** one reason we should never stop praying.

Why can we be sure that our heavenly Father will give us good gifts?

Work   together to make a Prayer and Praise Tree:

Cut a trunk and branches from brown construction paper.
Tape the trunk and branches to a wall in a hallway or garage.
Cut green paper into leaf shapes.
Write prayer requests on some leaf shapes.
Write praises for answers to prayer on other leaves.
Tape the leaves to the tree.
Touch each prayer request leaf and pray about that request together.

Add   praise and prayer leaves to the tree over the next several months.

Place   praises for answered prayer next to the matching prayer request leaves.

Watch   your praises grow!

Playing Favorites?

Get Set   Collect two outfits from the closet of the largest person in your family—one dressy outfit and one of shabby work clothes. Set out a few dollar bills and some change.

Go!

Ask   one person to put on the dressy clothes and another to put on the work clothes.

Who would you rather go out to eat with—someone in dressy clothes or someone in shabby work clothes? Why?

Give   the dollar bills to the person in dressy clothes; give the change to the person in shabby clothes.

Who would you rather go shopping with?
Do you sometimes treat people differently because of what they have or wear?

Read   James 2:1–9.

Does Jesus have favorites?
What does Jesus see when he looks at people?
What would Jesus want us to see in other people?

Pray,   asking God's blessing on those who have little money and few possessions.

Super Friend

Kenny hurriedly put on his blue-and-red bathrobe, tied a belt around his waist, and placed a baseball hat backwards on his head. "Here comes Super Friend!" he announced from behind his bedroom door.

Cassie, his three-year-old sister, peeked around the hall closet, waiting for Kenny's bedroom door to open. "Help!" she hollered. "A T-Rex is going to get me!"

"Super Friend to the rescue," called Kenny, leaping into the hall. He ran to his sister and bent down so she could climb up on his back.

"Hurry, young maiden. We must escape!" He hooked his arms around her legs while she wound her arms around his neck. He ran down the hall, around the living room, and into the kitchen, carrying his little sister.

"My hero!" she shrieked, bobbing up and down on his back.

Exhausted, Kenny collapsed on the sofa. "You are safe now and far away from the T-Rex," he assured her with a hug. She smiled at him and ran off to play with her dolls.

When Kenny went to bed that night, he told his father, "I know Jesus wants me to love my little sister. I'm trying to be the best brother I can be. Whenever I make Cassie happy, I feel that Jesus is happy, too."

"Love is patient and kind. Love is not jealous or boastful or proud or rude." *(1 Corinthians 13:4–5)*

How is Kenny like Jesus?
What would Jesus say about the way you
treat younger children?

Too Mean to Love

Jill took a plate of cookies to the new family next door. She smiled at a girl about her age. "Want to play?" Jill asked.

"Forget it, Fatso."

The words cut Jill's heart like a knife. She rushed back home in tears.

The next day Jill wanted to disappear when the new girl was ushered into her fourth-grade class and assigned the seat next to her. The teacher said, "Please welcome our new student, Gertie." The students snickered. Gertie scowled.

Jill winced, imagining the names Gertie would be called at recess. Sure enough, the children on the playground chanted, "Dirty Gertie, can't be purty."

Gertie swore at her taunters and played by herself.

Jill walked over to her. "Want to play tetherball?"

"I have enough problems without hanging around *you!*" said Gertie.

The next few weeks Jill tried to be kind to Gertie for Jesus' sake. One day Jill asked, "Would you go to Sunday school with me?"

Gertie sneered and walked away. Jill continued smiling and being friendly. Then one day Gertie surprised Jill by saying, "I guess I'll go to Sunday school with you."

That Sunday was Easter. Gertie listened carefully to the story of Jesus' dying on the cross and rising again. After class she told Jill, "Jesus couldn't love me. I'm too mean."

"That's why Jesus died," said Jill. "He took the punishment for everything we've done wrong. Jesus knows all about us and still loves us."

"Even me?" asked Gertie.

"Even you!" said Jill, giving Gertie a big hug.

Gertie asked Jesus to be her Savior. She continued to go to Sunday school with Jill. Soon Gertie's bad language and attitude changed. Everyone said Gertie was a new person!

Jesus said, "Therefore, go and make disciples of all the nations.... Teach these new disciples to obey all the commands I have given you."
(Matthew 28:19, 20)

Who is difficult for you to love?
How could you share Jesus with that person?

Better Than a Party

"But I want to go out too!" wailed Melissa. "It's not fair! I don't want to stay home because my ear hurts." She laid her head on the kitchen table and sobbed.

Larry tried on the mask for his costume for the Pumpkin Party. "Woof!" he said. "Guess what I am."

She glanced up and wailed, "I want to be a dalmatian puppy, too! I don't want to miss the Pumpkin Party!"

Larry fastened a black-spotted sheet around his waist and left for church with a carload of friends. Melissa played with her dollhouse a while, but nothing seemed fun. Later in the evening, the door burst open and Larry returned, carrying a full sack.

Taking off his outfit, he told his sister, "Melissa! Put on my costume and come upstairs! Bring your treat bag and knock on the first bedroom door."

Melissa put on the outfit, climbed the stairs, and knocked on the door. It opened and there stood Larry wearing his father's jacket and hat. "Hello, little doggie. You look great! I have a surprise for you!" He pulled something out of his coat pocket and dropped it in her sack. Melissa looked in and saw a huge orange-and-yellow lollipop.

"Go to my neighbor," Larry said, dashing into the bathroom.

Melissa laughed as she knocked on the bathroom door.

Larry peeked out wearing a shower cap and his mother's bathrobe. "You caught me in the shower! But here's a treat for you." He tossed some gum into Melissa's bag. Dashing to the linen closet, Larry repeated his performance, then went back to the first room again as Melissa followed.

She finally scrambled downstairs, calling, "Mom, see what Larry did for me! It was more fun than any Pumpkin Party I've ever been to!"

Jesus said, "I command you to love each other in the same way that I love you." *(John 15:12)*

Where can you show the love of Jesus to others today? What are you willing to do to make others happy?

A New Start

Thomas squared his shoulders and entered the fourth-grade classroom in his new school. *If I look scared, the kids will pick on me,* he thought. He still remembered how a kid named Jack had shut him in a box at the beginning of first grade.

"School starts in ten minutes," said the teacher. Thomas took the seat she pointed out and tried to look busy putting his books away. The rest of the kids chatted in groups. No one talked to him.

This desk is almost as big as the box Jack trapped me in, he thought. Thomas shuddered, remembering the panic he felt when Jack sat on the box, nearly squashing him.

"Hey, Tommy!"

Thomas looked up. His archenemy, Jack, was standing at the back of the room and grinning.

"It's me, Jack! I knew you in first grade." A skinny kid with freckles ran up and offered Thomas a high five.

He's just a little wimp! thought Thomas. *I must be a head taller than he is. How come I thought he was such a tough guy? I could finally get even...* Thomas smiled. *Or I could do what Jesus wants me to do and finally forgive him.*

Thomas turned to Jack with a smile and slapped a high five. "It's great to see you, Jack," he said. "I'm going to need a friend in this school."

Jesus said, "If you refuse to forgive others, your Father [in heaven] will not forgive you." *(Matthew 6:15)*

 *Why does Jesus want you to be a forgiving person?*

Encouraging Words

Jessica watched the new fourth-grade teacher write out her name on the blackboard: Mrs. Wilson. *I wonder what she's like,* thought Jessica.

Mrs. Wilson said, "I'm new and I don't know anyone at this school. As a way for me to get to know you, we'll do something special. Every morning this month, I will put a student's name on the board. You will each write one nice thing about him or her. Then that student will stand at the front of the class as you read your papers aloud."

A murmur ran through the class. Jessica leaned over to Denise and whispered, "It beats doing math or science!"

That morning, Mrs. Wilson wrote *Candace Avery* on the board. Candy was popular and most of the students wrote things like *pretty, smart,* and *nice* on their papers. Candy smiled. And Jessica felt good complimenting her.

The next day *Jessica Barnhart* was written on the board. At first Jessica was a little nervous. It embarrassed her when she heard others say she was a *fun* and *caring* person, but she felt a warm glow inside the rest of the day.

Wednesday morning, *Clint Basher* appeared on the board. When they saw the class bully's name, the students sighed and moaned. A few threw down their pencils and refused to write anything.

"Everyone must participate," said Mrs. Wilson.

Clint stood defiantly at the front of the room. *Nice brown eyes, good soccer player, clean fingernails, nice to his dog,* said his classmates. As the students handed Clint their papers, he grew less and less cocky. He didn't even pick a fight at recess. After school, he carried Mrs. Wilson's briefcase to her car for her.

"Mrs. Wilson had us do what Jesus would do," said Jessica to Denise. "It sure makes a difference!"

"Accept each other just as Christ has accepted you." *(Romans 15:7)*

How does Jesus' love change people?
Who could you accept and encourage today?

A Gift of Love

Get Set Collect paper, pencils, Bibles, scissors, ribbon, gift wrap, tape, and cardboard tubes from bathroom tissue or paper towels. Fill a bowl with sticks of gum, wrapped candies, and change. You'll also need large cups, root beer, ice cream, and spoons.

Go!

Read 1 Corinthians 16:14.

Take turns telling how others have shown Jesus' love to you.

Plan a surprise to bless your neighbors.

Make a small gift of love for each of your guests:

Cut pieces of wrapping paper larger than the cardboard tubes.

Wrap the tubes in the paper and secure with tape.

Twist the paper on one end of the tube only and use the ribbon to tie it.

Fill the tube with small treats.

Write favorite Bible verses on slips of paper and place a verse in each tube.

Twist and tie the other end of the paper.

Invite neighbors to join you for a root beer float. Place a "love gift" by each guest's cup.

Forgiving Hearts

Get Set   Collect as many heart-shaped items as you can find, such as greeting cards, candy, boxes, jewelry, wall plaques, wreaths, buttons, or pillows.

Go!   Let each person *choose* a heart-shaped item to hold.

What comes to mind when you think of the word <u>heart</u>?

Read   Psalm 51:1–4, 10–13.

What kind of a heart did King David want?
How do we get a "clean heart"?
When you ask God to forgive you, what happens to your sin?

Read   Micah 7:18–20.

Share   a time when someone forgave you.

What was that like?

Read   Luke 23:34.

What was the first thing Jesus said when he was on the cross?

Place   all the heart items in the center of the table.

Ask   yourself:

Is my heart clean? Is there anyone I haven't forgiven?

Pray   silently, thanking Jesus for his forgiveness. Pray for someone you have a hard time forgiving. Pray for someone who may be holding a grudge against you.

The Rock Collection

"Look at this beautiful rock!" said Nicole. "This is perfect for my collection." She placed it in the glass jar with several other special rocks she'd gathered during the past year.

"Let me help you collect some more," offered Jenna. "The tide washed in a whole bunch of new rocks this morning. I'll use my bucket to pick up lots of pretty ones for you."

The two girls ran along the curvy line of rocks, broken shells, and seaweed left by the retreating ocean tide. They explored the shoreline, collecting the shiniest and most colorful rocks they could find. Soon Nicole's glass jar was half full of rocks of all shapes, sizes, and colors.

Some time later Jenna came running barefoot through the sand. She lifted up her bucket and said, "Here's my great addition to your collection." Laughing, she dumped the contents of her bucket on top of Nicole's beautiful rocks.

Nicole gasped. Jenna's bucket was filled with *trash*—old bottle caps, stinky lobster legs, tangled seaweed, and dirty sand! Jenna giggled and ran farther up the beach, where she started building a sand castle.

Nicole dumped everything out of her jar and tried to pick out her special rocks. Finally, gathering what she could, she ran home in tears. She didn't know why Jenna deliberately messed up her collection. As she cried into her pillow, Nicole kept remembering one thing: Jesus wanted her to forgive, even though Jenna had played a nasty trick.

Later she told Jenna, "You thought your joke was funny, but you really hurt my feelings and made me angry. I've been praying about it a lot, and with Jesus' help, I have forgiven you."

Peter asked Jesus, "How often should I forgive someone who sins against me? Seven times?"

"No!" Jesus replied, "seventy times seven!" *(Matthew 18:21–22)*

When have you found it hard to forgive someone? Why does Jesus want us to forgive everyone?

Cody's Stepmother

Cody's stepmother, Janet, sliced a thick slab of ham and offered it to Cody.

"I'm not hungry," he lied. His stomach rumbled loudly. Janet glanced at his dad.

"Cody, you never eat anything when you come over here," his dad said. Cody looked at his plate.

"I'll have a couple olives," Cody said. He had opened the can of olives himself. Janet hadn't touched them.

Janet passed the scalloped potatoes to Cody. The smell made his mouth water. He handed the bowl of potatoes to his dad without taking any.

Putting down her fork, Janet cleared her throat. "Cody," she said, "I've been wanting to talk to you."

Cody couldn't look at her. If Dad hadn't met Janet three years ago, he'd still be married to Mom. And Cody would have a family. Cody hated Janet.

"Your dad and I started attending church." Out of the corner of his eye he saw Janet take his dad's hand. "We both accepted Jesus into our hearts last week and Jesus forgave us for the terrible things we've done." Janet's voice broke.

"I can't undo all the hurt I've caused you," she told him, "but I want you to know how sorry I am. I'm praying that you can forgive me."

"I'm sorry, too," his dad said. Cody looked at him. Tears rolled down his dad's cheeks. "Can you forgive me, Cody?"

Cody's heart pounded. Maybe he could forgive his dad...but Janet? Cody knew Jesus had forgiven him. And he knew Jesus expected him to forgive both his dad and Janet. But he didn't think he could forgive without Jesus' help.

"I'll try. I'm praying that Jesus will help me forgive...both of you." Cody and Janet smiled at each other. And Cody reached for the steaming dish of scalloped potatoes.

"Forgive us our sins, just as we have forgiven those who have sinned against us." *(Matthew 6:12)*

Who does Jesus want you to forgive?
Do you believe Jesus can help you forgive?

Bitter Revenge

"Hit a homer!" Ian shouted.

Kent slammed the baseball to left field and took off running. He touched first base and headed to second. Sam, the second baseman, caught the ball thrown in by the left fielder. He whirled to put Kent out. His glove hit Kent hard, knocking him to the ground before he touched second base.

Kent rolled on the ground in pain. Ian ran out and helped him up. Kent struggled to his feet, rushed Sam at second base, and punched him right in the face.

Ian had never seen Kent so wild. He grabbed Kent's arms to keep him from hitting again.

With his nose bleeding, Sam started kicking. He knocked Kent backwards and his cleated shoe stomped Kent's leg with a vengeance. Kent howled in pain.

By then coaches and parents had poured onto the field to stop the fighting.

As Sam was escorted off the field by his coach, he yelled back at Kent, "That will teach you to hit me!"

Kent hollered back, "I'll get you for this!"

Weeks later, Ian told his father, "Kent used to be fun to play with, but now all he thinks about is getting revenge. He and Sam hate each other. All I can do is pray they will learn to forgive."

"Never pay back evil for evil.... Never avenge yourselves. Leave that to God." *(Romans 12:17, 19)*

When have you felt like paying back evil for evil?
What would Jesus say to people who won't forgive?

Unable to Forgive

Melissa sat in the courtroom beside her mom. She glared at the three teenagers who had broken into their house, slashed their leather couch, and spray painted red words all over their walls.

I hate them, she thought. *I hope the judge punishes them severely!*

The boy who had a lot of rings in his ears and nose turned and looked at her. Melissa locked eyes with him and glared. *Do you know how much I hate you?* She wished he knew what she was thinking.

"When you hate, you're a murderer in your heart." Those were Jesus' words in her mind! Melissa knew Jesus was speaking to her. She dropped her eyes. *I can't forgive them.* "I forgave my murderers," Jesus reminded her.

Melissa broke into a cold sweat. *But I can't forgive them!*

"Remember my words from the cross, 'Father, forgive these people, because they don't know what they are doing'? You must forgive, too."

Why? How?

"Because they didn't understand what they were doing."

They did!

"They knew they were hurting your family, but they didn't understand they were making choices that will separate them from me for eternity unless they repent."

Melissa understood. Separation from Jesus forever was much worse than a ruined house. She closed her eyes and prayed, *Dear Jesus, please forgive them. Forgive me for hating them and help me forgive them, too.*

"Remember, the Lord forgave you, so you must forgive others."
(Colossians 3:13)

When is it hardest for you to forgive?
Do you believe Jesus can speak to you as he spoke to Melissa?

A Heart Full of Hate

Jimmy squirmed in his Sunday school chair. He was sorry he'd stayed overnight with Lee. Instead of getting to sleep in, he'd had to get up and go to church with Lee's family.

His ears perked up when the teacher asked, "Does anyone here hate your brother?"

Jimmy's eyes narrowed. *Yeah!* he thought. *I do!* He felt the rage simmer in his stomach. He elbowed Lee and leaned over to whisper, "Someday I'll get even with Hank. I'll hurt him worse than he's hurt me."

"God is love," explained the teacher. "Real love is that God loved us and sent his Son as a sacrifice for us. Jesus loved us so much that he died for everything we've done wrong."

Jimmy's heart began to soften. *Jesus loves me? All I know is hate,* he thought. *Mom left us. Dad works all the time. Hank beats me up and locks me in my room for hours.*

The teacher continued, "God says that if we have hate in our hearts, we are murderers."

I'm not a murderer! Jimmy thought. *My brother is!*

The teacher held up a black construction-paper heart. "All of us have hearts filled with selfishness and hatred. We've all failed to love others like we should. But forgiveness from Jesus can clean every sinful heart."

Jimmy frowned. *Maybe I am a murderer…. I don't want to be. Would Jesus forgive me?*

Lee pulled on Jimmy's sleeve. "Stop hating Hank," he said quietly. "Come to Jesus. He'll forgive you. And he'll help you forgive Hank."

Jimmy sighed. Lee was right. When the teacher asked who wanted to give their heart to Jesus, Jimmy raised his hand. *I need you, Jesus,* he prayed. *Help me receive your love…and stop hating Hank.*

Jesus said, "There is joy in the presence of God's angels when even one sinner repents." *(Luke 15:10)*

Does Jesus expect us to forgive those who keep on hurting us?
How can we do that?

105

Popcorn Forgiveness

Get Set   Make four quarts of lightly salted popcorn. Set out a heavy pan, molasses, sugar, vinegar, baking soda, and a candy thermometer.

Go!

Why is it so important to forgive other people?

Read   Matthew 18:21–35.

What happened to the servant who would not forgive?

Make   a treat that shows how unforgiveness can harm us.

> Combine in a heavy pan:
>> 1¼ cup light molasses
>> 2 cups sugar
>> ⅔ cup water
>> 2 teaspoons vinegar
>
> Cook to the hard ball stage (250 degrees).
> Remove from heat.
> Add 1 teaspoon baking soda and mix thoroughly.
> (Watch out! It bubbles up.)
> Pour the mixture over popcorn and form into balls.

How was the baking soda in the mixture like unforgiveness in our hearts?

Share   a popcorn ball with someone you've had trouble forgiving.

All in Good Time

Get Set   You'll need a box of uncooked macaroni.

Go!

Ask   everyone to name their three favorite foods.

Open   a box of macaroni and try eating it uncooked.

Offer   the uncooked macaroni to others.

When will this macaroni taste best?
What can macaroni teach us about prayer?

Read   Genesis 12:1–4; 17:1–6; 21:1–3.

How many years did Abraham wait for a son?
When have you had to wait for God's answer to your prayer?
Why doesn't God always answer our prayers quickly?
Can you think of times when people won't wait for God to answer
their prayers?
Why is it important to patiently wait for God's answers to our prayers?

Pray   together about a concern you've been bringing to God for a
long time. Ask God to give you patience and faith that he hears and will
answer your prayers.

Gretchen's Secret

Gretchen peered into the church office. "Hi, Mom!"

Her mother looked up with a smile. "It's good to see you! Do you have much homework tonight?"

"No," said Gretchen. "I came to help you fold Sunday's bulletins."

"Don't worry about them. It only takes me fifteen minutes to fold them all."

"But I want to help, Mom. I'll do it in the church kitchen." Gretchen took the stack of bulletins into the kitchen, sat down at a table, and began folding. She creased each bulletin slowly and carefully.

Soon Mother looked in. "Are you about finished?" she asked.

"No, Mother. It will take a while yet."

"Why don't I help you?" said Mother.

"Are you in a hurry to get them?" asked Gretchen.

"Well, no. I guess not." Her mother paused.

"I don't mind doing it," said Gretchen. "I'll bring them back when I'm done."

"Is it hard for you to fold them?" quizzed her mother.

Gretchen laughed. "Mother, if you must know, I'm doing what Jesus said: 'Go away and pray secretly.' I hoped this kitchen would be like a secret closet for me. I'm praying for everyone who will open these bulletins on Sunday morning."

Jesus said, "When you pray, go away by yourself, shut the door behind you, and pray to your Father secretly. Then your Father, who knows all secrets, will reward you." *(Matthew 6:6)*

Where can you pray "secretly"?
Why does Jesus want us to pray secretly?

Cammi's Prayer

Sitting at a table in the orphanage in Vietnam, seven-year-old Cammi overheard a visiting family tell the orphanage director, "We don't want to adopt a child over four years of age. We want a younger boy or girl."

Because she was older than the rest of the children, Cammi felt crushed. *Won't anyone choose me?* she wondered. Adoption seemed hopeless. But that night as Cammi spread out her sleeping mat, she remembered what a minister once said.

"Jesus said, 'When you pray, go into your room, and when you have shut your door, pray to your Father who is in the secret place.... Your Father who sees in secret will reward you openly.'"

After the other children had fallen asleep, Cammi got up, knelt beside her mat, and prayed. "Dear Father in heaven, you know that I need a family to take care of me here on earth. Please give me an American family I can live with. I ask this in Jesus' name, amen."

Cammi prayed that same prayer every night for months.

One day the head of the orphanage came to Cammi. "Someone in America wants to adopt an older girl. We'll send you if you're willing."

Cammi clapped her hands for joy. Her prayers were answered! She flew to America and became part of a Christian family with eight children, five of whom had been adopted.

When she learned English, Cammi told her new parents how she had prayed for a family. And she learned the reason why they'd adopted her. Her new mother said, "I heard God's voice tell me, 'I have another child for you in Vietnam and I want you to bring *her* here immediately.'"

Jesus said, "Ask, using my name, and you will receive, and you will have abundant joy." *(John 16:24)*

What have you prayed about for a long time? How can Cammi's story encourage you?

Emergency Prayer

On his way home from soccer practice, Nick stopped at the convenience store to buy pop and a hot dog. Nick had noticed a group of boys following him but didn't think much about it. When Nick reached into the cooler and took out a bottle of pop, someone grabbed him by the shoulder and spun him around. He couldn't believe his eyes—it was his old friend Bryan!

"How's it going, man? Haven't seen you for a long time," Nick said. Bryan introduced Nick to three of his new friends. As they continued talking, Nick noticed that the friends were sneaking pop cans into their jacket pockets.

"Here, have one," said the biggest kid, handing Nick a can of pop.

"I only have money for this bottle," said Nick, holding out his pop. Nick's heart was beating hard, but he tried not to show how scared he was feeling.

"Then stick it in your pocket!" insisted the boy.

"What if they catch us?" asked Nick.

"Don't worry, man," said the boy.

Nick didn't know what he should do. *Dear Jesus,* he prayed silently, *I'm in trouble. I don't know how to get out of this mess. I need your help. Please, Jesus, help me!*

Just then one of the cashiers came around the corner. "Hey, you kids!" he said. "Are you going to pay for your sodas?" Suddenly Bryan and his friends ran off like sprinters at the Olympics.

Nick heaved a big sigh of relief. He knew Jesus sent that cashier in answer to his prayers. To this day, every time Nick shops at that convenience store and passes the aisle of pop, he remembers to thank God for answered prayer.

Jesus said, "Listen to me! You can pray for anything, and if you believe, you will have it." *(Mark 11:24)*

 *What would Jesus want you to trust him for today? Do you have faith that Jesus can help you the way he helped Nick?*

Prayer Assignment

Everyone else in the car chattered about the soccer tournament, but Kristin silently gazed out the backseat window. She felt exhausted. It had been a tough game and she didn't like losing.

Her father pulled up to the intersection and stopped the car, waiting for the light to turn green. A blue pickup pulled alongside them in the right turn lane. Kristin looked at the driver. He appeared unshaven and scruffy. Puffing on his cigarette, he exhaled the smoke in a long stream. It swirled inside the pickup cab.

Suddenly Kristin felt alert…as if something important were happening. She sat up straighter and tried to get a better look at the driver. He wore a denim shirt and appeared to be about twenty years old. But somehow she knew he wasn't happy.

Kristin's heart jumped as she sensed God's voice speaking three words to her: *Pray for him.*

Immediately she began praying quietly, "Dear Jesus, please be with this man. Help him get to know you. Help him find happiness in you. Be at work in his life. Give him a heart of faith to trust you. I pray in Jesus' name, amen."

The light turned green and the pickup turned the corner. Kristin smiled and thought, *I may never see this man again, but I won't forget him. I know he's my special assignment!*

Jesus said, "Everyone who asks, receives." *(Luke 11:10)*

Are you on "prayer alert" as Kristin was? Who is your special prayer assignment?

A Change in Byron

Reg tied his shoelaces while he listened to his friend. "I can't seem to stop lying," Byron confided while they waited for the bus. "My parents don't believe anything I say anymore. It's a big problem."

"Why do you lie?" Reg asked, feeling concerned.

"I'm not sure. When I explain something, it's so easy to exaggerate. Pretty soon I've made up a big story." Byron sat down on the curb and stared at the pavement. His shoulders slumped. "Now my parents don't trust anything I say. And they're taking away my privileges."

"What about my birthday party this weekend?" asked Reg. "Can you come?"

Byron kicked a stone with his foot. "I lied about not having any homework yesterday. Dad says I'm grounded for the rest of the week. And he said he won't sign me up for summer camp either."

Reg groaned silently. He wanted Byron at his party. He especially wanted Byron to be his bunkmate at camp. But he knew it was more important for Byron to stop lying. That night, Reg started praying. He never told Byron what he was doing.

The next night Reg read Jesus' words in the Bible: "If two of you agree down here on earth concerning anything you ask, my Father in heaven will do it for you" *(Matthew 18:19).* He immediately phoned his friend Kirk. They prayed together over the phone for Byron.

Two weeks later, Byron told Reg, "Guess what! My folks know I'm really trying to be truthful. Now we pray together before I leave for school. And look! Dad changed his mind—he signed my camp registration!"

Thank you, Jesus, Reg prayed. *You've worked in both Byron's heart and his parents'.*

"The Lord hears his people when they call to him for help." *(Psalm 34:17)*

What would Jesus want you to do for a friend who is lying?
Who can you agree with in prayer?

Seeds of Prayer

Get Set   Prepare a snack tray of crackers, bread, cream cheese, and butter. Add small bowls of sunflower, poppy, and sesame seeds. You'll also need knives and napkins.

Go!

Ask everyone to name the seeds they recognize.

Read   Psalm 126:5–6.

How is praying like planting seeds?
When you plant seeds, how long do you wait for a harvest?
Is prayer like that? Explain.

Pass   the snack tray and let everyone prepare snacks with the seeds of their choice.

Ask   everyone to tell about something they prayed about for a long time before they saw God's answer.

Ask   everyone to share a prayer that was answered quickly.

"Plant"   a seed of prayer by praying for someone you've never prayed for before.

Good Fruit

Get Set   Gather several kinds of canned and fresh fruit, a cutting board, knives, and a large serving bowl. Set out small bowls and spoons for everyone.

Go!

What's your favorite kind of fruit?

Read   Luke 6:43–45.

What kind of fruit is Jesus talking about?

As you work together to rinse and cut the fruit and place it in the serving bowl,   tell   about the good fruit you've seen in one another's lives during the past week.

Read   John 15:16.

How can we "bear fruit"?
What good things would please Jesus in our speech? our actions? our attitudes?

Pray   about being fruitful and doing what's right this week.

Enjoy   your fruit salad.

Encourage   and   affirm   one another this week when you see each other bearing good fruit at home.

Marked Bill

Tyler and Bill rode their bicycles into the alley behind Main Street. Suddenly a man wearing a ski mask and carrying a black bag burst through a back door. He ran into Tyler and they both went sprawling.

"Hey—" Tyler broke off midsentence. The man's black bag dropped on the pavement and fell open. A pile of green bills spilled out.

An alarm rang as the man scrambled to his feet, picked up the bag, and fled. He left the alley littered with money.

Tyler untangled himself from his bike and the two boys hurriedly scooped up the loose bills. "We're rich!" hollered Bill, waving a fistful of money in the air.

"Now I can get Mega Cops 3 for my computer," said Tyler, already playing the new computer game in his imagination. He stuffed a wad of bills into his backpack and jumped on his bike. Bill followed.

As the boys sped from the alley, a verse Tyler had learned at camp came to his mind. "Be sure that your sin will find you out" *(Numbers 32:23).* Tyler stopped his bike. "Bill, we can't keep this money. It would be stealing."

"You're right," said his friend reluctantly. The boys rode to the bank and returned the money.

"It pays to be honest," said the bank manager. "These bills are marked. The police would have picked you up if you had tried to spend them."

Tyler grinned at his friend. "And then you would have been a *marked Bill.*"

"Very funny!" said Bill.

Later that week, at a special school assembly, the bank officials thanked Tyler and Bill for their honesty. The officials donated money to the school library fund and ordered pizza for the entire school in the boys' honor.

"The Lord hates cheating, but he delights in honesty." *(Proverbs 11:1)*

Have you ever tried to get away with something? What does Jesus want us to do when we're tempted?

The Magazine Ad

Lennie opened the door to his mother's home office and asked, "Mom? Are you busy?" With a worried look on his face, Lennie added, "I need to show you something right away."

"Come on in, son."

"I...well, I...could you come up the street with me?" he asked, feeling upset. "It won't take long."

His mother followed him silently up the block.

"It's over here, Mom." Lennie scrambled down into the ditch that ran alongside the main street. He quickly found what he was looking for and climbed back out.

"What is it?" asked Mother.

Lennie handed her a page that had been ripped out of a men's magazine. It featured a woman who wasn't wearing very much.

"Where did this come from?" Mother asked.

"Walking home after school today, Erik pulled it out of his book bag and handed it to me. I wouldn't take it. And I told him to get rid of it. At first Erik got angry at me, but then he decided that he didn't want it either. So he threw it in the ditch and went home."

"Lennie, you did what Jesus would want you to do. You stood for what was right even when Erik got mad."

"I don't want any other kid to find it. Let's throw it in the garbage where it belongs," said Lennie.

"Make every effort to live a pure and blameless life." *(2 Peter 3:14)*

WWJD *How have you helped someone else do what was right? What would Jesus have told Erik?*

To Snitch or Not to Snitch

At lunch recess when Troy and Ellis turned the corner of the school building, Troy nearly ran into a fifth grader who quickly dropped his hand to his side. That didn't stop a trail of smoke from wafting skyward or hide the smell of cigarettes.

Troy and Ellis walked away quickly.

"Just pretend we didn't see Mike," said Ellis.

"But it's against school rules. We're supposed to report it," protested Troy.

"And get beat up? Mike saw us. Anyway, it's snitching. There's nothing lower than a snitch."

Troy had trouble concentrating on his afternoon math lessons. *Which is worse,* he wondered, *disobeying school rules or being disloyal to a friend?*

Troy and Ellis argued about it all the way home from school.

Ellis said, "Mike's not trying to get anyone else to smoke. If he wants to die of lung cancer, that's his business."

Troy remembered the book of matches Mike had left on the ground. "What if he leaves his matches where some little kid picks them up?" he asked. "Someone might get burned or set the school on fire!"

Troy knew Jesus would want him to obey those in authority over him. He didn't feel particularly excited about it, but he knew he had to do the right thing.

Before school the next morning, Troy convinced Ellis to go with him to the principal's office to report what they'd seen.

"For the Lord's sake, accept all authority." *(1 Peter 2:13)*

When have you had to make a choice like Troy's? What would Jesus want you to do?

Strawberry Surprise

Amber stood up and rubbed her back. She'd never realized picking strawberries was such hard work—and this was only her first day! Still, she was determined to stick with it.

The older girl picking berries next to her smiled sympathetically. "Pretty tough, isn't it? This is my third year picking strawberries. I've learned to fill my crate faster and make more money."

"How?" asked Amber eagerly.

The girl glanced around. Then she picked up some small stones, placed them in the bottom of the half-quart basket, and piled strawberries on top.

"But that's cheating," said Amber.

The girl shrugged her shoulders. "Can I help it if farmers are dumb?"

By the time Amber had picked three more baskets of strawberries, she wanted to quit. *Maybe it wouldn't hurt to put a few stones in the bottom*, she thought. By the seventh basket, Amber was putting big rocks in the baskets and arranging the strawberries on top.

Finally Amber lugged her crate to the supervisor at the end of the field. Her heart sank when she saw it was her Sunday school teacher, Mrs. Leeper.

"Trying to make a little extra money, Amber?" asked Mrs. Leeper, smiling.

Amber nodded. Mrs. Leeper looked surprised when she took the crate from Amber. "This seems a bit heavy for strawberries." She pulled out a basket, removed the strawberries on top and exposed a mound of rocks. "Oh, Amber," she said quietly.

Amber hung her head.

"I can't pay you for this crate," said Mrs. Leeper. "It would be cheating the farmer and the customer."

"I'm so ashamed, Mrs. Leeper. I know Jesus wants me to work for my money and be honest. I won't put rocks in the strawberry baskets again."

"I'm sure you won't, Amber," said Mrs. Leeper. "Here's a new crate."

"The Lord demands fairness in every business deal." *(Proverbs 16:11)*

What would you say to someone who was cheating? How does Jesus want you to do your work?

A Deadly Poison

"I can't believe Haley won the short story contest," Tiffany said to her friend Rhonda.

Rhonda agreed. "She only won because she's the teacher's pet. Your story is much better."

"I bet she copied it from that big book at the library I saw her reading. If she hadn't transferred to our school before Christmas, I would have won first place instead of second."

At lunch, Tiffany heard Rhonda tell a friend that Haley had copied her story from a book. She felt a little twinge of her conscience, but she ignored it.

Tiffany groaned when the teacher assigned Haley to be her science partner. However, as the two girls did their science project together, Tiffany and Haley became friends.

One day Haley said, "You know, I really liked your short story, Tiffany."

A classmate at the next table heard her and said, "Tiffany should have won the contest. She didn't copy her story from a book!"

A look of pained surprise crossed Haley's face. Tiffany grew hot with shame. Her jealous words had spread like a virus throughout the class and were now returning to poison her new friendship with Haley.

Tiffany swallowed hard. She knew she had to tell the truth—right now! It's what Jesus would want her to do. She cleared her throat, then spoke loudly so everyone at the surrounding tables could hear.

"I was jealous when Haley won the short story award so I said she copied her story. But it's not true. I lied." Tiffany looked over at Haley. "I'm sorry. Will you forgive me? I really want to be friends."

Haley's eye were brimming with tears. "I never thought you'd do something like this. It really hurts! But I forgive you. Next time, make sure the stories you tell are true!"

"Don't speak evil against each other." *(James 4:11)*

Have your words ever caused trouble for others? When have you asked someone to forgive you for what you said?

Loves and Hates

Get Set Set out paper, pencils, and colored pencils or markers.

Go!

Hand out the drawing materials.

Ask everyone to **write** or **draw** three things they love.

Then have them **write** or **draw** three things they hate.

Did you know that the Bible tells us what God hates?

Read Proverbs 6:16–19.

Let everyone **name** the seven things God hates.

Have you ever done something God hates?
When do you find it is the hardest to do what is right?

Pray: Dear God, forgive us for all the times we don't tell the truth. Forgive us for not getting along with each other. Forgive us for being mean and selfish. Thank you for being willing to forgive us each time we fail. Pour your love into our hearts and help us live for you, not for ourselves. In Jesus' name we pray, amen.

Help Wanted!

Get Set Gather a red marker, bandages, soap, rubbing alcohol, and other items to treat wounds.

Go!

Ask for a volunteer.

Use the red marker to **draw** a line on the volunteer's arm to represent a wound.

Have someone **read** Luke 10:30–37 as the rest of you wash and dress the volunteer's "wound."

How does it feel to be cared for?
How does it feel to care for someone?

Tell about a time when you were hurt and someone cared for you.

Tell about a time when you cared for someone who was hurt.

When have you been hurt on the inside, where others can't see?
Who was a Good Samaritan to you then?
Is there a person or family to whom you could be a Good Samaritan?

Decide as a family what you will do for them.

Begin helping right now by praying for them.

Week
15

Beulah's Best Gift

"Lyla won't be in class today," announced the teacher of a small school in Nigeria. "Her home burned down last night."

"Oh, no!" exclaimed eleven-year-old Beulah. "Are they all safe? Did they get their things out?"

"The fire spread rapidly," said the teacher. "Everyone escaped, but their house and all their belongings were completely destroyed."

Beulah couldn't concentrate on her schoolwork the rest of the day. Lyla's family had been poor *before* the fire. Now they had nothing at all. *Dear Jesus, show me what I can do for this family,* she prayed. *Mother and I don't have much, but we have more than they do right now.*

After school Beulah hurried home. "Oh, Mother!" she cried, running into the kitchen. "Lyla's house burned, along with all her family's belongings. I want to give her one of my dresses to wear. It will show her that I love her and that God loves her. What else could we share with them?"

Though they had little enough of their own, Beulah and her mother packed a box with Beulah's best dress, some thread, and three pieces of cloth for sewing. They shared one of their wool blankets, along with several spoons and wooden bowls from their cupboard. Then they visited Lyla's family, who gratefully received all of the gifts.

The next day at school Beulah explained to her classmates what she had done. "When I gave my dress to Lyla, I felt so happy. It was even more fun than getting a present on my birthday!"

Lyla's good deed was contagious! That afternoon, many other students went home to find something to share with Lyla's family.

"Give generously to those in need, always being ready to share with others whatever God has given them." *(1 Timothy 6:18)*

What made Lyla's gifts so special?
What would Jesus want you to share with others today?

A Job for Christine

"Mommy, how can I earn some money?" asked Christine. She frowned and wrinkled her brows, trying to think of some work she could do. "Everybody says a six-year-old can't accomplish much! But I would be a good worker…if I just got the right job."

"Tell me," said Mother as she ran a rolling pin over the soft biscuit dough, "why do you want to make money?"

"Remember the missionary we heard last week? He said that new Christians in many parts of the world need Bibles. But a Bible costs them more than a whole month's wages!" Christine added quietly, "The man said it cost eight dollars to send a Bible. I think Jesus wants me to help them."

As Christine's mother slid the pan of biscuits into the oven, the phone rang. It was a neighbor. "We have to drive to Idaho," he said. "Our grandpa is in the hospital. We'll put our dog in the backyard, but he needs fresh water and food every day while we're gone. Would one of your kids like a job?"

"Yes," said Mother. "I'll send my daughter right over."

Every day for two weeks, Christine faithfully cared for the neighbors' dog. She also faithfully prayed for the new Christian who would receive the Bible she'd send.

"Whenever we have the opportunity, we should do good to everyone, especially to our Christian brothers and sisters." *(Galatians 6:10)*

How would Jesus want you to help Christians in faraway places?
Do you know someone who needs a Bible? How could you help?

Heather's Gift

Heather listened attentively to the missionary from Albania.

"Our country is among the poorest in the world. No one has money for clothes or food. The children in our orphanage are thankful for bread and soup and a place to sleep. They love to hear about Jesus. They would be grateful for a pencil and a few pieces of paper to write on. There are no toys in our orphanage. Please pray for all the children. We want to take back food, clothing, and medicine for them."

What could I do for the orphans? Heather wondered that night when she climbed into bed. *Bless those children, Jesus,* she prayed. *Help the people who deliver food and clothing. Show me what I can do.*

The next morning Heather brought her new doll to the kitchen. She asked her mother, "Would it be all right with you if I gave away this doll? I bought it with my birthday money. I want to send it to a girl in Albania."

Her mother silently stirred the oatmeal.

"I know what you're thinking, Mother. We spent hours looking for this doll. And it's a collector's doll, so it's worth more. But I want to give my *best* doll, not some old doll I don't care about." She looked earnestly at her mother. "Shouldn't we give Jesus our *best?*"

"Yes, dear," said her mother. "You can give your special doll. I know Jesus will bless your gift." She hugged her daughter tightly and smiled.

Heather twirled around with her doll. "Wouldn't it be fun to see that little girl's face when they hand her my doll? I can't wait to meet her someday up in heaven!"

"Don't forget to do good and to share what you have with those in need, for such sacrifices are very pleasing to God." *(Hebrews 13:16)*

When have you given away something that was important to you?
What things are hardest for you to share?

Camel Walk

Twelve-year-old Chino, a boy in Nigeria, listened attentively to Pastor Mayboll's report.

"During last night's flash flood, many church members lost their homes and all they own. They are setting up makeshift tents at the edge of town. Before you leave church today, please let us know if you can help in any way."

Chino put his hand in his pocket and felt the five small coins he'd earned last week. The coins would pay for one week's rides on the bus to his school. *Oh, Jesus. How would you want me to help these families?* he prayed.

His younger sister nudged him. "We could give some of our school supplies to the children. And if you grind the corn, I'll make some cornbread for them."

"Okay," whispered Chino. He kept thinking about the coins in his pocket. If he gave a coin, it meant that he would have to walk one hour to school and an hour back home.

"Look!" said Leela. "There's Ammon and his family. Their home must have been flooded. Their shoes and pant legs are still muddy."

Chino decided to give all he had. He walked to the front of the church. Reaching in his pocket, he took out five silver coins and handed them to Pastor Mayboll. "I will give this week's bus money," said Chino. "And when I earn five more coins next Saturday, I'll give them also."

"How will you get to school?" asked Pastor.

"I will walk…like a camel does. God gave me strong legs. I want to help my fellow Christians. And Jesus says we should give our best gift."

In the end, Chino Iwuchukwu of Nigeria voluntarily gave all his bus money for an entire month. He walked two hours to school and back every day.

Jesus said, "Sell what you have and give to those in need." *(Luke 12:33)*

When have you sacrificed to help others?
Who has given up time and money for you?

Spin the Globe

"I need another turn," insisted Traci. "My finger landed on the Pacific Ocean. I can't pray for the ocean! Spin the globe one more time."

Traci's father smiled. "Maybe you *can* pray about the Pacific Ocean. Do you know how many ships are sailing out there right now? Thousands of sailors make their home on ships. God may be telling you to pray for the sailors."

"Spin it one more time," said Traci. "If my finger lands on the ocean again, then I'll pray for them."

Father held the top of the globe with one hand and twirled it with his other hand. Traci closed her eyes, stuck out her finger, and stopped the globe from turning. When she opened her eyes, she moaned. "Not again!"

"You're in the Pacific Ocean," said her brother. "Now let me have a turn."

Father set the world spinning again and Benjamin stuck out his finger to stop it.

"Siberia!" he said excitedly. "That's one of the coldest spots in the world. People up there need prayer."

Father took his turn and landed on Indonesia.

"We all have a prayer challenge this week," he said. "Let's get busy and pray."

The three of them bowed by the table and began to pray for their special prayer assignments.

"I urge you, first of all, to pray for all people.... Plead for God's mercy upon them." *(1 Timothy 2:1)*

WWJD   *What group of people does Jesus want you to pray for?*

Assignment: The World

Get Set   You'll need a blindfold and a world map or globe.

Go!

To find your Good Samaritan prayer assignment:

Put on   the blindfold.

Spin   the globe.

Touch   the globe to stop it from spinning.

If you're using a map, *have* someone spin you, then stop you and face you toward the map. *Point* to a spot on the map.

Write down the name of the place where your finger rests. (If you land on the ocean, re-spin the globe. If you land on the ocean again, pray for those who sail in its waters.)
When everyone has had a turn, *pray* for your assignments.

Ask   Jesus to bless your fellow Christians in that land.

Pray   for Christian churches, pastors, and leaders of that country.

Ask   the Lord to open all the people's hearts to Jesus.

Keep   your prayer assignment for a week.

Serve or Be Served?

Get Set Make a crown from poster board covered with foil. Cut straws into different lengths. You'll need one straw for each person. You'll also need a dish towel.

Go!

Draw straws.

Crown the person with the longest straw king or queen.

Explain that he or she will "rule" for the next two minutes.

Give the dish towel to the person with the shortest straw. He or she will be the servant.

Have the servant **fold** and **hang** the dish towel on his or her arm.

Have the king or queen **give** the servant several commands.

At the end of three minutes, **announce** that the king or queen and servant must switch roles.

Have the new king or queen **give** the servant several commands.

Read Matthew 20:20–21, 25–28.

Who is more important, a king, a queen, or a servant? Explain.
How did Jesus, the greatest king who ever lived, serve everyone on earth?
Who did Jesus say was the "greatest" in God's kingdom?
So what should you do if you want to be great?

Pray and thank Jesus for serving us. Ask him to show you ways to serve today.

131

Jimmy to the Rescue

Jimmy peered anxiously up the street. "I wonder what's happened to the bus," he said to the elderly man standing beside him at the bus stop. "My game starts in half an hour. Coach isn't going to like this."

The old man reassured him, "The bus should be here soon. Where are you heading?"

"To the ball field across town. I'm already late because I had to help Mom with my baby brother this morning. If I don't make it for pregame practice, I won't get to play in the tournament."

Just then the bus arrived. Jimmy had one foot on the step when he heard someone cry out in pain. Glancing up, he saw an elderly lady lying in the crosswalk. *Oh no!* Jimmy thought. *I don't have time to stop and help. Besides, somebody else will go help her.*

In his heart, Jimmy knew what Jesus would do. So he stepped off the bus and ran into the street just before the light changed. No one else had gone to the old woman's aid. She couldn't get up by herself. The traffic stopped and waited as Jimmy gently took her arm and helped her to her feet.

After he walked her to the safety of the sidewalk, he looked back and saw his bus still waiting at the corner. The driver waved at him to come. He raced to the bus and climbed aboard amid cheers from the other riders.

"Why did you risk missing your tournament?" asked the elderly man.

Jimmy answered, "All I could think of was my Sunday school teacher saying that Jesus wants me to love God and love other people."

"Love does no wrong to anyone, so love satisfies all of God's requirements." *(Romans 13:10)*

When have you given your time to help someone in need?
When have others given up their plans and done what Jesus would do—for you?

Wise Little Brother

When Brenda saw her mother drive up to the school, she ran out and quickly jumped in the car. "Thanks for coming to get me, Mom," she said breathlessly. "I'm tired of those big sixth-graders pestering me when I walk home."

Her five-year-old brother pressed his nose against the car window. He smiled and waved. Brenda couldn't understand what he was muttering.

"What do you want, Joey?" she asked.

"Nothing," he answered.

"There's Randy and his stupid friends. I hate them," Brenda complained. "And those show-off girls who hang out with the troublemaker boys act so smart."

Joey mumbled again as he smiled and waved.

"I can't wait until I'm a sixth-grader," said Brenda. "Then nobody will pick on me."

Glancing at Joey, Brenda noticed him waving again. "What in the world are you doing?"

"I'm saying hi to Jesus," answered Joey.

"But why are you waving at those stupid kids?"

"Daddy told me that whatever we do to someone, we do it to Jesus," explained Joey. "I want to do something for Jesus."

Brenda closed her eyes and prayed silently, *Dear Jesus, I forgot what you said. And I've been mean to everyone I don't like. Please forgive me. Help me treat others like I would treat you.*

Jesus said, "Beware that you don't despise a single one of these little ones." *(Matthew 18:10)*

How do you treat other children you don't like? What kind of attitude does Jesus want you to have toward people who are hard to like?

Whitney's Sister

Whitney looked up from her math homework to smile at her four-year-old sister. Kendra was sitting in the middle of the family room floor with wooden blocks heaped in piles around her. Her eyes were closed, her hands were folded, and her lips moved.

"What's the matter, Kendra?" Whitney asked.

Kendra opened her eyes. "My castle crashed. I wanted to yell and throw my blocks. I asked Jesus if I should."

"What did Jesus say?" asked Whitney.

"You're silly." Kendra giggled. "You know Jesus wouldn't throw blocks and yell."

Kendra started building another tower of blocks and Whitney returned to her math homework. The teacher had assigned two long pages for tomorrow.

Whitney had noticed a big difference in Kendra lately. Her teacher at Kingdom Kids Preschool told the children to stop and ask, "What would Jesus do?" every time they got angry. Kendra used to scream, throw blocks, and sometimes even bang her head on the floor. Now she spent a lot of time talking to Jesus with her hands folded and her eyes closed.

Can a four-year-old really be a Christian? wondered Whitney.

She shut her book and slammed it on the table. "I can't believe the stupid teacher assigns so much homework!" she complained. "It just isn't fair. I'm going to call Jeff and get the answers from him."

Whitney noticed Kendra close her eyes and fold her hands. Her lips moved for a moment; then she looked up and asked, "Whitney, is that what Jesus would want you to do?"

Ouch, thought Whitney. Maybe a four-year-old can be a Christian. Maybe I'm the one who needs to be closer to Jesus!

"Anyone who becomes as humble as this little child is the greatest in the Kingdom of Heaven." *(Matthew 18:4)*

What would Jesus want you to do to be closer to him?
When have you stopped and asked Jesus what you should do?

Airport Attitude

Mark turned sideways and draped his knees over the arm of the airport chair. He groaned out loud and glared at the lady standing behind the ticket counter. He wished he could tell her how mad he felt.

"Stop squirming," his mom said.

"But our plane was scheduled to leave two hours ago," Mark complained.

Mom sighed. "Everyone's tired," she said. "Not just you."

"I asked Jesus to make our plane leave on time so I wouldn't miss my soccer game," said Mark. "I don't understand why this flight is delayed."

"I don't either," said Mom, "but Jesus has a reason for everything."

Mark lay down on the floor and used his carry-on bag as a pillow. A minute later he sat up and asked, "So what's his reason?"

"Jesus doesn't always tell us."

"I don't understand why Jesus wouldn't answer my prayer," said Mark.

"Now boarding flight 973," the lady behind the ticket counter announced.

Mark hoisted his bag onto his shoulder. "Finally," he said in disgust.

A worried-looking man wearing a dark suit hurried toward them.

"Did I miss flight 973?" he asked the lady behind the counter.

"No," she said, smiling. "It's just ready to leave."

"Thank the Lord," the man said, his voice choked with tears. "My son was in a terrible accident. This is the last flight until morning. If this plane hadn't been delayed, I wouldn't be able to get home to him. This is an answer to my prayers."

Mark's eyes filled with tears. He silently asked Jesus to forgive him for praying selfishly. Thank you for allowing me to see why you answered my prayer a different way than I wanted, he prayed. That man's son is a lot more important than a soccer game.

"When you do ask, you don't get it because your whole motive is wrong—you want only what will give you pleasure." *(James 4:3)*

Why does Jesus sometimes answer our prayers in different ways than we expect?

135

The Name Game

"Hey, elephant ears," Lennie called to Vince, who was standing in line waiting for the school bus. "Can you fly?" Lennie asked with a smirk.

Vince looked down at his shoes while Lennie's friends laughed.

Barbara Black and Laura Plimp lined up next to Vince.

"If it isn't Barbara Blackhead and Laura Blimp," said Lucas. His buddies snickered.

"Shut up, Lucas," said Laura.

Barbara tried to kick Lucas, but he jumped back, laughing.

On the bus, Lennie's older brother, Patrick, sat down next to him. "You were mean to those kids."

"Mean?" Lennie was surprised.

"The names you called them."

"We were just having fun."

"How much fun were Vince and Barbara and Laura having?"

"Oh, come on. They're just thin-skinned. They need to toughen up a little."

"It looked like you were building yourself up at those kids' expense." Lennie shifted uncomfortably. "Yeah, maybe."

"I don't remember Jesus telling us to do that," said Patrick.

Lennie thought of the pastor's sermon last week about building up others, not tearing them down. He sighed and hung his head. He liked being clever, but Jesus said loving others was more important. Lucas prayed silently, "Dear Jesus, I want to obey you. Help me say positive things to the kids at school. Amen."

Then Lennie told Patrick, "You're right. Jesus says to do just the opposite."

"Try to build each other up." *(Romans 14:19)*

Who can you build up today?
What will you say?

Be-Glad-for-Each-Other Day!

Get Set   Gather large sheets of butcher paper or newsprint, markers, tape, and scissors.

Go!

Tape   sheets of paper together until you have sheets large enough to trace each person's outline.

Use markers to   *trace*   around each other.

Cut   out the shapes and tape them on each person's bedroom door.

Read   John 13:34–35.

How do we show love in our family?
Why is showing love so important?
How can we do a better job of showing love for each other?

Write   encouraging and loving words on everyone's paper shape. Leave the shapes up for several days so everyone is reminded how much they are loved and appreciated.

God's Show-and-Tell

Get Set You'll need an empty picture frame and a flashlight.

Go!

Ask each person to return in three minutes with a Show-and-Tell item that tells something about God.

Have each person **share** about what they brought and what it tells them about God.

Listen for what the Bible tells us about another of God's Show-and-Tells.

Read Matthew 5:14–16.

Who is God's Show-and-Tell?
How can we live so that people will praise our Father in heaven?

Place the picture frame in front of someone's face.

Shine the flashlight on that person's face.

Read Matthew 5:16, inserting that person's name at the beginning of the verse.

Let the "framed" person **tell** how he or she will shine for Jesus this week.

Repeat this process with each person.

Sing "This Little Light of Mine."

Pray that the Lord will help you shine and bring glory to him.

Erin's Example

Tears came to Erin's eyes as she looked around the crowded soccer park. This happened every Sunday. Hundreds of soccer players flocked to the park for tournaments instead of attending church—and she was one of them. She felt terrible about it, but she didn't have a choice.

Erin's dad insisted that she play high-level club soccer so she would be good enough to earn a college scholarship someday. And everyone who played club soccer had to do it on Sunday.

Please forgive me, Jesus, she prayed. *Show me how to honor you even though I'm here on your special day.*

Erin walked over to the shade tree where her teammates chatted. She put down her bag, waiting for the field to clear. All her teammates hoped for scholarships by the time they got to high school. They all chose to play soccer instead of attending church. Erin wondered if any of the girls were Christians.

Jesus, show me how to worship you here, she prayed.

She sat in the shade and tried to pray, but her teammates' voices distracted her.

Erin looked around. "Does anyone want to pray?" she asked boldly. She didn't care if they thought she was weird.

Two girls joined Erin for prayer that morning. By the end of the season most of the team met for prayer before every game and three of them became Christians.

"Remember to observe the Sabbath day by keeping it holy."
(Exodus 20:8)

 *How do you keep the Sabbath special for the Lord?*

Amy's Quiet Witness

Rinnggg! A bell signaled the end of class. Amy felt frustrated. She needed more time in the library to work on her science report. Wadding up her scratch paper, she headed for the nearest wastebasket.

"Out of my way!" yelled Brandon, shoving past her. He threw a handful of crumpled papers at the wastebasket. One hit its target. The rest scattered across the floor by the teacher's desk.

"Ha, ha!" Brandon laughed. "It's *your* fault that I missed, Amy. Pick up the papers or you'll be in trouble!" Then he hurried out the door with his buddies.

Amy turned to go back to her table. Then she switched directions, went back, and began picking up the scattered papers.

"What a mess," she said to herself. *Dear Jesus, please work in Brandon's heart. I'm picking up these papers with the prayer that you will do something to change him.*

"I saw what happened," said the teacher, returning to her desk. "You don't have to clean up Brandon's mess."

Amy smiled. "I know." She finished putting the papers in the wastebasket.

"I've been watching you since school started," said her teacher. "You seem different from the other students. Like now...I don't think anyone else would have picked up after Brandon."

Help me be a good witness for you, Jesus, Amy prayed silently. Then she told her teacher, "I want to follow Jesus and do what he would do. I think he would show love to Brandon. I'm trying to do that, too."

The teacher smiled. "You sound a lot like my brother who keeps talking to me about God. I seem to keep learning a little more about Jesus all the time."

"In everything you do, stay away from complaining and arguing.... Let your lives shine brightly." *(Philippians 2:14, 15)*

How can you "shine" as a quiet witness with the things you do?
When is it hardest to let your actions speak for Jesus?

Igor's Decision

"I'm glad you're coming with me to this vacation Bible school," Igor told his two younger sisters on the way to the mission church. "I want to see what Pastor Vladimir will teach about God."

On the first day of vacation Bible school, Igor and his sisters felt nervous. They refused to say anything, even their names. But they listened attentively while Pastor Vladimir explained that Jesus died and rose from the dead to save us from our sins. Pastor gave Igor a Bible and a page of Bible verses and songs. "Please read about Jesus," he told Igor. "You will learn how much he loves you!"

Every evening Igor read the Bible to his sisters. At the end of the week he confided, "I asked Jesus to be my Savior." Soon his sisters became Christians also. Their attitudes toward each other changed.

"I'm going to live for Jesus," Igor told his sisters. "I don't want to tease you and be mean to you anymore. Jesus will help us enjoy each other!" Instead of arguing, they began to work and pray together. They even began to smile and sing as they helped around the house.

In the beginning, Igor's parents weren't interested in the Bible. But they listened as Igor read the Bible, and they watched their children's behavior change.

At the end of the two-week vacation Bible school, Igor's parents walked to church and asked if they could pay for their children to be in the next session. "We see a big difference in our children's behavior," they told the pastor.

Many parents in the former Soviet Union are coming to Jesus as they see their children trust Jesus and do what he would do.

"For though your hearts were once full of darkness, now you are full of light from the Lord, and your behavior should show it!" *(Ephesians 5:8)*

 *How could you help someone in your family learn to know Jesus?*

Pizza Prayer

Diana laughed and talked with the other kids as they waited for their pizza. This was their soccer team's first winning season in three years and they were celebrating. As soon as the coaches set out pitchers of pop and three large pizzas, everyone started grabbing the food.

Diana looked at the slice of pepperoni pizza on her napkin, then at Kayla who was sitting next to her. Although she always prayed before eating, Diana felt funny about bowing her head in front of her teammates. Kayla was the most popular player on the team and Diana was hoping they could be friends. But what if Kayla laughed at her?

"And you shall be my witnesses.…" Those familiar Bible words slipped into Diana's mind. And she remembered she had been asking Jesus to help her get over her fear of talking about him to her friends. This was her opportunity!

Knowing it was what Jesus wanted her to do, Diana hesitated a moment, then bowed her head and prayed silently.

When Diana looked up, Kayla asked, "Are you feeling okay?"

"Sure," said Diana. "I was just thanking God for my pizza."

Kayla rolled her eyes, but Diana glowed inside. She had obeyed Jesus and been a witness for him. Next time she'd be prepared to say more.

"Let your conversation be gracious and effective so that you will have the right answer for everyone." *(Colossians 4:6)*

 *How does Jesus want you to be a witness when you eat out?*

Mr. Goody-Goody

John climbed to the top of the monkey bars. Chelsea followed him.

"Why did you tell the teacher that you cheated on the math test?" she asked. "You could have gotten an A."

"Well," John said, "I felt bad because I knew Jesus didn't want me to cheat. So I admitted to Mrs. Lindbloom that I looked at some of Eric's answers."

"I don't understand you," said Chelsea. "You never swear either. Why not?"

"Because I'm a Christian," said John, swinging from the top bar. "Jesus loves me and died for me. I don't want to use his name to swear."

The bell sounded, ending recess. John let go of the bar, jumped down to the sawdust underneath, and headed to class. Chelsea tagged along.

"Ramon is so mean. He's always pestering you," she said. "Why don't you slug him?"

"It's not what Jesus would want me to do, Chelsea. Can't you understand?"

"No! I think you're stupid," she said as they entered the classroom. "I'm going to call you Mr. Goody-Goody from now on!"

Sitting down in his seat, John had a hard time not getting mad. He thought of an even worse name he could call her. *Dear Jesus,* he prayed, *help me forgive her. I know you don't want me to get even with her and call her names. Help me!*

At the end of the day, John gathered up his books and headed for the bus.

"Good-bye, Mr. Goody-Goody," chanted Chelsea.

"Good-bye, Chelsea," said John in a kind voice. Boarding the bus, he silently prayed. *Thank you, Jesus. You helped me show love to Chelsea instead of getting revenge. I'm glad it feels so good to do what is right.*

"God blesses you when you are mocked.... Be very glad! For a great reward awaits you in heaven." *(Matthew 5:11, 12)*

When has someone mocked you for being a Christian?
What does Jesus want you to do when others make fun of you?

Catch the Glow

Get Set You'll need matches, as well as candles of many shapes and sizes.

Go!

Place a candle in front of each person.

Give the youngest child the smallest candle and the oldest person the tallest.

Turn off the lights and *light* the candles.

Do the smallest candles give less light than the taller ones?
Do the largest candles have the biggest flame?
Which candle has the brightest flame? (All burn about the same.)

Read Matthew 5:14–16. *Memorize* the passage together.

What do the candles teach us about ourselves?
How did you shine for Jesus this week?
When have you seen someone else's light shining this week?

Pray for the youngest person, then *blow out* his or her candle. Pray for the next child, and so on.

When all the candles are out, hold hands and *pray* that Jesus will help all of you be lights in this dark world.

Week
18

The Best Medicine

Get Set   Set the following items on a tray: a Bible, a bottle of vitamin C, cough drops, aspirin or other bottled medicines, a fever thermometer, and a book of jokes.

Go!

Pass   the tray and let each person take one thing from it.

Take turns telling   how the thing you're holding can make you feel better.

Read   Proverbs 17:22.

What does the Bible say is like medicine?
How would a happy heart help you?

Read   what Jesus said in John 16:33.

Why should we be happy and peaceful?
What things in your life tend to make you sad?

Read   God's promise in Romans 8:28.

How can we be cheerful, even when things go wrong?

Pray   together about problems that are worrying you. Ask Jesus to give you happy, trusting hearts.

Read   from the joke book—it's good medicine!

Wheelchair Summer

"Don't put any weight on that leg!" cautioned Bentley's mother. She helped him out of the car and into the wheelchair.

"I hate wheelchairs!" complained Bentley. He slumped down while Mother pushed him into the house. "This will be the worst summer vacation ever! No camp, no swimming, no hiking trips…"

"We'll all help you, Bentley. You'll do a lot more than you think."

"I'm stuck in this wheelchair all summer. And the doctor said I may still need another operation on my leg." He sullenly watched the neighbor boys playing outside in their tree house. "I suppose you think I have a bad attitude, don't you, Mom?" he asked.

"Yes," said Mother. "And your attitude is more important than your leg."

"I know," admitted Bentley. "I don't want to spend the summer being a grouch. I just wonder why Jesus let this happen to me."

"When people asked Jesus why a man was born blind, Jesus said it was so God's power could be seen in the blind man."

"How could God's power be seen in me?" asked Bentley.

"That's a question you can ask Jesus," Mother replied.

From then on, Bentley prayed every day. "Dear Jesus, show your power in my life. Help my attitude and heal my leg."

Determined not to gripe or be bitter, Bentley learned to play basketball from his wheelchair. He practiced drawing and learned to paint watercolors. A friend taught him to play chess. On top of all that, he learned to type and use a computer. It was a busy summer!

Everyone in the neighborhood was impressed with Bentley's cheerful attitude and his consideration for others. The elderly man next door told Bentley's parents, "Your son's great attitude has challenged me to quit complaining, to do what I can, and to be thankful!"

"Whenever trouble comes your way, let it be an opportunity for joy."
(James 1:2)

How is your attitude? What do you tend to complain about?
How can God's power be seen in you during your time of trouble?

Wrong Call!

The swim center echoed with cheers for the preteen swim team heading into their final lap. Lisa was leading, but Shelley and Monique kept edging forward.

In the final yards, Lisa knew her friends were closing in. The crowd roared while the girls swam hard to get to the end of the pool first. Lisa made a final thrust and touched the wall. Looking over her shoulder, she saw Shelley finish a second later and then Monique.

Shelley shouted and held up her arm in victory, claiming first place. Lisa frowned. She had touched the wall first. Surely the judge saw it, too.

But the judge reached down and handed Shelley the gold medal and Monique the silver.

Lisa's parents and several other adults hurried down the bleachers to the railing around the pool. They called to the judge, saying, "Lisa touched the side of the pool first!"

The judge wouldn't listen.

Lisa climbed out of the pool and walked over to the railing. Her parents reached across and hugged her. "You were first, dear. We saw it. We'll make sure the judge reviews this race."

Smiling through her tears, Lisa shook her head. "Don't say any more. Shelley is my best friend. Her friendship is more important to me than any gold medal. You and I and Jesus know I was first. That's all that counts."

"Remember to live peaceably with each other." *(1 Thessalonians 5:13)*

How important is winning to you?
What would Jesus say to Lisa?

The Ruined Basketball Court

Ken dribbled his ball down the street, racing ahead of his buddies. Turning the corner, he came to a abrupt halt. "What's going on?" he yelled.

He couldn't believe what he saw—a bulldozer was tearing up the neighborhood basketball court! Waving his arms, Ken headed to the bulldozed lot with his friends following close behind.

"This isn't fair! Who messed everything up?"

"Where's the hoop? Our tournament is next week! How will we practice?" The man on the bulldozer ignored them and continued demolishing the court. He left without any explanation. Upset and angry, the boys trudged home.

"Our tournament will be a disaster," said Ken to his parents. "We need to practice this week. Can you help us, Dad?"

Ken's father made several phone calls and found out what happened. "Someone is trying to clean up the empty neighborhood lot behind the grocery store," he said. "It was full of old tree stumps and gopher holes. And the basketball hoop was rusted and bent anyway."

"That didn't bother us when we played," protested Ken. "Now our neighborhood team has no place to play. We'll lose the city tournament for sure!"

"Wait a minute. Would Jesus want you to give up? Are you going to be bitter and angry about circumstances that can't be changed?" asked his father.

Ken felt too upset to talk and stormed off to his room. He didn't feel like reading his Bible, but he opened it anyway. *You know what's happened, Jesus,* he prayed. *Help us keep our team together. I'm trusting you to work this out for good, even if it looks impossible.*

See tomorrow's devotion for this story's ending.

"Trust in the Lord with all your heart; do not depend on your own understanding. Seek his will in all you do, and he will direct your paths." *(Proverbs 3:5–6)*

What does Jesus want you to do when things go wrong?
How can you live for Jesus in the midst of disappointment?

Surprise Ending

Deep in thought, Ken ran home after school. He knew today's basketball practice was crucial. The neighborhood team had to learn to work as a unit or else disband.

Ever since their local basketball court had been demolished, they hadn't played well as a team. Ken wondered what could help. They desperately needed a place to practice.

Cutting across the lot behind the grocery store, Ken came to an abrupt stop. He couldn't believe his eyes! There, on the very place the boys used to practice, was a new slab of cement—a slab about the size of a basketball court!

Two men were removing the forms around the hardened cement. Ken went over to talk with them.

"What are you doing to this lot?" he asked.

"The owner wanted to clean up this area and build something to benefit the neighborhood kids. He ordered a cement basketball court and two new hoops. We're getting ready to set those up right now. Did you used to play here?" they asked.

Ken nodded his head. He was thankful that he had trusted God instead of getting angry and bitter about circumstances he didn't understand!

"Wait till the team hears about this!" he exclaimed and took off running to find his friends.

"Glory be to God! By his mighty power at work within us, he is able to accomplish infinitely more than we would ever dare to ask or hope." *(Ephesians 3:20)*

When has Jesus surprised you with a special answer to your prayers?

No Quitters

Katie slumped down on the sofa. "I don't want to go to gymnastics class," she said. Her father stood at the door with his coat on, waiting to drive her to class.

"Why do you feel that way?" he asked.

"It's too hard! The exercises wear me out and I can't do them right. None of the other eleven-year-olds are as clumsy as I am. You should see me try to do flips and somersaults. Others watch me and laugh."

"So you want to quit?" asked Dad.

"Yes. I'm tired of being a flop in class."

Her father took off his coat and sat down beside Katie. "Have you asked Jesus to help you?" he asked quietly. "Did you talk to Jesus about your decision to quit?"

"No," Katie mumbled. She didn't want to ask Jesus. She was afraid he would tell her to stay in class.

"Jesus loves you," said Dad. "I'll pray with you. Let's ask Jesus what you should do."

Katie bowed her head and prayed, "Jesus, help me know what to do. I'm so miserable in gymnastics. Can I quit? Or will you help me get better?"

Katie was silent for a few minutes. Then she said, "I could go to gymnastics a little longer with Jesus' help. If I can't improve, then maybe I should quit. But I'll give it another try...*if* you keep praying for me, Dad."

Father hugged her. "You're learning a lesson some grown-ups haven't learned: Don't give up when things are tough. Keep praying. Jesus will help you."

Katie decided to try her class for another month. During that time, she started getting better. She is still in gymnastics class and continues to improve.

"I can do everything with the help of Christ who gives me the strength I need." *(Philippians 4:13)*

 *Why would Jesus want you to learn not to give up when things are hard?*

The Other Side

Get Set You'll need a piece of embroidery or cross-stitching. (You might find an embroidered pillow case in your linen closet.) You'll also need a sliced lemon. Hide a pitcher of lemonade in the refrigerator.

Go!

Pass around the item that has been embroidered or cross-stitched.

Turn it inside out and **look** at the under side.

Point out the messy cut strings and ugly knots.

Why is this side of the piece so ugly?
How are these knots and strings like our lives?

Hold up the embroidered piece so everyone sees only the underside.

If our lives seem like this right now, when will they look like this?
(**Turn** the stitching to the right side.)

Read Isaiah 55:8–12.

How are God's thoughts different from our thoughts?
Why can we trust God to work out every problem?

Give everyone a slice of lemon to taste.

How is tasting a lemon like facing a difficult problem?
Trusting God changes lemons into...

Serve lemonade to everyone!

Smelly Stuff

Get Set On a tray, set out several items that have a strong odor, such as aftershave lotion, perfumes or colognes, hand cream, window cleaner, shampoo, a scented candle, furniture polish, fingernail polish remover, ammonia, and vinegar. You'll also need a blindfold.

Go!

Ask for a volunteer and *blindfold* him or her.

Take turns waving the various items from the tray under the volunteer's nose.

Have the volunteer *give* a thumbs-up if the fragrance is pleasant or a thumbs-down if the fragrance is unpleasant.

Place the pleasant-smelling items on one side of the table and the unpleasant items on the other.

Which of these would you like to smell like?

Have everyone *try on* a fragrance.

Read 2 Corinthians 2:14–16.

What kind of "fragrance" is these verses talking about?
What kinds of attitudes and actions make you "smell sweet"?
What would make you smell rotten?
How can all of us be like a fragrant perfume this week to those who don't know Jesus?

Light the scented candle and *pray* that the fragrance of your life will draw others to Jesus this week.

A Bonnet for Becca

Jenny walked into Becca's hospital room, not sure what to say to her best friend. Becca had recently lost her left leg because of cancer. Now her hair was falling out because of the medicine she was taking.

Jenny handed her a stuffed frog, Becca's favorite animal. Becca grinned. "Ribbet! Thanks!"

"And here's a box of cards from everyone in fourth grade, even Jonah Striker. Everybody at school misses you. They want to know when you'll be back."

Becca's face flushed. "Why?" she asked, turning her head away. "So they can stare at a freak with one leg and a bald head?"

Jenny sat there, not knowing what to say. Silently she prayed, *How can I help her, Jesus?* When Jenny's mother picked her up later at the hospital entrance, Jenny told her what Becca had said. Mother's eyes filled with tears.

On the way home, Mother stopped at a fabric store. "Jesus would want us to help make Becca's first days back at school good ones," said Mother.

After finding a pattern for a prairie dress and bonnet, they chose a yellow-and-brown calico material and yellow ribbon to match. Then they went home and started to sew.

Three weeks later, Jenny's mom drove the girls to school. Jenny jumped out of the van, handed Becca her crutches, and helped her step down. Then Jenny arranged Becca's long calico skirt to hide the missing leg. She smoothed her own skirt and adjusted both their bonnets. "What do you think, Mom?" she asked. "Do we look like twins?"

"You look like Mary and Laura from *Little House on the Prairie!* Have a good day, girls."

"We will!" Becca said with a big smile.

And Jenny knew they would.

Jesus said, "Do for others as you would like them to do for you."
(Luke 6:31)

How could you help a friend who's having a hard time?
Put yourself in that person's place. What do you think would help the most?

The New Brother

Five-year-old Wayne rubbed the satin binding of his blankie and listened to his mother talk on the phone. He wondered if it was the call they'd been waiting for.

When Mother hung up the phone, she threw her arms around Wayne and laughed. "Your new baby brother just arrived in the world! We need to go pick him up today!" She twirled Wayne around excitedly.

"Oh, Mama, when can I see him? What does he look like?" Wayne had been asking for a baby brother or sister for over two years. He could hardly believe a new baby would finally arrive at their house.

Wayne's father hurried home from the office to pick up Grandmother. She was going to stay with Wayne while he and Wayne's mother drove to the hospital in Seattle.

Wayne watched his mother finish packing the suitcases. She held up some baby overalls and a shirt. "Here's the outfit I got him to wear," she said. "And here's his first toy—a fluffy rabbit. Now all we have to do is pick up your new brother."

Just as his parents got in the car to leave, Wayne came running out of the house.

"Here!" He shoved his treasured blankie into his mother's hands. "This is my most special gift for my brother. Tell him I can't wait to play with him," said Wayne.

"God is love, and all who live in love live in God, and God lives in them." *(1 John 4:16)*

What treasures would Jesus want you to share?

A Different Thanksgiving

Hannah scooped mashed potatoes from a large pot, put them on a paper plate, and handed the plate to her dad. He added a slice of turkey. Last Thanksgiving Hannah would never have dreamed she'd be spending this Thanksgiving at Seattle's Gospel Mission serving dinner to the homeless. But last Thanksgiving her mother had been alive. She bit her lower lip to keep it from trembling.

Fifteen minutes later, Hannah untied the apron covering her sweater and jeans, picked up a plate of food, and looked over the crowded room for a place to sit. The only empty spot was next to a man neatly dressed in faded clothes.

When she sat down, he asked her, "Does your family serve here every year?"

"No. My Dad made me come." She wiped the tears welling up in her eyes. "My mom's dead. And we can't afford to drive to Grandma's."

"Not a lot to give thanks for this year?"

She shook her head.

"I've been there," he said. "I lost my family and my business in one year. Didn't feel too thankful last Thanksgiving."

"You're thankful now?"

He nodded. "I've learned to think about what I have, not what I've lost. Jesus has given me friends to love—Red-Eye Randy," he said, nodding across the table toward a bleary-eyed man, "and Two-Bag Nellie." The old woman next to him rummaged through her shopping bags. "Then there's Mrs. Gilbert and her boy at the next table and Chong Lee." He pointed to a teenager with a gold ring in his nose.

"I get the message," said Hannah. "Happiness comes when we give." She noticed the child sitting across from her. "Need help cutting your meat?" Hannah asked with a smile. It was time to start giving to others.

Jesus said, "If you give, you will receive." *(Luke 6:38)*

Who do you love and care for?
Do you focus on your own problems or try to help others?

The Empty Shoe Boxes

Jacob finished sweeping fallen leaves off the driveway and headed up the walkway to the house, sweeping as he went. Exhausted, he went inside and collapsed on a kitchen chair.

"I give up!" he said to his mother. "For weeks I've washed the car, cleaned house, vacuumed, and trimmed hedges. I'll never earn enough money to fill my empty shoe boxes."

"I know you feel discouraged," said Mother. "But think of the two children overseas who need the soap and combs and toothbrushes. They would be so excited to receive art supplies, notepads, and some toys to play with!"

Jacob munched on an apple while he looked around the kitchen. "I've never known what's it's like to have no food. I can't imagine being without soap, a toothbrush, or a toy."

His face lit up as he thought about what his gifts would mean to two children who lived in a poor country. "What is all this work I'm doing once a year compared to what people in Africa, Asia, and Bosnia have to do every day? They work much harder and have almost nothing! I *can't* give up!" He grabbed the broom and headed for the neighbors' house. "I'll ask Mr. Higbee if I can sweep his driveway. I want to fill those boxes on Monday!"

After washing several neighbors' cars, Jacob finally went shopping. He bought toothbrushes, combs, wash cloths, soap, bouncy balls, dolls, stickers, and markers. That evening, he wrapped each shoe box in Christmas paper he'd bought and filled them to overflowing with gifts.

When he delivered the beautiful boxes to his schoolteacher, Jacob said, "I'm thankful I didn't give up. I chose to do what Jesus would have done—give to others. And it's made me happier than getting a gift myself!"

"Don't give reluctantly...for God loves the person who gives cheerfully." *(2 Corinthians 9:7)*

What are you willing to give to someone in need? Time...money...belongings?

Mindy's Sacrifice

A feeling of satisfaction washed over Mindy. She sang the last note of her solo while fifty voices swelled around her for the Christmas program's finale. The music ended and the choir bowed to the audience.

Mindy glanced to her right. Her friend Leah stood beside her.

Mindy smiled. Choir was Leah's chance to do something right for once. Mindy had talked her into joining. What could she mess up? If she forgot the words, she could mouth them. And no one would ever notice her slightly off-key voice.

A movement to her right started Mindy's heart pounding. What was Leah doing? Leah, all alone, marched toward the steps to exit the stage. Mindy's body stiffened. Every day for the last week, the choir had practiced waiting for the curtain to close. How could Leah mess up? How could she not notice the rest of the choir waiting in place? Mindy shot up a quick prayer. *Please Jesus, help her realize and come back.*

Scattered laughter rippled through the audience. It was too late now. Even if Leah came back and waited with the choir, she would be totally humiliated.

Jesus, show me how to help her, prayed Mindy.

Taking a deep breath, Mindy strode toward Leah. Together they walked down the stage steps and the curtain closed behind them. Mindy knew Leah wouldn't be so embarrassed if she had a friend.

"Our purpose is to please God, not people." *(1 Thessalonians 2:4)*

Why do you think Mindy's sacrifice pleased God?

Hidden Sweets

Get Set Gather chocolate kisses, a paper bag, note paper, envelopes, and colored pencils.

Go!

Have each person *write* his or her name on a slip of paper and drop it into the bag.

Draw names.

Read John 15:9–13.

Let everyone *tell* how the person whose name they're holding shows love to other members of your family.

Hand out envelopes, note paper, and colored pencils. Have everyone *write* their person's name on an envelope, then *make* an appreciation card for that person.

Place the appreciation notes and a few chocolate kisses in the envelopes, then *hide* the envelopes around the house.

Go on an envelope hunt, then *read* the notes and *enjoy* the candy.

Have everyone *pray* for the person who wrote and hid their note.

Sign on the Doorpost

Get Set Gather a tiny gift box, scissors, a pen with gold ink, and a brown grocery bag.

Go!

Explain: As a boy, Jesus probably had a mezuzah (muh-ZOO-sah) fastened to the doorpost of his home. It was a small box that contained Deuteronomy 6:4–9 and 11:13–21 on a small parchment scroll. The words were a reminder of God's protection. Every time Jewish people entered their homes, they would touch the mezuzah and say, "May God protect my going out and coming in now and forever." To make your own mezuzah:

Cut a long strip from the grocery bag. Make it narrow enough to fit in the box.

Using the gold pen, **copy** Deuteronomy 6:5 onto the strip.

Roll it up into a scroll.

Place the scroll in the small box.

Tape the mezuzah to a frame of a door.

Read Deuteronomy 6:4–9 and 11:13–21.

Pray together for God's blessing on your home. Ask God to help you remember to do what Jesus would do each time you enter and leave your home.

A Friend for Mr. Montrose

"Mr. Montrose is a lousy teacher," whispered Jake. "Nobody likes him and his stupid science class."

Chad nodded and watched the teacher closely. He thought Mr. Montrose had taught a couple of interesting lessons. But he was downright ugly—a skinny, balding man with a large nose.

If I want to be cool in this new middle school, Chad thought, *I'll have to make sure I don't have anything to do with this teacher.*

At the close of science lab, Mr. Montrose picked up everyone's papers. As he was carrying the stack back to his desk for grading, Jake suddenly shoved his book bag out in the aisle. Mr. Montrose tripped and went sprawling on the floor at the end of the row of desks. Papers flew everywhere.

The class burst out laughing. But Chad knew what Jesus wanted him to do. He got up from his seat and collected the scattered papers. Even though he knew the other students were laughing at him, he straightened out the lab reports and laid them on the teacher's desk.

Mr. Montrose stared in disbelief at his young helper. He hadn't expected anyone to help pick up the mess.

"Trying to be the teacher's pet?" asked Jake when Chad returned to his seat. "Why didn't you let him pick up his own mess?"

Chad didn't say anything. He was more concerned about what Jesus thought than what others thought.

"So our aim is to please [the Lord] always." *(2 Corinthians 5:9)*

 *How can you please Jesus today?*

The Snowball Raid

The tallest boy looked back at Jeremy. "Okay, shrimp," he said. "You can come with us…*if* you do what we say. Understand?"

"Wait for me!" shouted Jeremy, grabbing a handful of snow and running down the street toward the older boys. As he packed the snow tightly, his heart pounded with excitement. He would show them that his aim was as good as theirs and that he could throw hard, too. Maybe after this snowball raid they'd accept him into their group instead of making jokes about him.

The boys turned the corner and headed down a side street.

"Let's use this street. We can run down the alley if we have to get away fast," said Jake.

When several cars turned down the street, Jake yelled his orders: "Give it to them!"

A flurry of snowballs flew through the air, splattering doors and windows of passing cars. The boys roared with laughter.

"Hey, did you see that last driver's face?"

"Yeah! We sure scared her! She couldn't even drive straight after we blasted her!"

But Jeremy had seen another face in the back window…a little girl with red curls. Her eyes were filled with fear and her mouth hung open in fright. She looked terrified.

Her face startled Jeremy. *Would Jesus want me to throw these snowballs?* he wondered. *No, he wouldn't. I can't do this anymore.* "Jesus, help me!" he prayed.

Jeremy shivered in the cold, wondering what to say to the other boys. Finally he spoke up. "It's no fun scaring little kids. It's wrong and I'm leaving." And with that, Jeremy turned and went home. He didn't care anymore what older boys said about him.

Jesus said, "I assure you, when you did it to one of the least of these my brothers and sisters, you were doing it to me!" *(Matthew 25:40)*

What do you think Jesus meant by these words?

New "Friends"

Sam sighed and packed up his book bag. He dreaded walking home alone. After two weeks in this new school, he still didn't know anyone very well.

Please help me, Jesus, he prayed. *I need some friends.*

When Sam walked out the front door of the school, two boys called to him. "Hey, Sam! Come with us to the store and we'll walk home with you."

Sam excitedly waved, crossed the street, and followed them. *They might be my first friends,* he thought. He hurried over to the next block where the boys stood waiting outside the deli.

"We're glad you came, Sam. Now we're gonna let you in on a little secret," one boy said in a low whisper. "Every day after school we come here and pick up a few extra treats. We'll let you be part of our special group."

"I...I didn't bring any money," Sam started to explain.

The tallest boy interrupted. "Hey—it's time. The cashier is busy with a lot of customers. Let's get to work. I'll get the chips and dip. Jenkins will get the pop. Sam, you sneak some gum and candy." He grabbed Sam's coat sleeve and warned, "Stand behind the shelves where the cashier can't see you. And if you do get caught, pretend you don't know us—do you understand?"

Sam's mouth dropped open. He never dreamed these new friends would ask him to shoplift! He sent up a quick prayer, saying, *Help me, Jesus!*

"Hey, guys," Sam said, "I like giving things away. I'm no good at taking things from people. Jesus says that I'm not supposed to steal. So good-bye, I have to go."

With that Sam took off and sprinted for home.

"Get rid of your evil deeds. Shed them like dirty clothes." *(Romans 13:12)*

Is there something you're doing that Jesus would want you to stop?
When have you refused to take something that wasn't yours?

Overflowing Sink

"Whoa!" hollered Caleb. His feet skidded across the wet floor as he hurried into the boys restroom.

Two older boys laughed loudly when Caleb slipped. One sink was already overflowing onto the floor. The boys quickly grabbed more paper towels from the dispenser, stuffed them into a second sink, and turned the faucet on full blast.

The troublemakers peeked out the restroom door into the hall. "Let's get out of here fast, before a teacher shows up!" said one boy.

"We'll let you clog the third sink—have fun!" they said, rushing out of the restroom.

Caleb surveyed the mess left behind. "Watch out!" he warned a younger boy who stepped into the restroom. "Don't fall on these wet floors." Turning off the faucets, Caleb reached into the sinks and pulled out the towels that were clogging the drains.

"What a waste of water and money," he said. "But I was just like them last year. I used to think it was fun to cause trouble. That was before I gave my life to Jesus."

Picking up other paper towels littering the floor, he prayed for the boys. "They need you, Jesus. Work in their hearts so they will know how much you love them. Help them learn to live for you and do what's right."

"Do not let any part of your body become a tool of wickedness, to be used for sinning." *(Romans 6:13)*

 *What would Jesus say to someone who was vandalizing?*

Mrs. Keizer's Class

Dan slumped sideways in his chair facing away from the teacher who droned on about some multiplication problem. Who cared! Kyle was right—Mrs. Keizer was a bore.

Dan watched Kyle fold his math paper into an airplane and float it across three rows of desks. Two girls giggled and whispered. Another boy wrote on his desk. It was a typical day in Mrs. Keizer's class.

"Then if you number from zero to ten the other way," Mrs. Keizer said, demonstrating on the board, "you have the answers to the 'nines' multiplication tables."

"Cool!" Dan blurted out. Everyone stared at him. "Well, it will help *me,*" Dan muttered.

Kyle rolled his eyes and turned away.

"You know I need help memorizing my multiplication tables," Dan whispered to Kyle, defending himself. But he knew he would suffer for this. Nobody was supposed to even *listen* to Mrs. Keizer.

It didn't used to be like this. Everyone used to like Mrs. Keizer. That changed when Kyle came. Kyle hated Mrs. Keizer. Since he was popular, the other kids started hating Mrs. Keizer, too. One by one they started saying cruel things behind her back. Then they started laughing at her in class.

Dan had joined in with everyone else. He knew if you wanted to be accepted, you *didn't* cooperate with Mrs. Keizer.

But Dan knew that wasn't what Jesus would do.

"Mrs. Keizer," Dan said after class, "I liked that lesson."

Out of the corner of his eye Dan saw Kyle shake his head, stomp to the door, and slam it behind him. Maybe Kyle wouldn't be his friend any more. Or maybe he could influence Kyle to make better choices.

No matter what happened, Dan had definitely decided—he would be nice to Mrs. Keizer.

"Watch out that no bitter root...rises up.... Many are corrupted by its poison." *(Hebrews 12:15)*

What would Jesus say about following the crowd? Who does Jesus want you to be nicer to?

The Right Voice

Get Set Rearrange the furniture in one or two rooms to make an obstacle course. You'll need a granola bar for each person and a blindfold.

Go!

Blindfold a volunteer.

Explain that if the volunteer can go through the entire obstacle course without touching anything, he or she will win a granola bar.

Promise to coach the volunteer. *Tell* him or her to listen for your voice. As the volunteer enters the obstacle course, have other family members *call out* false instructions.

Encourage the blindfolded person to listen only to your voice.

Call out a steady stream of clear, careful instructions.

If necessary, *allow* the volunteer to go through the course more than once in order to win the prize.

Continue until everyone has successfully completed the course.

Sit in a circle and *enjoy* your treat.

How was doing the obstacle course like trying to live for Jesus?
When is it easiest to "follow the crowd" and hardest to follow Jesus?
How can we encourage one another to follow Jesus?

Pray for God's strength to live for Jesus and listen to his voice.

A Handful of Prayer

Get Set   All you need are your fingers!

Go!

Read   Ephesians 6:18.

Explain: We can use our fingers to help us remember how to pray "all kinds" of prayers.

Press   the tips of your little fingers together. Little fingers help us remember to pray for little children. **Pray** for the youngest members of your family, for little ones at church and in your neighborhood.

Put   ring fingers together. Rings join people in marriage to form families. **Pray** for your family at home and for those who live farther away.

Touch   the tips of your middle fingers. Our middle fingers are tallest so they remind us of our leaders. **Pray** that God will give wisdom to the leaders of your school, church, community, and country.

Put   pointer fingers together. Think of people you can point to everyday—schoolmates, store clerks, neighborhood friends. **Pray** for them.

Touch   your thumbs together and you're pointing back to yourself!

Pray   that God will help you live for him and do what Jesus would do each day.

A Loving Friend

Jennifer couldn't understand why Anne seemed grumpy and tired again. "Let's join the kids playing softball," encouraged Jennifer. But Anne sat in the swing, saying nothing.

"What a loser!" said Jennifer. "All you do is sit on that swing! I don't know what your problem is, but I'm going to join a team."

"Go ahead!" shouted Anne. "I don't have to do what you want!"

"You can do nothing—see if I care!" Jennifer shouted back.

Anne jumped out of the swing and started toward the classroom. Jennifer turned to go to the softball field—until she heard a muffled sob. It was Anne!

Jennifer felt terrible. *Why did I say those mean things?* she wondered. She ran after Anne, saying, "Don't be upset. Please forgive me!"

Anne sat down on the grass and cried. "I'm sorry, too." She dried her tears and continued, "I suppose I should tell you the truth. Everything's going wrong in my life. Mom and Dad don't want to live together any longer. And the doctor just called and said my blood tests show that I have leukemia. I can't play softball—I'm too sick. I need to start treatments that could make my hair fall out."

Suddenly the way Anne had been behaving recently made sense. Jennifer said, "I'm sorry all those things are happening. Jesus is here to go through it with you, and so am I. Come home with me after school and we'll pray together. Nothing is too difficult for Jesus."

A month later, Jennifer told her pastor, "One of the biggest blessings of my life has been to pray after school with Anne. Her parents are back together and are going to counseling. Her treatments at the hospital are working and she hasn't lost any hair. Now when we get together after school, we just praise God!"

"Most important of all, continue to show deep love for each other."
(1 Peter 4:8)

 *How would Jesus want you to help someone going through a difficult time?*

A New Heart

Sheila's father picked her up and hugged her. "Your new baby brother may not live," he whispered. "Let's pray for his little heart."

Emergency surgery had been needed to repair a hole in Joshua's heart, which had only one valve instead of four. Several surgeries later, doctors warned his parents that Joshua wouldn't live. But Sheila prayed daily, "Jesus, please heal my brother's heart."

Joshua continued to live, and he grew bigger and stronger. When he began crawling, he got into everything—especially Sheila's things! Then he learned to walk and run. Everyone was amazed at his health and strength.

Sheila went along to the doctor's office for Joshua's twenty-four-month medical exam. She took her toy doctor kit. While they waited, Sheila got out her little stethoscope and listened to Joshua's heart. He giggled and laughed, unaware of the miracles that had already happened in his life.

"Jesus is healing you, Joshua," Sheila said confidently. "Your heart sounds better."

When the doctor came in, Sheila watched him listen to her brother's heart.

"Doctor, do you hear Jesus in Joshua's heart?" she asked. "Jesus is making Joshua's heart well. I know Jesus lives there, because Jesus lives in my heart, too."

"Be strong and courageous! Do not be afraid or discouraged. For the Lord your God is with you wherever you go." *(Joshua 1:9)*

Are you confident that Jesus lives in you? How can you keep from being discouraged during difficult times?

Boozey Joe

"Anybody for a game of Parcheesi?" asked Dad, pulling the game out of the closet.

"Yeah!" Tricia and her younger brother Ben shouted together. Tricia loved family night. No matter how busy Dad was during the week pastoring their inner-city church, he always stayed home on Friday nights to be with the family.

Mother walked into the living room and asked, "Should we make milk shakes or banana splits after the game?" Suddenly someone pounded forcefully on the door.

"Who could that be?" Mother wondered aloud.

When their father opened the door to the apartment, Boozey Joe stumbled in.

With a wild look in his eyes, he pulled a gun from his pocket and waved it in the air. "I could kill you if I wanted to!" he yelled.

Tricia caught her breath and grabbed Ben's hand. "Dear Jesus, keep us safe," she prayed quietly. "And help Boozey Joe know your love." Slowly she inched over to her mother.

Boozey Joe looked at the two children. Then he dropped the gun and fell at their father's feet, crying. "Pray for me, Pastor," he sobbed. "Pray for me."

"Come, children," said their mother softly. "Let's go to the bedroom. Boozey Joe is drunk. We'll let Dad deal with him."

When they reached the bedroom, their mother shut the door. She hugged them closely and asked, "Were you afraid?"

"We're okay, Mom," said Tricia. "It's Boozey Joe who needs help. He needs Jesus. Can we pray for him?" All three of them knelt by the bed and asked God to protect their dad and make Boozey Joe a new man in Christ.

Boozey Joe accepted Jesus that night. And with Jesus' help, he quit drinking. Later he became one of the leaders in their church!

"Those who become Christians become new persons.... The old life is gone. A new life has begun!" *(2 Corinthians 5:17)*

Do you know someone who needs a new life in Jesus? Could you pray for them now?

Toby's Prayer

Toby heard the television news report that a man had fallen from a cliff at Multnomah Falls. Rescuers were searching for him in the trees and underbrush. Toby set his peanut butter cookies and glass of milk on the kitchen counter.

Scott, Toby's scout leader, had gone to hike at the falls that morning. *Could it be Scott?* Toby wondered. *Scott isn't a Christian.*

Without saying a word, Toby hurried to his room and knelt by his bed. "Dear Jesus," Toby prayed, "is that Scott? Whoever it is, please protect him. Keep him alive. Help the rescuers find him. And let him know you love him."

Toby went downstairs and continued to pray silently. He couldn't eat his cookies. An hour passed. A news flash reported that rescuers were still searching.

Mom called Toby to set the table for dinner. He turned the television up so he could hear any news about the rescue. Toby prayed as he folded napkins. *Comfort him and help him not be afraid,* he prayed.

The television announced another special report. Toby went to watch. They had found the man who fell at the bottom of the gorge. They didn't know if he would live. Cameras zoomed in on his face as paramedics carried him to the ambulance. It was Scott!

Dear Jesus, please don't let Scott die, Toby prayed.

Over the next few weeks, Scott lay in a coma. Toby visited him several times. At home, Toby prayed faithfully every day for him.

Two months after the accident, Scott came out of his coma. A week later, Toby and his dad talked to Scott about Jesus.

Scott tells people today that he probably would never have become a Christian had it not been for the accident…and Toby's prayers.

"I love the Lord because he hears and answers my prayers." *(Psalm 116:1)*

When has Jesus shown you how he answered your prayers?
Have you ever prayed about an accident you heard on the news?

179

Carolyn's Reward

"Hi, Carolyn," Ronnie said. He kissed his twenty-year-old cousin on the cheek. "Your new wheelchair is fancy!"

Ronnie saw the muscles around Carolyn's eyes tense in agreement. Ten years ago she could have answered. Two years ago she would have smiled to respond. She couldn't do that anymore. A rare disease called Neiman Picks had changed her. Through her T-shirt Ronnie could see the bulge of her feeding tube.

Ronnie saw Carolyn's eyes fasten on the pages in his hand. He smiled. "I brought you three new prayer pages," he told her. Ronnie took the three-ring binder from her lap and inserted the pages. Mom had helped him punch three holes in the paper and then laminate it. Now it wouldn't rip when Carolyn struggled to turn the pages with her curled-up hands.

"Pretty exciting, huh?" he asked.

Carolyn laboriously lifted her head, then let it drop to her chest to say, "Yes."

"This page asks prayer for a kid in my class whose parents are getting a divorce," he said.

Carolyn squinted her eyes to read it, then shut them. Ronnie knew she was already praying for his friend. She spent hours praying. A lot of people thought Carolyn's life was wasted. Ronnie knew better.

"You help more people than anyone I know," Ronnie said. "When you get to heaven, you'll be amazed at all the things your prayers have accomplished."

"Pray…. Then your Father…will reward you." *(Matthew 6:6)*

How often do you pray for others?
Who would Jesus want you to pray for?

Prayers in the News

Get Set Make a video recording of a national newscast. Then gather your family around your television for a unique time of prayer.

Go!

Read 1 Timothy 2:1–2.

Watch the first news story.

Pause the tape and stop to pray for the people in that story.

Continue the tape, pausing after each news item to pray.

Challenge family members to find Bible verses or stories that teach about the issues in each story.

Discuss how things would be different if everyone pledged to do what Jesus would do.

Decide if there's any further action you'd like to take as a family.

Would it be helpful to write a letter to a person in government? to send money to a mission organization in a needy country? to write an encouraging note to a person or organization that suffered a loss?

Assign one news item to each person for further prayer throughout the week.

Trinkets and Treasures

Get Set Prepare a fancy dessert such as a cake or pie, decorated cookies, or banana splits. Place servings on individual plates, but don't make enough for everyone—plan to keep one plate empty. Ask everyone to choose one thing they treasure to bring to devotions.

Go!

Have each person *tell* about what he or she brought and why it is important.

Read Mark 10:17–23.

Can our earthly treasures ever be too important to us?
How could earthly treasures keep us from doing what God wants?

Read Luke 21:1–4.

How was the widow different from the rich young man?
What treasures should we be most concerned about?
What's one thing our family treasures that we might give up in order to send money to help others know Jesus?

Serve the desserts.

Give one person the empty plate.

Share part of your treasured dessert with that person.

Encourage others to do the same.

How does sharing a treasure make it even more valuable than when we keep it ourselves?

Close with prayer, asking God to bless you with a giving heart.

The Bride Doll

From the top of the stairs, Marissa listened to her parents' conversation. She heard her mom crying.

"We can't afford presents this year," said Dad.

"But Marissa keeps begging for a bride doll," Mom said.

"She'll have to understand that until God provides a job…" Dad's voice trailed off and Mom finished for him, "we're fortunate to have a home and food."

Dad nodded. Mom gazed into his face and stroked his cheek. "We can make Christmas fun. Things don't matter."

Marissa swallowed hard and tiptoed back to her room. She understood, she really did. It was just that she had dreamed of a bride doll for months.

She stopped at Mom and Dad's room to gaze at Mom's wedding dress hanging in her closet. It was white satin decorated with pearls and it still fit Mom. Their wedding picture sat on the dresser. Marissa wanted a doll that looked like that.

The next few days flew past. Cookie smells filled the house. Marissa and Mom decorated with popcorn and holly. They folded origami swans from colorful magazine pages and strung them into chains. Marissa tried not to think about the bride doll.

Christmas morning, Marissa awakened to the aroma of pancakes and the sound of "Joy to the World" coming from the stereo. Downstairs she could hear Mom and Dad giggling. Marissa ran downstairs, thanking Jesus for all her blessings. The bride doll really didn't matter.

Beneath the tree sat one of Marissa's dolls. It wore a magnificent bridal gown of satin and pearls. Tears streamed from her eyes as Marissa knelt to stroke her doll's elegant dress.

"You cut up your wedding dress," she whispered, "for me."

Tears shone in Mom's eyes. "*You* are more important than things," she said.

"We love each other as a result of [God] loving us first." *(1 John 4:19)*

What did Jesus sacrifice for you? How does Mom's sacrifice remind you of Jesus?

The Greatest Gift

Jimmy undressed, put on the long white gown, and lay down on the hospital bed. He couldn't stop praying for his little sister. Jimmy loved Grace and he loved being a big brother. Now Grace was very sick with a rare blood disease.

The doctors had explained the seriousness of her illness to Jimmy. They told him how important it was for her to receive several pints of donated blood. When they discovered that Jimmy's blood was a perfect match for his sister's, they asked Jimmy, "Would you help your sister by giving her some of your blood?"

It hadn't taken him long to answer. He was willing to do anything for his little sister.

Jimmy heard the door open, and the doctor entered the room. While the doctor sterilized Jimmy's arm and inserted a tube, Jimmy continued to silently pray for Grace.

When the nine-year-old saw his blood begin to flow through the long tube, Jimmy looked up and quietly asked the doctor, "How long will it take for me to die?"

The doctor was startled. "Die? Who said you were going to die? We're just going to take some of your blood. Your healthy body will replace it in a few days. You'll be just fine!"

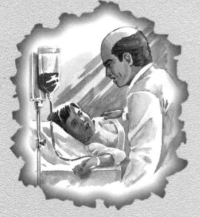

"Christ gave up his life for us. And so we also ought to give up our lives for our Christian friends." *(1 John 3:16)*

In what way was Jimmy like Jesus?
Would you be willing to give your life so someone else could live?

185

Jennifer's Gift

Jennifer colored a paper rainbow and taped it inside an empty shoe box.

"What are you making?" asked Keeta, her Vietnamese friend.

"A gift for my dad. It's his birthday today." Just a couple of months before, Jennifer's mother had walked out on the family. Jennifer knew how important it was to show her dad how much she loved him.

"It's my father's birthday too," said Keeta. "I picked some yellow flowers on the playground that I'll give him." She had carefully taped the flowers together and tied them with a piece of yarn.

The teacher walked by and said, "I asked you earlier to put your art project away until free time, Jennifer. This is math hour."

The rest of the morning, Jennifer worked on her shoe box whenever she had a free minute.

When the class gathered for story time, one boy snatched the bouquet of dandelions off Keeta's desk. Keeta's eyes welled up with tears.

"Give her back those flowers!" Jennifer ordered.

The boy snapped off all the golden tops and threw them on the desk.

Keeta covered her face and cried.

Running back to her desk, Jennifer got the shoe box she'd been working on for so long. She brought it to Keeta and said, "I know you don't have a mother either. Give this to your father. I can always make another one."

"Don't think only about your own affairs, but be interested in others, too, and what they are doing." *(Philippians 2:4)*

How was Jennifer unselfish?
How would Jesus encourage you to be unselfish today?

Learning from Annie

"Help! I'm stuck!" Rachel's little sister, Annie, tried to push her foot into the armhole of her bunny costume. She couldn't keep up with her sister and brothers as they changed into their animal outfits.

"Just a minute and I'll help you," offered Rachel. She was used to assisting her Down syndrome sister. She knew Annie's uncoordinated hands and fingers took twice as long to do everything.

When they finished dressing, their father walked down the street with them. They collected all kinds of treats at their neighbors' houses. Rachel's brothers couldn't hurry fast enough from one house to the other to get a new treat.

But Rachel noticed what Annie did at each house. Annie was delighted to receive treats, but she didn't hurry away like her brothers did. She took extra time to talk to each neighbor. She would pet their cats or dogs and comment on the pansies still blooming in their flower boxes. Before she left, she would flash a radiant smile and say, "Thank you very much!"

Rachel waited patiently at each house until Annie finished talking. She realized, *Annie isn't just thinking about getting treats, she is loving and caring for those who are giving! She is wiser than we are!*

For the first time Rachel saw her sister in a new light. Although Annie couldn't read and write, she seemed more understanding, considerate, and loving than other children. She cared about the people who lived in each house, not just about the treats they handed out.

"You should remember the words of the Lord Jesus: 'It is more blessed to give than to receive.'" *(Acts 20:35)*

 When have you been more interested in "getting" than giving?
How do you act when you receive a gift? What would Jesus want you to do?

Floored by Love

Ramon sighed as he scrubbed the peeling linoleum floor in the kitchen. "No matter how much we wash this floor, it always looks dirty," he told his mother.

The doorbell rang. "Ramon! Answer the door!" Ramon's dad shouted over the blaring TV. Ramon dropped the scrub brush and went to answer it.

"Pastor Garcia!" said Ramon. His heart soared. "Have you come to tell my father about Jesus' love? He won't listen to me."

Pastor Garcia smiled. "Buenos dias, Ramon."

Ramon stared at the group of men who were with the pastor. They carried trowels, putty knives, a large roll of flooring, and a bucket labeled "Floor Adhesive."

"Who is it?" yelled Ramon's father, stomping to the door.

Pastor Garcia extended his hand. "I am Jose Garcia, pastor of the church your son attends. We heard you could use a new kitchen floor."

Ramon prayed silently, *Dear Jesus, do not let my father turn these men away.*

"We cannot afford a new floor. Good-bye," said Ramon's father as he turned to shut the door.

"We will do it for free," said Pastor Garcia.

Narrowing his eyes, Ramon's father asked, "Why would you do that?"

"Because people who love Jesus help their neighbors," said Pastor.

Ramon excitedly watched the men remove the old, chipped floor, then lay the new linoleum. And he watched his father, who stood by with a puzzled expression on his face.

When the workers left, the family gathered to admire the new kitchen floor. Ramon's father said, "I'm amazed at what those men did!"

"Why don't you come to church with me tomorrow?" asked Ramon.

"We will all go," said Ramon's father. "Maybe there is something to this Jesus stuff."

Ramon felt as if he would burst with joy. Now his whole family would hear about Jesus!

"Love your neighbor as yourself." *(Matthew 19:19)*

Which neighbor needs your love?
How could you help a neighbor and share
Jesus' love?

Dinner to Go!

Get Set Gather everyone in the kitchen to prepare a surprise lunch for a neighbor. You'll need a large basket (or box lined with wrapping paper), colorful paper napkins, a large glass jar, and a variety of food.

Go!

Read 1 John 4:7–12.

Explain: Today we're going to show Jesus' love in a very practical way—by making a surprise lunch for a neighbor. (You may want to prepare your own lunch at the same time!)

Decide which neighbor to treat.

Make heart-shaped sandwiches by cutting bread, lunch meat, and cheese with a heart cookie cutter.

Add plastic zipper bags filled with pretzels and cookies.

Wash fresh fruit.

Pour iced tea or lemonade into the glass jar.

Arrange the lunch in the basket.

Write a simple card saying: "With love from the [your last name] family."

Add a favorite Bible verse to the back of the card.

Deliver the lunch to your neighbor's door, **ring** the doorbell, then **run** away!

Fruit of the Spirit

Get Set Set out nine different varieties of fruit. You may want to use some canned or frozen fruit. You'll also need knives, a can opener, a cutting board, and a bowl and spoon for each person.

Go!

Read Galatians 5:16–23.

Explain: We're going to choose a fruit to represent each fruit of the spirit. Each time we discuss a fruit of the spirit and choose a fruit, we'll add that fruit to our bowls.

How can we show more love to others?
Do you think people see us as joyful Christians? Why or why not?
How could we have more peace in our home?
When do we need more patience?
What is the kindness level in our family?
How do our lives show goodness?
When do we need to work on being more gentle?
Are we faithful in the things we need to do?
When could we use more self-control?

Pray: Dear Lord, please allow your Holy Spirit to work in our lives so that we show the kind of fruit that brings glory to you. Bless us and make us a blessing wherever we go. In Jesus' name, amen.

Enjoy your fruit cups!

Hail to the King and Queen!

"Mom!" Jon stomped his feet angrily. "Paul and Elizabeth never play what I want! They ignore me when I tell them what to do!"

"What's going on?" Mother asked.

"I brought these out of the dress-up box so we could act out some stories." Jon held up three red capes. "But they won't play superheroes! They just keep digging in the sandbox."

"Maybe you could play with them in the sandbox," suggested Mother.

"No!" Jon stomped off into the living room.

Later, Mother peeked into the living room to see what he was doing. She found the room rearranged with two large chairs in the center, surrounded by stuffed animals. Jon was pulling quilts out of the closet.

"What's happening?" she asked.

He flashed a smile. "I got a great idea! Just watch!" He went outside and soon came back—leading his younger brother and sister.

"Make way!" he announced loudly. "Here are the new king and queen!" Paul and Elizabeth wore big grins as they marched to the front room and sat down on their "thrones."

Jon addressed them as "Your Highness" and "Your Majesty" as he draped colorful afghans and quilts over their shoulders and laps. Using items from the dress-up box, he put crowns on their heads, gave each of them a broken broomstick for a royal scepter, and laid down a carpet of blankets in front of their chairs.

"Get the camera, Mom! We need a picture of this lovely queen and king! And I need to be in the picture, too. I'm their servant."

After the photo shoot, Jon told his mother, "I decided to please them and not insist on my own way. Please leave the royal throne room the way it is so I can show Dad. I can't wait to tell him about all our fun today!"

"We should please others…. For even Christ didn't please himself."
(Romans 15:2, 3)

 *How can you please your family members today?*

What Katie Did

Giggling, Katie snatched Trisha's bear and dashed off across the playground.

"Give it back!" Trisha yelled.

Katie, who was in a teasing mood, clutched the furry white bear by its plaid jacket and sprinted through the sandbox and past the monkey bars. Finally she turned back toward Trisha, who was looking furious. Katie felt sick.

"That's my show-and-tell bear," Trisha screamed. "Give it back right now!"

The playground fell silent. The girls faced each other with the entire fourth grade looking on.

Katie heard herself saying, "Here, take your dumb bear." She tossed the bear to Trisha, but it fell short of its target and landed right in a mud puddle.

"I hate you!" Trisha screamed. Katie felt awful.

Several girls rushed over to Trisha. One lifted the dripping bear from the dirty water and held it in front of her.

Katie realized that everyone was mad at her. She had never felt so alone.

Then she heard a voice behind her. "Everyone does stupid things sometimes." It was Billy.

"As stupid as what I just did?" asked Katie.

"Yep. The best way to fix a mess is to ask yourself what Jesus would do."

"Jesus would want me to apologize and clean up Trisha's bear, wouldn't he?"

Billy smiled and nodded.

"That's what I'll do," said Katie, feeling better. "Right away!"

Jesus said, "I have given you an example to follow. Do as I have done to you." *(John 13:15)*

How does it feel to right a wrong by doing what Jesus wants you to do?

A New Father

As Brad sorted through his camping gear, he turned to his friend. "Alex, you didn't really invite Jake to the church's father-son camp-out, did you?"

"Yes. Why shouldn't I?"

"He beats up on people. And his mouth is like a sewer."

"He's not a Christian, Brad. What do you expect?"

"But he'll wreck the weekend for everyone. Besides, it's a father-son deal. He doesn't have a father."

"My dad says that's why he does mean things. He needs to know his heavenly Father."

On the ride out to the campsite, Jake punched Alex in the stomach. Later, Jake swore when he tried to set up his tent and it collapsed.

"I warned you," Brad whispered to Alex.

All weekend Jake made trouble. He was caught swiping another boy's hunting knife. Then Jake disappeared after dinner and Brad had to do his dish-washing job. Brad felt really mad.

After the campfire Saturday night, Brad saw Alex's dad pick up his flashlight, put an arm around Jake's shoulder, and disappear with him down one of the trails.

Alex said, "Dad's going to talk to Jake about Jesus. Come on, let's pray." As the two friends prayed, Brad felt ashamed of his bad attitude toward Jake. Brad prayed for forgiveness; then he asked God to soften Jake's heart so he could accept God's love.

Later that night, Jake found Alex and Brad. With a big smile on his face, Jake said, "Guess what? Now God is my Father. If Alex's dad could love me when I did bad things, God can, too. And God will give me the power to change and do good things!"

Suddenly Brad realized that this was the best camping trip ever.

"You must be compassionate, just as your Father is compassionate."
(Luke 6:36)

How do you show others that you care for them? Do you take time to pray for those who need Jesus?

The Flying Horse

"I'm the artist of the family, not Tony!" Stacie complained to her twin sister, Karen.

"But he won the contest," said Karen. "First place in the whole second grade."

"He painted a stupid flying horse. But it doesn't even look like a horse."

"Mom and Dad think it's good. That's what bugs me," said Karen.

"It belongs in the garbage can," Stacie said. The two nine-year-olds giggled.

The next day Tony brought "The Flying Horse" home from the school art contest display. It was rolled in a special tube for artwork.

Mom and Dad talked it over after dinner and decided to frame it for Mom's office. "Go get it, Tony, so we can measure it," Mom said.

Tony returned empty-handed. "I put it on my bed. Now it isn't there!"

Karen snickered. "Maybe it flew away. It was a flying horse, wasn't it?"

Mom said, "Girls? Do you know where it is?"

Stacie kicked Karen under the table. "Ow! Um...we didn't do anything wrong, Mom," said Karen. "We thought it was trash and threw it in the garbage."

Tony wailed while Mom and Dad fished his painting out of the garbage can.

Dad took the twins to their bedroom. "I want you to be like Jesus," said Dad, "full of love for other people — especially your little brother." The twins watched tears fill their father's eyes.

"Jealousy is ugly," he said. "If you want to become beautiful women like Mom, beauty must begin in your hearts."

Tears ran down the twins' cheeks. They realized they'd been jealous of their brother. Hugging their dad, they confessed, "We're sorry. We'll ask Tony to forgive us and ask Jesus to help us love him more."

"Anger is cruel, and wrath is like a flood, but who can survive the destructiveness of jealousy?" *(Proverbs 27:4)*

Why is jealousy so harmful?
What would Jesus want you to do if you feel jealous?

Computer Battle

Aaron felt himself getting madder and madder. His little brother Jeff was playing on the computer again! It seemed like Jeff always started to play computer games just when Aaron had finished his homework and had a few minutes to play.

"It's my turn for a change," he told Jeff firmly. "You can play when I'm at baseball practice later this afternoon."

"But I'm in the middle of a great game," Jeff protested. "I can't stop now!"

"Too bad! Get off…or else!"

"Quit threatening me! I'll tell Dad," Jeff warned. "Then you'll be grounded from using the computer and I'll get it all to myself."

Aaron couldn't take it anymore. He grabbed his brother by the collar and yanked his shirt. "I said, GET OFF!"

Jeff started crying. "You're hurting my neck. Leave me alone!"

Seeing the red welt on Jeff's neck shocked Aaron. He let go of Jeff's collar and sat down beside him. Aaron knew deep inside how selfish he was acting. He wasn't thinking of his brother's feelings— only his own.

Feeling convicted, Aaron said quietly, "Jeff, please forgive me. I've been pretty selfish ever since we got this new computer game. I know Jesus wants me to care about you. This game will wear out, but you'll always be my brother. Let's shake hands and make up."

"Live a life filled with love for others, following the example of Christ." *(Ephesians 5:2)*

When are you tempted to be selfish?
How does Jesus want you to treat your brother or sister?

Indoor Olympic Tryouts!

Get Set Set out one of each of the following items for each person: a balloon, a piece of bubble gum, and a raw potato. You'll also need washable markers and several paper wads.

Go!

Read 2 Timothy 4:6–8.

What race did Paul finish?
What prize would he win?
What prize can we look forward to as we run our race for the Lord?

Explain: We're going to have fun with some wacky races!

See who can be the first to:

Blow up a balloon, tie it, then pop it by sitting on it.
Throw three paper wads over your shoulder into a wastebasket.
Chew a piece of bubble gum and blow a big bubble.
Hold a potato between your knees and run all the way around the house.

Applaud everyone's efforts.

How can we be like Paul and run a race for God?
How can we encourage one another to do our very best for the Lord?

Use a washable marker to **draw** a "#1" on each person's hand.

Pledge to help one another do your very best as you run your race for the Lord.

Only You!

Get Set Preheat the oven to 400 degrees. Set out flour, baking powder, salt, shortening, milk, cinnamon, sugar, and margarine. You'll also need measuring spoons and cups, a mixing bowl, two knives, a cookie sheet, and a rolling pin.

Go!

Gather everyone in the kitchen to make yummy pinwheel biscuits.

Have everyone **choose** one or two ingredients to be in charge of.

Work together to make biscuits according to the following recipe:

In a bowl, stir together 2 cups flour, 4 teaspoons baking powder, ½ teaspoon salt.
Use two knives to cut in 8 tablespoons shortening.
Stir in ½ cup milk.
Dust the counter with flour and set the biscuit dough on the counter.
Roll it to a thickness of about ½ inch.
Spread it with margarine.
Mix ½ teaspoon cinnamon and ⅓ cup sugar. Sprinkle it over the dough.
Roll the dough like a jelly roll and cut off 1-inch slices.
Place the slices on a cookie sheet and bake at 450 degrees for 10–12 minutes.

While the pinwheels bake, **read** 1 Corinthians 12:12–18.

How are God's people like ingredients in a recipe?
Can one ingredient do another ingredient's work? Explain.
What special work does God have for you to do?

Before you eat the pinwheels, **pray:** Thank you, Lord, for making each of us special and giving us jobs that only we can do. Help us do those jobs well for you. In Jesus name, amen.

Bad Hair Day

Cedra stared at herself in the bathroom mirror. She felt like crying. "I look like a clown!" she wailed. Her friend, Beth, stared at the magazine picture and then at Cedra's frizzy hair. Beth wrinkled her nose.

"My mom will kill me!" said Cedra.

Just then Cedra's mom called from downstairs, "Cedra, I'm home! Where are you?"

"Oops!" said Beth, slipping out the door. "I think I'd better go."

Cedra's mom came into the bathroom. "What did you do to your hair?"

Cedra burst into tears. "I wanted to be pretty like the models in Beth's magazine."

"Oh, honey," said her mom, hugging her. "I just heard an interview with a top fashion model. She said she felt ugly because photographers touched up her pictures. She knows her natural beauty can't compete with their 'improved' photographs."

"Really? A supermodel said that?"

Her mom tapped the magazine. "This isn't reality, sweetheart, it's fake. Beauty is a wonderful gift, but Jesus cares more about what we're like on the inside."

Cedra wiped her eyes. "I guess I've been letting magazines and TV tell me what's important instead of listening to Jesus." She looked in the mirror and sighed. "I'll never be a supermodel, but I can let Jesus make me beautiful on the inside!"

"People judge by outward appearance, but the Lord looks at a person's thoughts and intentions." *(1 Samuel 16:7)*

Why doesn't Jesus want us to judge ourselves and others by how we look?

The Face in the Mirror

Randy picked up his toothbrush and looked into the mirror. "You dope," he muttered. "You're so stupid. Your ears stick out, your nose is ugly, and nobody likes you...including me!"

Five-year-old Joey stopped at the door and listened. "Who are you talking to, Randy?" he asked, looking around.

"Myself!" Randy snapped. "And it's none of your business, so get out of here!"

Joey looked perplexed. "Why do you talk mean to yourself?"

"You don't know very much, do you?" Randy asked, frowning. "Haven't you ever felt ugly and stupid?" He could feel his face getting red.

"But didn't God make you?" Joey asked. "Aren't you special—like me?"

Randy silently brushed his teeth. He didn't want to look at Joey or answer his question.

Joey wrapped his arms around Randy's waist. "I love you, Randy!" he exclaimed. "You're the bestest brother in the whole world! I think you're special, and I know God does, too. Don't talk mean to yourself."

Putting down the toothbrush, Randy hugged him back. "Thanks, kid," he said softly. "Sometimes I forget what God says about me. Then I start feeling miserable about how I look and what I can't do right. Thanks for reminding me how God thinks of me."

Joey grinned. "Remember when I couldn't catch a baseball? You took me out and played with me. You told me, 'God doesn't make any junk!' and you helped me learn to catch."

Thanks, Lord, for my little brother, Randy prayed. *And thanks for making me. I want to be thankful for everything you made— even myself!*

"O Lord, you...know everything about me.... Thank you for making me so wonderfully complex! Your workmanship is marvelous."
(Psalm 139:1, 14)

How does Jesus want you to feel about yourself? What can you do to help others see themselves as wonderfully made?

Laura's Sparrow

Jessie noticed that her big sister wasn't eating any breakfast. "Are you feeling okay, Laura?" she asked. "Did I do something to make you mad or upset?"

Laura slowly stirred her cereal. She looked at her kid sister and tried to smile. "No, it's nothing about you. You've been kind of nice lately," she teased. "It's just that I'm feeling afraid and worried."

"About what?" asked Jessie.

"About everything! Schoolwork, Mom and Dad arguing with each other, my hair, Kate not being my friend anymore. You name it, I'm worried about it."

Looking out the kitchen window, Jessie prayed silently. *Dear Jesus, help Laura know that you care for her.* A flutter of wings caught her eye as a little sparrow landed on the windowsill. It cocked its head and looked inside.

"Laura, look!" Jessie pointed to the sparrow. "That little bird is peeking in our window. I think Jesus sent him to tell you something."

"What would a sparrow have to say to me?"

Jessie ran to her room and returned with her Bible. "Listen!" she said, opening to the book of Matthew. "Jesus said, 'Not even a sparrow, worth only half a penny, can fall to the ground without your Father knowing it. And the very hairs on your head are all numbered. So don't be afraid.'"

As Laura gazed at the sparrow, tears welled up in her eyes. "Do you think Jesus would send a sparrow to remind me not to be worried and afraid?"

"Well, have you ever seen a bird sit at our window and look in? I prayed that Jesus would help you. And I believe he sent a little messenger to cheer you up!"

Jesus said, "Don't be afraid; you are more valuable to [God] than a whole flock of sparrows." *(Matthew 10:31)*

Why doesn't Jesus want us to worry?
What would Jesus want you to remember when
you feel worried?

Week
24

Fingerprints

The twelve-year-old twins took turns pressing their thumbs on the ink pad, then on white paper.

"Our thumbprints look alike to me," said Mark. "How are we supposed to see the difference and divide all our fingerprints into seven basic patterns? I can't see two different patterns. This is a dumb assignment!"

"Use this magnifying glass," Myron urged. "Watch for different directions in the swirls of your fingerprints." After handing the magnifying glass to his brother, he inked the fingers on his right hand and pressed them onto the paper.

"The curves of my thumb print swirl up, then curve back," Mark observed. "But how can every fingerprint be different from all the others in the world?"

"They're like snowflakes," said his twin. "Every snowflake is different. Why can't fingerprints be different? God is big enough to make everyone and everything unique. God knows all about us and how we're special."

"Most people can't tell us apart," Mark said with a grin.

"God wouldn't get us mixed up. God even knows what we're thinking."

"We usually do everything together," Mark said quietly. "But I think I need to get to know God better. And that's something I need to do alone."

"I agree," said Myron. "I'm going to read my Bible and pray a while."

"Search me, O God, and know my heart; test me and know my thoughts." *(Psalm 139:23)*

How much time do you spend getting to know Jesus?
What would Jesus say about your thoughts?

Never a Failure

Janelle slowly set her school books on the kitchen counter. She avoided her mother's eyes, knowing "FAILURE" was stamped all over her face.

Her mom stopped stirring the spaghetti sauce. "How did tryouts go for the sixth-grade play?"

"Megan got the lead. I'm only the understudy." Janelle choked on the words.

"Oh, honey, I'm so sorry. I know you really prepared for the tryouts." She put her arms around Janelle and held her tight.

"Megan deserved it," Janelle whispered. "She's so much better than I am."

Janelle cried softly as Mom stroked her hair. "Mom, I'm not *best* at anything! Not at spelling, or piano, or tennis, or even kickball. It's just not worth trying anymore."

"Well, you make a pretty fantastic salad," her mom teased gently. "Think you could cut up some tomatoes and cucumbers?"

Janelle gave a shaky laugh, dried her eyes, and reached for a cutting board.

That evening as she tucked Janelle into bed, Mom asked, "Honey, do you remember the story Jesus told about the servants who were given talents? One had ten talents, one had five, and the other had one."

"Yes. But wasn't that about money?" asked Janelle.

"In Jesus' country a talent meant a sum of money. But I think the story could apply to the special abilities we each have been given by God."

Janelle asked, "Didn't the master want his servants to use their gifts, not bury them?"

"That's right. In our world, people tend to reward only those who are the best. But Jesus promised to reward those who faithfully use whatever he's given them."

"Mom, I'm going to be the best understudy the school ever had!"

Her mom hugged her and smiled. "That will please Jesus. Please him and you'll never be a failure."

Jesus said, "Well done, my good and faithful servant." *(Matthew 25:23)*

How do you faithfully use the talents Jesus has given you?

Egg-straordinary Individuals

Get Set You'll need slips of paper, a basket, markers, aluminum foil, and one hard-boiled egg for each person.

Go!

Have everyone **write** his or her name on a slip of paper and place it in a basket.

Explain: There's a passage in the Bible that says we have some pretty special people living in this house.

Read 1 Peter 2:9–10.

According to these verses, who are we?
What does it mean to be a royal priesthood?
What is the job God has given us to do?

Explain: God sees us as a royal priesthood, but we don't always see ourselves or each other that way. Let's have some fun celebrating the fact that God has made each of us an egg-straordinary individual.

Have each person **take** a name from the basket, then use markers to **draw** that person's portrait on a hard-boiled egg.

Use aluminum foil to **mold** crowns for each egg.

Present the crowned eggs to one another as you finish this sentence: "[Name], you're egg-straordinary because…"

Pray, thanking God for each unique individual in your family.

If you wish, **make** royal egg salad!

The Sin Trap

Get Set   You'll need a ball of yarn and a pair of scissors.

Go!

Have everyone *stand* in a tight circle.

Explain: I'm going to read the Ten Commandments. If you've ever broken any one of them, loop the yarn around yourself, then pass it to the next person. Keep looping and passing as I read.

Read Exodus 20:1–17.

Keep looping and passing the yarn as you ask: *What are some small ways we may disobey these commandments each day?*

Hold the ball of yarn.

Invite everyone to pull away and try to break free.

How do our wrong choices trap us?
How can we get free?

Read Jesus' words in John 8:35–36.

Pray: Jesus, when we make wrong choices, please help us to turn to you for forgiveness. Thank you for being willing to take our sins and set us free. Amen.

Cut the yarn with scissors to set everyone free.

Keep the pieces of yarn that were holding you as a reminder that the choices you make every day can trap you or set you free.

The Watch

"Hey, is this your green-and-blue striped towel under here?" asked Matt. He and Patrick had finished their swimming lesson and were changing their clothes.

"No, I already stuffed my towel in my backpack," said Patrick.

"Then I'll take it to the lost and found," said Matt as he reached for the towel. "Wait a minute—there's a watch underneath the towel."

"Let me see it," said Patrick. He scooted over on the bench and snatched the watch away from Matt. "This is just exactly what I need. I don't have a watch."

"Is that what you would want if someone found something you'd lost? I would want them to be honest and hand it in. Give it back to me. I'm taking it to the main office."

"That's stupid," protested Patrick, handing it to Matt. "You found it. Why don't you just keep it and say it's yours?"

"Because it belongs to somebody else. I'm not going to keep it and lie." Matt thought for a moment. "If nobody comes back and claims it, maybe the office will give it back to me. I'll leave my name and phone number with them, then wait and see what happens. But for now, I want to do what's right and hand it in to the pool office."

Read the conclusion of this story in Wednesday's devotion.

"So put away all falsehood and 'tell your neighbor the truth.'"
(Ephesians 4:25)

What would you have done if you were Matt?
What would Jesus say to Patrick?

Week
25

Nate's Choice

Nate pulled on his basketball shirt before practice. Justin slid onto the bench beside him.

"Hey, Nate, have you seen the movie *Evil Eye*?" asked Justin. "The special effects are awesome!"

"How did you see it? It's rated R." Nate had seen the movie advertised on TV. There seemed to be lots of violence and bad language.

"My older brother rented the video. Some of the guys on the team are coming home with me after practice to watch it. Wanna come?"

Derek, the star forward on their city league team, said loudly, "Not preacher boy here. It might pollute his mind."

"Sure, I'll come," said Nate, ignoring the quiet warning voice inside him. Nate was tired of being made fun of and called "preacher boy." Just once he wanted to be like his friends and join in their fun.

As the boys walked to Justin's house after practice, a verse from Psalms popped into Nate's head: "I will set no wicked thing before my eye." *It's only once,* he argued to himself.

The boys joked while they drank soda and ate a package of cookies. But Nate wasn't having fun. As Justin popped the video into the recorder, snatches of a verse from Philippians ran through Nate's mind: "Whatever is right, whatever is pure...think on these things."

When the violent opening scenes of the movie flashed on the TV screen, Nate knew he couldn't stay—no matter what names the guys called him.

"I'm leaving," said Nate. "Thanks for inviting me, Justin, but Jesus wouldn't watch this and neither will I."

As Nate left the room, Derek hooted, "I told you he wouldn't stay!" But Nate felt good inside. He had done what Jesus would do.

"I will refuse to look at anything vile and vulgar." *(Psalm 101:3)*

When have your friends wanted to do something wrong?
Which TV shows or movies would Jesus want you to stop watching?

Patrick's Lie

"Come back in thirty days. If someone hasn't claimed the watch, you can have it," the pool manager told Matt.

Matt marked the days on his calendar. As soon as thirty days had passed he visited the pool office again.

"I'm Matt Hadley and I've come back to check on the watch I found here last month. Has anyone claimed it?" he asked.

The lady behind the counter asked the lifeguard on duty, "Didn't someone come early today and get the watch that was here?"

"Yes," said the lifeguard. "When we opened, a boy came in and said he was Matt Hadley. The watch hadn't been claimed, so I gave it to him."

Matt remembered how much Patrick wanted the watch. "Was that boy short and skinny with black curly hair?" he asked.

"Yes," said the lifeguard.

Matt was furious! He hurriedly biked to Patrick's house.

When Patrick answered the door, Matt saw the watch on his wrist. "Why did you claim that watch, Patrick? I was the one who found it."

"Oh, I just wanted to borrow it and see what an expensive watch would feel like. I'll give it back to you at school tomorrow."

Two weeks later, Matt told his mother, "I'll never see that watch again. Patrick wore it all last week and promised to give it to me on Friday. This week he kept saying that he forgot to bring it to school. Today he told me his cousin took it to California."

"What are you going to do about it?" asked Mother.

"I'm going to forgive him, Mom, like God forgives me when I don't deserve it. I just pray that Patrick will get right with God. Nothing's more important than that."

Jesus said, "If you forgive those who sin against you, your heavenly Father will forgive you." *(Matthew 6:14)*

 *What would you have said to Patrick?*
Do you think Matt did what Jesus would do?

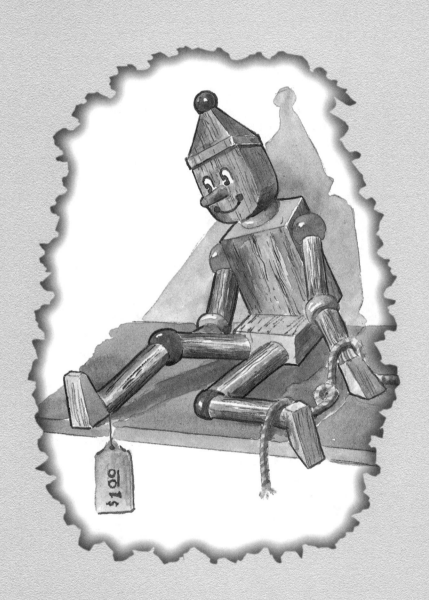

Puppet Problem

Cari wandered through the resale shop looking at the used toys while her mom searched the racks for a brown skirt. Cari picked up a brightly painted wooden puppet with a white cord dangling from its back.

When Cari pulled the cord, the dangling arms and legs shot out straight and stiff. When she released the cord, the arms and legs went limp. Cari pulled the cord over and over, making the little man dance.

Without warning, the cord snapped. The puppet's arms and legs went slack.

Cari glanced around to see if anyone else had seen what happened. No one was looking her way. Quickly she put the little puppet back on the shelf and moved down the aisle, looking at other toys.

You broke something that wasn't yours, her conscience told her.

"It was an accident. Besides, it was only worth a buck," she argued back silently.

You should pay for it.

"Nobody will know," she thought.

You will know and so will God.

Just then her mother walked up. She had found a skirt. "Ready to go, Cari?" she asked.

Cari sighed. "Mom?" She reached out for the limp puppet. "I accidentally broke this."

"What are you going to do about it?"

"I'll pay for it."

Her mother hugged her. "I'm proud of you. That's what Jesus would do."

Jesus said, "Do not steal." *(Matthew 19:18)*

 *Have you ever broken anything and not paid for it? What would Jesus want you do to?*

Horsey's Drink

Ty walked into the family room just in time to hear his sister Tori whisper to her rocking horse, "You thirsty, Horsey?" Tori thought stuffed bears and plastic horses had feelings, just like people. She loved her rocking horse almost as much as she loved her big brother.

Ty tried not to smile. "Hey, Tori, your horsey looks thirsty," he said. He loved teasing her. "Why don't you give it a drink?"

Tori slid from her rocking horse and patted its neck. "I'll give you a drink, horsey," she said and hurried to the kitchen to find a pan for water.

"Here, use this." Ty grinned as he handed Tori a wicker basket that usually held bananas on the kitchen table.

"Thanks, Ty."

Ty felt a twinge of conscience as Tori headed for the sink. But what happened next was so funny that he decided to keep quiet. Tori pulled a chair over to the sink, filled the basket with water and started back to her horse. She didn't notice the water leaking. After placing the basket on the floor under her horse's nose she smiled, climbed back on, and started to rock. Ty could tell she felt proud of herself.

Just then Mom came in. "What's this mess?" she asked.

"Horsey drank his water," Tori said.

Mom looked upset. "No, honey, look! There's water all over the floor!"

Tori looked at the basket, then at the floor, then at Ty. Her eyes overflowed with tears.

Ty's heart overflowed with regret. "It's my fault, Mom. Don't blame Tori."

Tori started rocking to comfort herself.

"I'm sorry, Tori," he said. "Please forgive me. I'll clean it up." While Ty got the mop, he asked Jesus to help him be more kind to his sister.

"Live a life of steady goodness so that only good deeds will pour forth." *(James 3:13)*

Do you think Jesus cares if we tease people? Are there ways to tease that aren't hurtful?

Chalk It Up!

Get Set   You'll need chalk and a garden hose attached to a water spigot.

Go!

Gather   outside by a sidewalk or paved driveway.

Give   everyone a piece of chalk.

Draw or **write** on the sidewalk one good choice that you made this week.

Draw or **write** about one not-so-good choice you made this week.

Invite   everyone to explain what they drew or wrote.

Read   Matthew 16:26–27.

How will Jesus reward us for our good choices?
What can we do about our bad choices?

Pray   and thank Jesus for helping you make good choices. Ask his forgiveness for the bad choices you've made.

Turn on   the hose and wash away the words and pictures that represent your bad choices.
(If it's a nice warm day, this would be a great time for a friendly water fight!)

What's the Right Way?

Get Set   Set out a road map, a sharp knife, a lightbulb, crackers, and a cookbook. Write the following Bible references on slips of paper: Psalm 25:4–6; Psalm 119:105; John 3:16–17; Galatians 5:22–23; Hebrews 4:12–13; Hebrews 5:11–14.

Go!

Explain: The Bible is many things to us. We'll take turns looking up the Bible verses to discover how the Bible is like each of the things on the table.

Take turns   looking up and reading each Bible passage.

Discuss   how each passage relates the Bible to one of the items on the table.

Check   your answers against the list given below and   *discuss*   the questions.

> Psalm 25:4–6. *How is the Bible like a map?*
> Psalm 119:105. *How is the Bible like a lightbulb?*
> John 3:16–17. *How is the Bible like good news?*
> Galatians 5:22–23. *How is the Bible like a recipe book?*
> Hebrews 4:12–13. *How is the Bible like a sharp knife?*
> Hebrews 5:11–14. *How is the Bible like food for our souls?*

Explain: Since the Bible is our guidebook for so many things, it would be nice to know how it ends.

Read   Revelation 21–22.

Praise   God for a wonderful ending to a wonderful book!

Praises in the Snow

"I love spending Christmas Eve on the mountain!" Megan said. She tipped her head back and stuck out her tongue to catch a snowflake. Then she stooped to adjust the boots on her cross-country skis. When she stood up, her family had disappeared from sight. How could they vanish so quickly? Hadn't they noticed she had fallen behind? She could just barely hear their voices up ahead.

"Wait!" she yelled, but the snow swallowed her voice.

Large snowflakes began to drift around her. A deer crossed the trail and disappeared into the forest. Megan pulled her green knit hat down over her ears, leaned into the snow, and pumped her legs and arms as hard as she could. She knew she was in trouble if she couldn't catch her family.

Within minutes it was nearly dark. Snow covered all signs of the trail. She wondered if she was even on the trail. She felt terrified. "Jesus, save me!" she prayed.

Wait here for help.

Megan stopped. "Where did that thought come from?" she wondered. Trembling with cold and fear, she'd never felt so alone.

Sing and dance your praises to me.

"Oh, I will, Jesus," said Megan. "Thank you for letting me know you are with me." Megan began to sing and bounce around. "Praise you, Jesus," she sang, lifting her mittened hands.

All during that long, lonely Christmas Eve night, Megan sang songs of praise to the Lord and danced to keep warm. When she felt afraid, she imagined Jesus wrapping his arms around her. Finally the snow stopped and the stars twinkled above her. She thought of the star that led the wise men to Jesus.

As dawn painted the Christmas sky, she spotted a rescue helicopter. Megan jumped up and down, waving her green hat. "Thank you, Jesus," she prayed. "You are faithful."

"The Lord your God is merciful—he will not abandon you or destroy you." *(Deuteronomy 4:31)*

Why did Jesus want Megan to think about him? How did Jesus help her?

The Lost Boy

Waiting for the hike to begin, Matthew thought about his parents and little sister. He missed them. He'd just begun first grade at a boarding school for missionary children in Africa, and his family was hundreds of miles away.

"Stay close together," the school director instructed. "We don't want anyone getting lost in the high brush."

Matthew found himself at the end of the line. As the group hiked into the foothills, he struggled through waist-high grass, trying to keep up with the bigger kids.

Then Matthew noticed a beautiful butterfly perched on a nearby bush. He crept closer and watched it, not realizing that the other hikers had turned off the main trail onto a different path.

When Matthew looked up, there was no one around. At first he felt scared. He didn't know where to go. *Help me know what to do, Jesus,* he prayed. Then a thought popped into his mind: *If I try to find the others, I may get really lost. But if I turn around, I think I can find my way back to the school.*

Later Matthew told his parents what happened. "Jesus gave me wisdom to make the right choice. He kept me calm and he did help me find my way back to the school."

"In my distress I prayed to the Lord, and the Lord answered me and rescued me." *(Psalm 118:5)*

Have you ever been lost? What did you do? What does Jesus want you to do when you need help?

Running Away

"Dad's always mad at me no matter what I do," Rosie mumbled to her Raggedy Ann doll. Her stomach quivered and tears rolled down her cheeks.

"If my homework isn't perfect, he gets angry. When I don't get an A, he yells at me. And he wants me to be good at sports like he is. But I'm a klutz."

Rosie set her doll aside, blew her nose, and walked slowly downstairs to practice the piano. Playing the piano wasn't easy for Rosie like it was for her father. It was especially hard to see the notes when tears clouded her eyes.

Even while she practiced, her dad criticized. "You're playing too loud…You make so many mistakes…Why are we paying your teacher? You never learn anything!"

After practice, Rosie went to her room and packed a small bag with some clothes and her doll. She didn't want to run away, but she felt she couldn't live at home any more. She tiptoed out the door and hid behind the hedge in the backyard.

Watching the stars twinkle overhead, Rosie prayed, "What shall I do, Jesus? Where can I go?" She wondered how Jesus would answer her prayer.

Slowly but surely, Rosie began to relax and feel peaceful inside. *Maybe Jesus doesn't want me to run away*, she thought. *Maybe he wants to help me.* She couldn't count on her earthly father's love and approval, but she knew she could count on Jesus and her heavenly Father.

"Thank you for loving me, Jesus. I'll go back inside. Help me not to get so upset at Daddy. And help him learn to know you."

Rosie stuck it out at home, depending on Jesus and praying for her father. After five years, when Rosie was twelve years old, her father became a Christian. Little by little he learned not to be so critical.

"When you go through…great trouble, I will be with you." *(Isaiah 43:2)*

*When have you felt like giving up?
How can you depend on Jesus for help?*

Attitude Adjustment

March 21, the day Michael had dreaded for months, finally arrived. He woke up and immediately rolled out of bed. His knees felt cold on the wooden floor. He knew he couldn't face today without Jesus. He needed lots of help and strength. And he needed courage.

"Jesus, I thank you for staying by me and caring about me. You know how tough it is to leave all my cousins and my school friends here in California. When we're packing today, help me not be grouchy and irritable. Give me a better attitude about moving. I want to trust that you'll have great friends for me in Oregon."

He looked out his window into the sunlit backyard and remembered the good times he'd had with his dog Butch. Memories of birthday parties and neighborhood games flooded his mind.

Why did Dad have to get a job transfer to Portland? he wondered.

"I'm going to miss this home, Jesus," he prayed. "I'm glad you're my best friend. Help me like my new home…and help me find new friends. I'm thanking you ahead of time. Amen."

All day Michael helped load the moving van. Then it was time to say good-bye to all the relatives and neighbors. Some of them knew it was hard for Michael. They gathered around him and prayed.

On the second day of their drive to Oregon, his father commented, "Michael, I've been concerned about you. I know you didn't want this move, but I'm happy to see that your attitude has changed."

"I didn't have a good attitude, Dad. But since I prayed and others prayed too, Jesus gave me a new attitude. And he'll help me in our new home."

"Don't worry about anything; instead, pray about everything. Tell God what you need." *(Philippians 4:6)*

What attitudes in your life do you need help changing?
Do you pray about your attitude?

Look at Your Bracelet!

Laura hung up the phone and ran to her mother in the kitchen. "Grandpa and Grandma want to take me to the Blazers basketball game on Saturday. They have box-seat tickets! Isn't it great?"

Laura's mother looked at the calendar on the refrigerator. "Isn't that when you have practice for the Sunday school musical?" she asked.

"I can't believe it!" sighed Laura. "The one time I could see the Blazers and it has to be the same time as choir practice."

"Let's talk while we dry dishes," said Mother, handing Laura a towel. "Perhaps Grandpa can get tickets for another night. Or he could trade tickets for a night next month."

"No, he said he hoped I could go this Saturday because these are the only tickets he would get." Laura frowned. "I haven't missed any practices. Perhaps I can skip this one. Other kids have missed rehearsals and they still get to sing."

"What do you think you should do?" asked Mother.

"I don't know."

"You could take a good look at what you're wearing on your wrist," Mother suggested.

Glancing down at the burgundy bracelet on her wrist, Laura grinned. The white letters, WWJD, stood out boldly.

Laura smiled. "I'll do what Jesus would do. I'll go to my choir practice!"

"Try to find out what is pleasing to the Lord." *(Ephesians 5:10)*

How does Jesus want you to make decisions? When have you recently asked, "What would Jesus do?"

Heads or Tails?

Get Set You'll need a coin. Plan to take a walk or a drive for this devotion.

Go!

Read Psalm 32:8.

What does God promise? How does this make you feel?
Would you rather trust God or flip a coin when you make decisions?

Set off on a walk or a drive.

Take turns flipping a coin.

If you get heads, turn right at the next intersection.
If you get tails, turn left. (If you are driving, flip the coin well before you reach the intersection.)

Continue for ten minutes.

Find the nearest store and purchase a treat to take home.

Return home by the shortest route.

How is God's guidance different from flipping a coin?

Flip a coin to determine how you will pray.

Those who get heads, *thank* God for a specific blessing.

Those who get tails, *pray* for God's direction for your family's future.

Enjoy your treat.

Message on Your Wrist

Get Set You'll need multicolored plastic beads and half a leather shoelace for each person.

Go!

Read Luke 9:1–3, 6 and Luke 10:1–4.

What good news did the disciples share with people?

Make a good news bracelet to help you tell others about Jesus:

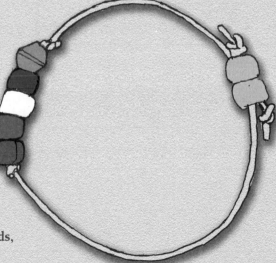

- Tie a knot about three inches from one end of the leather.
- Slip on a gray bead, then tie a knot.
- Slip on a red bead, then tie a knot.
- Slip on a white bead, then tie a knot.
- Slip on a green bead, then tie a knot.
- Slip on a blue bead, then tie a knot.
- Slip on two clear beads.
- Push the other end of the leather through the clear beads, then tie a knot.

Review the gospel message in colors from Week 3, Saturday (page 31).

Put on your bracelets and practice telling each other how each color tells part of the gospel story.

225

The Tetherball Game

The tetherball missed Rocky's fingers and swung past him. "Rats!" he said. "I can't hit anything." Rocky played tetherball against Brandon during recess every morning. Usually he beat Brandon easily. Not today.

Brandon whacked the ball again. The rope wound tightly around the pole, signaling the game's end. Onlookers cheered.

"Rats!" Rocky said for the fourth time.

"I won!" Brandon strutted around the pole holding his arms above his head.

Rocky paced, hands on hips. "One more game," he said. It killed him to lose to Brandon.

Brandon winked at the crowd. "Losers serve."

Rocky grabbed the ball and punched his frustration into a perfect looping serve, low enough for him to smack, then too high for Brandon to touch. Rocky whooped and laughed. Nothing beat winning.

Then the unthinkable happened. When Rocky swung for the hit that would end the game, he connected with the rope! An onlooker yelled, "Bobble!" Rocky opened his mouth to say "Rats!" but the Lord's name tumbled out instead!

Rocky stumbled away from the tetherball pole, shocked. He had never used the Lord's name in vain. Onlookers stared at him. They all knew he was a Christian.

Immediately, Rocky stopped and prayed aloud in front of everyone. "Jesus, please forgive me." Some things were more important than winning.

"Do not misuse the name of the Lord your God." *(Exodus 20:7)*

Why do some people use the Lord's name to swear? Have you used his name in vain? Did you ask his forgiveness?

Danny's Midnight Mission

Danny awoke with a start. Moonlight streamed through his window, and the frog-faced owls that lived in the highlands of Papua New Guinea made noises like the clop-clop of horses.

But that's not what had wakened him. Danny had a strong feeling that God wanted him to visit the chief of the valley who lived about a mile away. Quietly, Danny slipped into his clothes and ran down the trail. There was a bright moon, and trees cast shadows across his path as Danny walked to Chief Gadluwa's thatch-roofed house.

Knocking on the carved slat door, he thought, *I trust I'm doing the right thing.*

A voice inside the hut called, "Nu nai?" ("Who are you?")

Danny replied, "It's Danny, Missionary Connor's son."

The old chief and his two sons stepped out into the moonlight. "What do you want?" they demanded.

Danny took a deep breath. "Chief Gadluwa, God told me to come and tell you that although you have done bad things, he loves you. If you accept him into your life and be his man, he will not punish you. And someday he will take you to heaven to live with him."

He watched the chief's face. To his surprise, the old chief nodded his head. "I will do this." And he prayed with Danny and asked Jesus into his heart.

Afterward, Danny hurried home and slipped into bed. No one knew he had left or returned.

Seventeen years later, Danny returned to New Guinea as an adult. He learned that when Chief Gadluwa was baptized, he told everyone the story of how he'd given his life to Jesus one moonlit night when the little red boy came to his house. Grown-up Dan was glad he'd obeyed God's voice. (Dark-skinned natives didn't have a word for "pink." They called rosy-cheeked white children "red boy" or "red girl.")

"Your servant is listening." *(1 Samuel 3:10)*

Is anyone too young to tell someone about Jesus? Are you?

Angels' Wings

Little Rachel could barely see over the pew in front of her when she stood to sing with the congregation. The evening church service would soon be over and she would have to go to bed—in the dark.

Rachel prayed, *Dear Jesus, help me not to be afraid of the dark.*

The next line of the song caught her attention. "I can hear the brush of angels' wings...."

Angels' wings! What would they sound like? Rachel wondered. *Like the flapping of birds' wings? Like gentle breezes that make the leaves flutter?*

Rachel heard the pastor say, "May God's angels keep watch over you until we meet again." She imagined angels dressed in white robes folding their wings around her protectively.

At the end of the service, Rachel's friend Jamie ran toward her and held out a tiny wrapped package. Rachel smiled at her friend and asked, "Is it for me?"

Jamie nodded. Rachel unwrapped the package and found a glow-in-the-dark ring with a picture of an angel on it.

"Look at it when night comes. It will help you remember that God's angels are watching over you," whispered Jamie. "Then you won't feel so afraid."

That night when she climbed into bed, Rachel slipped the ring on her finger and turned out her light. The little angel glowed! Rachel looked at the tiny light and remembered, *God's angels are here.* She didn't feel afraid anymore.

When Rachel's mother came to her room for bedtime prayers, she exclaimed, "Why, Rachel, you turned off your light!"

"Shhh!" said Rachel, showing her mother the glowing angel ring. "I think I hear the brush of angel wings."

"For he orders his angels to protect you wherever you go." *(Psalm 91:11)*

Why doesn't Jesus want you to feel afraid? What does Jesus want you to remember when you're afraid of the dark?

Sink or Swim!

Heather stood in the shallow end of the swimming pool looking at all the little kids floating around her. She felt embarrassed being in the beginner class. She had never learned to swim because she'd always been afraid of the water. But this summer she was determined to learn.

Taking a deep breath, Heather lay back in the water, trying to follow her swimming teacher's instructions: "Arch your back and stick your tummy in the air."

Feeling heavy as a brick, Heather began to sink. She stood up quickly so her face wouldn't go underwater.

Her instructor came over and asked, "Having trouble? Here, try lying back on my hands."

Heather stretched out in the water, feeling the teacher's hands under her. She could float! But when the teacher took her hands away, Heather sank.

Her instructor quickly pulled her up. "Why did you float when my hands were under you?" she asked.

"You were holding me up," Heather answered.

"No, the water held you up."

Heather's teacher lay back on the water. "Watch," she said. "Although I weigh more than you do, the water supports me. Trust the water to hold you."

Like Jesus! thought Heather. *I can't see him, but I trust him anyway. He'll help me.* Heather tried again.

"You're floating!" said her teacher with an encouraging smile.

Happiness flooded Heather's heart. She knew she'd be swimming soon!

"When I am afraid, I put my trust in you." *(Psalm 56:3)*

 *What do you do when you are afraid?*

Becky's Witness

Becky wiped the sweat from her forehead and stood back to survey the wall she'd painted. "Building this extra hospital room is important, isn't it, Dad?"

He nodded and glanced at the line of people outside the El Bueno Pastor Hospital. "This village needs this hospital addition," he said. "I'm glad you came down here with me to help."

Later that day a crew leader gave all the workers some Spanish tracts. "Here are your booklets about Jesus," he explained. "I'll teach you what to say when you hand them out."

Becky listened carefully to the Spanish phrases. She practiced saying them while she painted.

All week, Becky shared her booklets with young Mexican girls who walked by the hospital where she was working. They smiled as she said in Spanish, "I have a book for you. It is about God."

On their last evening in San Quintin, Becky ate tostadas in a restaurant with her father and other mission workers. When she got up to leave, she slipped on her jacket. "What's this in my pocket?" she mumbled to herself. It was one last Spanish tract.

Should I give this to the waitress? Becky wondered. *She's busy working.*

As Becky headed to the exit, a Bible verse popped in her mind: "Work hard so God can approve you. Be a good worker, one who does not need to be ashamed and who correctly explains the word of truth."

I should be willing to share the gospel with anyone, anytime, she thought. She quickly ran back to the waitress, spoke her two Spanish sentences, and gave her the booklet.

"Muchas gracias," said the waitress, accepting it with a smile.

As they drove back to their hotel room, Becky prayed, *Jesus, I don't know if that waitress knew you, but at least she has a chance to know you now. Bless her as she reads it.*

Jesus said, "Preach the Good News to everyone, everywhere."
(Mark 16:15)

Who can you tell about Jesus? Who will you pray for?

Nature's Wonders

Get Set Pack a snack or a picnic lunch. You'll also need a blanket and a kitchen timer.

Go!

Walk or *drive* to a park or woods.

Sit together on the blanket and *read* Psalm 19:1–6.

What do the sun and sky tell us without saying a word?

Set the timer for *two* minutes.

Ask everyone to be silent and *observe* the colors and designs of God's world.

Set the timer again for *two* minutes.

Ask everyone to *close* their eyes and *listen* to the sounds of God's world.

What did you see and hear?

Set the timer for *five* minutes.

Search for one item from nature that tells about God. (Be sure not to disturb the homes of any of God's little creatures!)

When time is up, *share* what you've collected.

Close with a prayer of thanks to God for the wonders of creation.

Enjoy your snack.

Week
28

Bible Balloon Launch

Get Set You'll need one or two helium balloons for each person, strips of paper, pens, clear tape, a hole punch, and string.

Go!

Read Jesus' words in Mark 16:15–16, 19–20.

What does it meant to "preach the good news"?

Choose one or two good-news verses, such as John 3:16 or Romans 10:9.

Write those verses on slips of paper.

Carefully **cover** the paper with tape to make it waterproof.

Punch a hole in one end of each slip of paper.

Thread a piece of string through the hole.

Tie each verse to a balloon.

Find a good place to release the balloons.

Pray that the verses will touch the hearts of the people who find them.

Sing a favorite song as you *release* the balloons.

Gift for a Bully

Susie nervously reached into her book bag and took out the candy cane she'd brought to school that morning. Slipping it into her coat pocket, she prayed, "Dear Jesus, help me share this with someone who needs you. And help me explain it well."

Walking to the end of the playground, she thought, *The tough kids hang out by the track field. Maybe I could talk to someone who is alone.* It was scary just thinking about talking to an older boy.

The biggest bully in sixth grade walked by. Quickly holding up the candy for him to see, Susie prayed her voice wouldn't shake.

"Hey, Reggie, have you heard what the candy cane means?"

He stopped, eyeing her suspiciously. "No," he said.

Turning the cane upside down, Susie explained, "First of all, it's a J. That's J for Jesus 'cause it's his birthday we celebrate. And it's white because Jesus is the holy and sinless Son of God." She turned it right side up and continued, "It's a staff that shepherds use because Jesus called himself the good shepherd."

Reggie kept listening, so Susie continued. "These stripes are red for Jesus' love and for his blood. The little stripes remind me of the wounds in his hands, feet, and head. The big stripe reminds me of the cross where he died for us. This candy cane tells the whole reason why Jesus was born. Here—take it. Merry Christmas!"

Reggie took it without saying thanks. He walked off and started unwrapping it. Just then Skip joined him. Susie overheard Reggie tell his buddy, "Have you heard what the candy cane means?" To her delight, he turned the cane over and began explaining the Christmas message!

Jesus said, "If anyone acknowledges me publicly here on earth, I will openly acknowledge that person before my Father in heaven."
(Matthew 10:32)

 *Who could you tell about the candy cane gospel?*

Week
28

God's Jewels

Beth brought a plate of butter cookies to the patio table. She felt excited to be having a tea party with her best friend Heidi.

"Oh!" whispered Beth, "look at the hanging plants behind you. Two hummingbirds are having a nectar tea party!" The girls quietly watched the tiny birds dart in and out of the pink and white fuchsia blossoms.

"I didn't know hummingbirds were so beautiful," said Heidi. "Look how fast their wings beat!"

"My big brother studied them in biology. He said hummingbirds are called 'jewels in the sky.' Their wings beat about two hundred times per second."

"They work hard," observed Heidi.

"They need lots of food for energy," said Beth. "If we worked as hard as a hummingbird, we'd have to eat over 1,000 hamburgers a day!" Beth smiled. Every day she had been praying that Heidi would want to know about Jesus. Here was Beth's chance to share her faith.

"Hummingbirds remind me that God cares for me," said Beth. "If God made the smallest birds in the world so beautiful, I know he cares about everything in my life. Jesus said that even the hairs on our heads have been counted!"

"I'd like to learn about Jesus," said Heidi.

Beth felt delighted. "I'll help you. Let me get my Bible and I'll read you what Jesus said about sparrows."

Jesus said, "And the very hairs on your head are all numbered."
(Matthew 10:30)

 *How can you share Jesus with your friends?*

Double Detention

"Report to the headmaster immediately!" the teacher ordered.

Her heart pounding, Amanda walked to the main office of her African school. She began to pray softly, "Thank you, Jesus, for letting me talk to Rena about you. The teacher must have found out because another classmate overheard what I said."

The joy of talking about Jesus with another student far outweighed any fear Amanda had of punishment. She knew that the Muslim authorities in this region had forbidden Christians to talk about their faith. But nothing would stop her from telling others that Jesus loved them.

If my friend Tia hadn't told me about Jesus, I wouldn't be a Christian today, Amanda thought as she climbed the stairs. Opening the office door, Amanda whispered a quick prayer, "Help me tell of your love, Jesus…even here."

The headmaster was waiting. "We will not tolerate any talk of Christianity in our school!" he said harshly. "If you speak about this man Jesus you will be punished—do you understand?"

Amanda quietly answered, "Jesus loves me. He loves you, too. He gives joy to my heart. I just want to share his love and joy. Is that wrong?"

"Yes! It is an insult to Allah. You will destroy our community with your talk of Jesus," he said. "Report back here after school for your detention!"

Later Amanda explained her difficult situation to a missionary. "I refuse to be silent about Jesus. But I have received detention so often that the school officials now double it, making me stay four hours after school! They are ready to expel me. Please ask Christians to pray for me."

Jesus said, "God blesses those who are persecuted because they live for God, for the Kingdom of Heaven is theirs…. Be happy about it!" *(Matthew 5:10, 12)*

Have you ever been punished for talking about Jesus? How could you pray for Amanda and others like her?

Home Missionary

Martin sat on the front porch of his home in Papua New Guinea and watched the steam rise in the thick forest surrounding his home. The rain had stopped, but it was too wet to play outside.

His four-year-old sister Julie sat down beside him. "Where's Daddy?" she asked.

"He went to a new village," said Martin.

"What for?"

"To tell them about Jesus. That's what missionaries do." Martin was surprised his sister didn't already know that.

"What does he tell them about Jesus?" asked Julie.

"He tells them how Jesus died on the cross to forgive them. He helps them ask Jesus to be their Savior. Then he teaches them to live for Jesus." Sometimes Martin traveled with his father. He loved watching his dad talk to people about Jesus. He hoped God would let him do that someday.

Julie scooted closer to him. "How do you ask Jesus into your life?"

Martin paused to think. "You pray and tell him you want him in your life. You invite him in, like we invite people into our house."

"That's all?" she asked, surprised.

"Well, you tell him you're sorry for doing bad things. And you ask him to forgive you." Martin wanted to be sure he got it right. "Then you invite Jesus to come and live in your heart. He already lives in mine," Martin added.

Julie was very quiet. After a moment, Martin realized what was happening. "If you want to," he said gently, "you can pray to Jesus right now. I'll help you."

"Really? Right now? I want to!" Julie's eyes sparkled. She prayed and invited Jesus to come into her life.

A big bubble of joy grew in Martin's heart as he prayed, "Thank you, Jesus, for helping me be a missionary—to my own sister!"

Jesus said, "Look! Here I stand at the door and knock. If you hear me calling and open the door, I will come in." *(Revelation 3:20)*

What is it like to pray and ask Jesus into your life? Who can you tell about Jesus?

Food for a Hungry Heart

Jocelyn slammed the front door behind her and dropped her schoolbooks on a chair. "Mother, I'm home," she called.

The smell of freshly baked bread filled the house. "Mmm! Can I have some?" Jocelyn asked, walking into the kitchen.

"Sorry, it's not for you," said Mother, pulling another golden brown loaf from the oven.

"Aww. Not fair!" Jocelyn complained, her mouth watering.

"These loaves are for two first-time visitors who attended our church last Sunday. We want them to feel welcome."

Jocelyn bit into a juicy red apple. "I'd come back to church if you gave me a loaf of fresh bread."

Mother laughed. "That's what we're hoping. See, here's a pamphlet about our church that we send along with the bread."

"But what if they don't come back to church? They might never hear about Jesus again. Along with the bread, could we give something that tells about Jesus?"

"What do you have in mind?"

Jocelyn went to her room and brought back her calligraphy pen and colored pencils. An hour later she showed her mother the card she'd made. She had drawn a loaf of steaming bread and printed underneath, *Are you hungry for something to fill your soul? Try Jesus, the Bread of Life (John 6:35, The Bible).*

"It's perfect," exclaimed Mother, hugging her. "Together we've used the talents God gave us to tell someone about Jesus!"

Jesus said, "I am the bread of life." *(John 6:35)*

 *What special talent could you use to tell someone about Jesus?*

Sharing Cross

Get Set You'll need newspaper, pinking shears or regular scissors, solid-colored fabric, a permanent marker, fiberfill stuffing, and a needle and thread.

Go!

Cut a cross pattern from newspaper. Make it about twelve inches high and eight inches wide.

Draw around the cross pattern on a double thickness of solid-colored fabric.

Cut out the crosses then ask *invite* everyone to tell about people who told them about Jesus and helped them ask Jesus into their hearts.

As you share, *write* the names of those people on one of the fabric crosses.

Read Isaiah 52:7.

On the other fabric cross, *write* the names of people you've talked to about Jesus.

Put the two crosses together and take turns stitching them together around the edges. Leave a small opening.

As you *stuff* the cross with fiberfill, *thank* God for filling your hearts with Jesus' love.

Stitch the opening shut.

Continue to *add* names to the cross each time you tell someone about Jesus.

Decorated Dudes

Get Set You'll need sticky notes and pencils.

Go!

Look around the room.

What's the most valuable thing in it?

Read Psalm 8:3–8 and 1 Corinthians 6:20.

How much does God think we're worth?
What price did God pay for our salvation?
If God thinks we're so valuable, how should we treat each other?

Give everyone some sticky notes.

Write on the notes things you value about each other. For instance, you might write *patient* about your mother or *helpful* about your older sister.

Decorate each other with your notes!

Read what other people wrote about you.

Thank God for each other and **ask** him to help you treat each other as people of great value.

Little Brother

Nate stomped through the playground gate on his way to lunch recess. "I'm going to make the little turkey pay," he fumed. His younger brother Adam had gotten into his room again and messed up Nate's soccer trophies and medals.

Nate would teach him a lesson.

Is that what Jesus would do? Nate's conscience prodded him. Nate knew why Adam sneaked into his room to play. Adam missed him when he was away on soccer trips. Adam copied everything Nate did. He was Adam's role model.

My little brother is lots more important than a few trophies, Nate realized. *I should treat him the way Jesus wants me to.* Nate didn't feel mad anymore.

Scanning the school grounds, he spotted Adam across the field, all by himself. He stood there holding his soccer ball, watching the bigger boys play.

He's hoping they'll let him play, thought Nate. Adam looked lonely. Nate felt sorry about that. After all, Adam was his brother.

The biggest boy on the soccer field called out, "Hey, Nate, join my team!"

Nate saw Adam look over at him.

"Maybe later," Nate called, waving at the boy. He walked toward Adam and asked, "Want to kick the soccer ball around with me?"

The big smile that came to Adam's face erased the look of loneliness.

"If you love your neighbor, you will fulfill all the requirements of God's law." *(Romans 13:8)*

How did Nate demonstrate Jesus' love to his brother?

Short Fuse!

"It's my turn to play with Mega Hero," said Chad, pulling the helmeted action figure from his toy box.

His younger brother Lucas scowled. "You played with Mega Hero yesterday. I get to play with him today."

"I got him first!" insisted Chad, holding the toy above his head and backing away.

Lucas jumped up and tried to pry the action figure from Chad's hand. The boys tumbled to the floor. Chad exploded with anger. He hit Lucas in the face with the hard plastic figure.

Lucas bawled as blood trickled from his nose.

Horrified at what he had done, Chad asked, "Are you okay, Lucas? I'm sorry. Really I am. Don't tell Mom."

Lucas pushed Chad away and ran to his room, crying.

Chad sat down on his bed and thought about his temper. This wasn't the first time he'd lashed out without thinking of the consequences. He remembered the time he pushed a girl off the slide at school. Then there was Mom's favorite vase, which he'd smashed in a fit of anger. Now he'd hurt his own brother.

I don't want to be hurting people all the time. The thought frightened Chad. He remembered his Bible memory verse for the week: "Your anger can never make things right in God's sight" (James 1:20).

Chad knew he needed Jesus' help. He dropped to his knees beside his bed. "Dear Jesus, please forgive me for losing my temper. And please help me control it."

Chad prayed that prayer every night for months. He memorized Scripture verses about anger and about loving others. When he became angry, he counted to ten, then quoted Bible verses to himself. It took time, but Chad learned to let Jesus help him control his temper.

"Be…slow to get angry." *(James 1:19)*

Why does Jesus want you to control your temper? What can you do when you get angry?

Kip's Act of Friendship

"I'll beat you to the track," hollered Kip, racing his cabin mates down the hill. The camp's big tournament was about to begin. The prize for the winning team was a late-night pizza party and a swim in the camp pool.

Kip's team tried to decide who would compete in each event. Kip volunteered, "Mark me down for all individual races, relays, shot put, and javelin throw."

"You can't be in everything!" complained Randy. "What about the rest of us?"

"And what about Stewart?" asked Joe. "He needs a wheelchair relay."

"Be quiet," whispered Kip. "Here he comes."

There was an awkward silence as Stewart rolled up in his wheelchair. Kip didn't think Stewart looked very happy. There was nothing Stewart could do in the tournament.

Kip thought, *I sure wouldn't want to be left out of this track meet.*

"Is there something I can play?" asked Stewart. No one said anything. Stewart's face reddened and his eyes looked watery.

Suddenly a thought popped into Kip's mind: *Show Stewart the love of Jesus.*

What would Jesus do? Jesus would love Stewart and make sure he had a good time. Kip knew he needed to make a decision. He could either do what he wanted or what Jesus wanted.

"Hey, Stewart!" he said. "How about if you and I play a game of basketball? I'll hop on one foot while you use your wheelchair. When we're finished, we can come back here and watch the rest of the tournament."

Kip made Stewart's day. And the kindness he showed encouraged other campers to include Stewart in all the rest of the week's activities.

"Don't live to make a good impression on others. Be humble, thinking of others as better than yourself." *(Philippians 2:3)*

What would Jesus say to Kip?
How could you bring happiness to someone like
Stewart?

The Candy Bar

"Mmmm," said Penny, licking her lips.

Suzette glanced at her four-year-old sister in the backseat of the car. Penny's lips looked brown and sticky. She peered to see what Penny held in her hand. It looked like candy.

"Dad!" said Suzette. "I thought you weren't going to buy any sweets at the store!"

Dad looked surprised. "I didn't."

Suzette leaned over as far as she could, trying to see what Penny had in her hand. "It is a candy bar! Penny, where did you get that?"

Penny's eyes grew wide. "At...at the store," she said softly.

"*How* did you get that candy bar?" asked Dad.

"I took it out of the box on the shelf. Everyone else was taking some."

"You can't take things that don't belong to you—that's stealing," said Dad. "We'll go back so you can tell the clerk what you did. I'll loan you some money to pay for it. You can repay me out of your bank when we get home."

Penny looked like she was going to cry.

"When we do something wrong," explained Suzette gently, "Jesus wants us to be sorry and to ask for his forgiveness. He's always glad to forgive us." Then she added, "And I think Jesus would want me to hold your hand when you talk to the clerk."

Penny nodded and smiled through her tears.

"God has no favorites who can get away with evil." *(Colossians 3:25)*

What would Jesus want you to tell someone who was stealing?

Let the Children Come

Liza ran into the backyard to play. She stopped when she saw her younger sister, Tessie, standing on a wooden box. At her feet sat a circle of five-year-old boys and girls. Tessie held a large lesson book while she placed figures on an easel. Liza recognized the flannelgraph board their mother used to teach Sunday school.

Tessie is going to be in big trouble for playing with mother's stuff! thought Liza.

"Tessie! Put Mama's flannelgraph back right now. She's going to be mad!"

"Shh!" said Tessie, placing a figure of Jesus on the board. She told the children, "The Bible says, 'For God so loved the world that he gave his only Son, so that everyone who believes in him will not perish but have eternal—'"

Liza rushed over and snatched the book and flannelgraph figures from Tessie's hands. "Stop it now!"

The children in Tessie's audience jumped up and ran from the yard. Tears streamed down Tessie's face. "I was telling them about Jesus!" she protested.

Ignoring her sister, Liza picked up the easel and took it indoors.

But Liza's mother was not happy. "Tessie asked permission to use my things. You should have checked with me instead of acting bossy."

Liza put down the lesson book. It opened to a picture of Jesus blessing the children. Liza knew that story. The disciples tried to keep the children away from Jesus. *Just like I did today,* she realized.

She turned and hugged her sister. "Tessie, please forgive me. You didn't get to finish telling your friends about Jesus. I want to help you do that. Let's invite them to come back tomorrow. You tell them about Jesus and I'll serve cookies and juice."

Jesus said, "Let the children come to me. Don't stop them! For the Kingdom of Heaven belongs to such as these." *(Matthew 19:14)*

 *How does Jesus want you to treat younger children? How can you tell them about Jesus?*

Backward Night

Get Set Plan a meal that could be served backward—dessert first, salad last. Ask everyone to wear their clothes backward or inside out. Set the table with the silverware turned upside down. Write names backwards on place cards.

Go!

Have devotions before, instead of after, your backward meal.

Walk backward to the table. *Greet* each other with a "Good-bye!"

Read Mark 9:33–37.

Who is the greatest in God's sight? Why?
Which people today are considered to be the greatest?
Are servants considered great today?

Have everyone *name* one way they can serve other people.

Serve dessert first. Make sure it's upside down!

Put potatoes on your gravy, salad on your salad dressing.

Talk to each other in backwards sentences.

Serve each other by working on cleaning up the meal together.

Hot Spot Prayers

Get Set   Cut a large circle from red construction paper.

Go!

Read   Daniel 3:1–30.

How did Shadrach, Meshach, and Abednego get in a hot spot?
Was it their fault? Explain?

Place   the red circle on the floor.

Take turns   standing on the red circle.

Tell   about a time when you were in a hot spot.

How did God help you?
How did other Christians help you?
What does God want us to do when we find ourselves in a hot spot?
Why does God allow us to get into hot spots?
What good things happened because of Shadrach, Meshach, and Abednego being in a hot spot?

Name   someone you know who's in a hot spot right now.

Read   Psalm 55:16–17.

Pray   for God to help that person.

Plan   ways you can help and encourage that person.

Safe on the Rock

Troy tied on his rubber wet-vest, pulled on his snorkel mask, and jumped off the rocks into the ocean. He quickly paddled over to his dad and the diving instructor, who were already in the water. The enormous waves crashing on the boulders made Troy jittery.

Troy and his dad knew the instructions: swim out around the jetty, then float into the channel with the tide. Troy swam alongside his instructor, matching strokes against the rough incoming waves. Finally Troy reached the end of the jetty. Before he turned left to float toward the beach, he glanced around. He didn't see his father anywhere.

Where's Dad? Troy wondered. Treading water, he frantically signaled his instructor that something was wrong.

At last Troy spotted his dad bobbing in the water way back at the spot where they'd started. *What could have happened?* Troy's heart skipped a beat as he watched a wave slam his father up against the rocks. His dad scrambled to hang on to a rock but it was too slippery.

Dad is going to die! Troy thought. *Jesus, help him!*

Suddenly a huge wave crashed into the jetty. A swirling column of water lifted his dad up high. Troy watched him rise in the water—up, up, six feet in the air. Then his father spun around and landed safely on top of a large rock.

Troy couldn't believe his eyes! Sure enough—his dad was sitting on the rock, waving and signaling the two swimmers to keep going.

Praise and thanks filled Troy's heart. He floated ashore, thinking, *If God isn't ready for us to die, he can do anything to keep us alive!*

"The Lord protects me from danger.... He will place me out of reach on a high rock." *(Psalm 27:1, 5)*

*Do you pray first when you need help?
When has Jesus helped you?*

Stopping to Pray

Stephen burst through the front door and announced, "Jeremiah is missing! His parents haven't seen him for hours. They're asking everyone to help them search!"

"Come with me, Stephen," said his dad. They started up the nearby hillside together. Calling for Jeremiah, they searched behind every bush where the four-year-old might be hiding.

When they reached the hilltop, Stephen said, "Dad, it will be dark soon. Can we stop and pray?"

He and his father knelt in the grass and asked Jesus to help them find Jeremiah.

As Stephen got up, he noticed a small, faint trail used by small animals. It was just the right size for a little boy to follow. Stephen pulled out his flashlight and followed the trail under the brambles. His father couldn't make it through the underbrush—he was too tall.

But the narrow trail didn't go far. When Stephen turned around to head back, he heard a noise like a kitten's meow.

He pulled aside some brush and saw two little legs. It was Jeremiah! The little toddler couldn't talk—he'd cried until he lost his voice.

Stephen wrapped his arms around Jeremiah and said, "Don't be afraid. We'll take you home."

While Stephen's dad carried Jeremiah down the hill, Stephen wondered, *What if we hadn't stopped to pray?*

Jesus said, "Keep on asking, and you will be given what you ask for." *(Matthew 7:7)*

 *When have you been close to giving up? How did Jesus help you?*

Jillian's Choice

Kim's mouth fell open as she heard her friend's words. "God has never answered a single prayer I've ever prayed," Jillian said, "so I've stopped praying."

The two girls sat down in the grass, and Kim said quietly, "God answers my prayers."

"He doesn't answer mine," said Jillian. "I prayed that my parents wouldn't divorce, and they did. Then I prayed my dad wouldn't remarry. He did."

"I'm sorry," Kim said.

"I asked God to make my parents stop fighting," Jillian continued. "They still fight every time Dad picks me up."

"Can't you can think of one prayer God did answer?" asked Kim.

They didn't talk for a while. Kim searched the grass for clover and prayed silently for her friend. Jillian stared off into space. Kim knew she was thinking.

"Okay, I can think of one time," said Jillian. "I asked God to help find my cat when it got lost and he did." Kim smiled.

"He healed my cousin's leukemia, too," Jillian said. Tears filled her eyes. "But he didn't make my parents get back together."

Kim prayed that Jesus would give her the right words to say. "Do you remember the story of Adam and Eve? God made them in his own image. He gave them the special freedom to choose. He wanted them to obey, but he wouldn't force them—then they'd be robots. But they chose to disobey…"

Jillian continued Kim's thought. "And they had to separate from God."

Kim nodded. "You wanted both of your parents to stay with you and God wanted Adam and Eve to stay with him."

"It was almost like they divorced him, wasn't it?" Jillian said softly. "He must understand how I feel."

Kim put her arms around Jillian. "He does. Jesus wants you to choose to be with him."

"I'll start praying again," said Jillian.

"Choose today whom you will serve." *(Joshua 24:15)*

 *How can you show that you choose Jesus?*

Prayers of Faith

Nicole's mom hung up the phone. "Hong just accepted the Lord," she said, smiling.

"That's wonderful!" said Nicole. "But I'm shocked!"

"So am I!" said Mom.

Hong had lived with Nicole's family as a foreign exchange student when Nicole was born. Hong worshiped her Chinese ancestors the way most Buddhists did. After she finished college, she moved to Chicago. Nicole and her mom had prayed many years for Hong to accept Jesus.

"I didn't believe Hong would ever become a Christian," said Nicole. "I guess I didn't have much faith. When I prayed for her, I never believed it would really happen."

Mom hugged Nicole. "Me neither," she said. "A lot of times I thought we might as well stop praying."

"How did Jesus save her if neither of us had faith? Did he just save her without us?"

"He could have, but I think our prayers helped. Jesus said if we have enough faith we can actually move a mountain. When we kept on praying, it proved we had a teeny tiny bit of faith."

"You mean people who have no faith at all just stop praying?"

Mom nodded.

Nicole took her mom's hand. "Let's pray! And let's ask Jesus for more faith."

Jesus said, "If two of you agree…concerning anything you ask, my Father in heaven will do it for you." *(Matthew 18:19)*

Is there something you've nearly given up praying for?
What would Jesus tell you?

The String of Fish

"Where are the fish?" asked Brett.

Grandpa looked up from the log where he was reading his Bible and keeping an eye on his bobber. "They were right here," said Grandpa, "next to this log."

"Oh, no," Brett said. "The whole string is gone!"

Dad sloshed over in his hip wader boots. "Look downstream," he said. "They may have caught on something."

Dear Jesus, help us find our fish, Brett prayed. He ran along the bank looking for the string. Disappointment overwhelmed him. It was his special weekend with Dad and Grandpa. Now their whole afternoon seemed wasted.

"I'm sorry, Brett. I was the last one to put a fish on the string. I must not have anchored it well enough." Dad frowned. "This creek is too fast and deep. We'll never find those fish."

"It's okay, Dad," said Brett. "We'll catch more."

"Let's pray," said Grandpa. "The Lord can find our fish." Grandpa and Brett prayed, then returned to their fishing holes. Brett chose a rock near the middle of the rushing creek. Dad went upstream. Grandpa watched his bobber in a little pool. They fished for another hour but didn't get a single bite.

Brett moved to a bigger rock. *Please, Jesus, help me find the fish,* he prayed. Just then he glimpsed a silvery glint in the water. The string of ten fish was caught between the rocks! He reached over and scooped them out with his big net. "Dad! Grandpa!" he shouted as he scrambled to shore, holding up the fish for them to see.

"It's a miracle you found those fish, Brett," Dad said.

"That's what I prayed for," Brett replied.

"And God answers prayer!" added Grandpa with a smile.

"When you pray, I will listen." *(Jeremiah 29:12)*

How does Jesus want you to pray when things seem hopeless?

Popcorn Showers

Get Set You'll need unpopped popcorn, a popcorn popper, salt, and melted butter. (You'll also need oil if your popcorn popper requires it.) Give everyone a large bowl.

Go!

Have everyone **pour** a few kernels of popcorn into the popper.

Add oil if your popper requires it.

Leave the lid off and **turn on** the popper.

As the popcorn heats, **read** Ezekiel 34:26.

What blessings has God showered into our lives?
How do we show our thanks?
What everyday blessings do we take for granted?

As the popcorn starts to fly from the popper, **hold** out your bowls and try to **catch** it.

Combine all the popcorn in one bowl.

Pour salt and melted butter over it.

Sing your thanks with a favorite praise song.

Enjoy the blessing of freshly popped popcorn!

Week
31

Portrait Party

Get Set You'll need a kitchen timer, paper, and various drawing and painting materials such as pencils, watercolor paints, brushes, colored pencils, markers, or crayons.

Go!

Invite everyone to sit around a table.

Distribute paper and art materials.

Explain: Your assignment is to draw or paint a portrait of the person sitting across from you. You'll have only five minutes to work, so don't try to make it a masterpiece!

Set the timer for five minutes.

When the timer dings, take turns *giving* your portrait to the person you drew.

Have everyone *tell* that person what makes him or her unique and special.

Read 1 Timothy 5:8.

Why are families so important to God?
How can we better care for one another in our family?

Hang the portraits in a special place.

Pray and ask God to help you take good care of one another in your family.

Breaking Records

"Don't lose sight of Annie," Gina's dad told her before the race, "and you won't get lost."

Gina's running shoes pounded the trail. She had struggled to keep up with her friend, Annie, during the first half of the cross-country race. Could she continue to stay with her?

Annie loped along a few feet ahead of Gina. Gina matched Annie step for step. She concentrated on Annie's blond ponytail as it swung in a circle. She let Annie's strength pull her along. The rest of the runners trailed behind. *Jesus, please help me stay with her,* Gina prayed. *If Annie pulls out of sight, I might have trouble finding the trail.*

Gina kept pushing herself. Up ahead Annie seemed to stumble. Gina wondered if something was wrong. Gina pushed harder and closed the distance between them. Annie was wheezing!

"You okay?" Gina managed to gasp. Sweat drenched Gina's shirt.

Annie was fighting back tears. She looked at Gina with frightened eyes. The two girls ran side by side.

"Asthma?" Gina's every word took effort. Annie nodded in response. *Jesus, help Annie,* Gina prayed.

"Walk! I'll get help." Gina lengthened her stride and pushed her legs faster. She could get help for Annie at the finish line if she didn't get lost. Using every ounce of strength, Gina pushed ahead.

Jesus, please protect Annie. Help me stay on course. Gina's chest hurt and her legs ached. She wanted to quit. Instead, she fought and prayed harder than ever before in her life. She crossed the finish line and ran straight to Annie's parents to let them know that Annie needed help.

When Annie arrived, her parents were ready with her inhaler. Both girls had beaten the course record for their age group!

"May we shout for joy when we hear of your victory." *(Psalm 20:5)*

In what ways did both girls do what Jesus would do? When has Jesus let you help someone in trouble?

Friend or Foe?

Casey stood by the slide and watched Andrew run around the track with Jason, the new second grader.

I wish Jason had never come to this school, thought Casey. *He's taken away my best friend. Now I'm all alone at recess.*

Andrew used to play with Casey all the time. They were the best kick-ball twosome in the school. Now all Andrew did was follow Jason around the playground. Andrew never played kickball anymore.

"Jason is my worst enemy," muttered Casey. "What could I do to get even with him?"

"Hey!" hollered Andrew, running by and waving his arms. "Come and chase us, Casey!"

Suddenly it struck Casey. He thought *they* wouldn't play with him, but maybe the problem was that *he* wouldn't play with *them!* Maybe Jesus sent Jason to be a friend, not an enemy.

"Dear Jesus," Casey prayed, "help me be a friend. Help me change the way I think about Jason." Dropping the ball he held, Casey ran after them. They played and laughed all during recess.

Later Casey asked Jason, "Could we play some kickball tomorrow?"

"I'm not very good at it," Jason answered, "but I'll try…if you'll teach me."

Before long, the three boys became best friends. Casey was glad he'd given Jason a chance.

"Let God transform you into a new person by changing the way you think." *(Romans 12:2)*

 *Whom do you need to get to know better?*

The Orange Juice Disaster

Tiffany ran her hand over her sleeve, feeling the soft material. She knew she should be working on math, but she couldn't stop admiring her new birthday dress.

At lunchtime Tiffany turned to Kate and said, "I'll share my birthday cake with you."

Kate smiled, picked up her lunch sack, and followed Tiffany to the cafeteria. Tiffany was glad someone wanted to sit with her. She still felt shy after only one week in her new school.

Tiffany opened her lunch box and took out her sandwich and juice. She noticed that Kate was already eyeing the birthday cake hungrily. Anxious to please her new friend, Tiffany reached for the slice of cake. But as she lifted it out of her box, she bumped her juice bottle. Crash! The bottle fell over, splashing sticky orange juice all over the front of the new dress. Tiffany froze with embarrassment.

"I'll go with you to tell the teacher," said Kate. "She'll know what to do."

Their teacher was sitting at a nearby table. *Oh, no,* thought Tiffany. *The teacher is sitting by Heather, the most popular girl in class! She'll make fun of me when she sees what a mess I've made.*

"Teacher," said Kate, "we have a problem—"

Heather interrupted. "What in the *world* is that orange—" When Heather saw Tiffany's face, she stopped in the middle of her sentence, then said, "Tiffany, your dress is sooo pretty! Is it new?"

Tiffany blushed at Heather's compliment. "Yes, thanks. It's my birthday dress."

Heather smiled and stood up. "Come on. I'll help you wipe up that juice. We can use the hand dryer and it'll be dry in no time."

Thank you, Jesus, Tiffany prayed as she followed Heather to the rest room. *Heather seems so nice—maybe I'll make a new friend on my birthday.*

"Let everything you say be good and helpful...an encouragement to those who hear." *(Ephesians 4:29)*

 *Why does Jesus want you to be careful what you say to others?*

Oranges and Grapes

Kelvin loved visiting Aunt Nancy. She was always full of fun and energy. Kelvin didn't mind at all when she asked him to help her with grocery shopping. While Aunt Nancy shopped for meat, Kelvin wandered into the fruit section. It had been weeks since he'd had fresh fruit. Since his dad got laid off, there wasn't enough money to buy much fruit. They ate lots of macaroni, beans, and rice.

Kelvin picked up an orange and sniffed it. His mouth watered. He ran his finger around the curve of a shiny red apple. His stomach rumbled. He longed to pop just one strawberry into his mouth.

Kelvin looked up as Aunt Nancy approached. Had she seen him admiring the fruit? Kelvin didn't want her feeling sorry for him.

Aunt Nancy stacked some green beans in the cart. "Should we buy fruit?" she asked. "These look good." Aunt Nancy filled a plastic bag with green seedless grapes. "Would you bag some oranges?" she asked as she picked up a box of strawberries.

When they returned to Aunt Nancy's house, Kelvin helped unload the groceries. He piled a luscious-looking mound of fruit in a basket on the table.

"Help yourself to the fruit," Aunt Nancy said.

Kelvin offered a strawberry to Aunt Nancy first.

"I can't," she said, putting away a box of cereal. "I'm on a special diet."

Kelvin's eyes grew wide. "You mean all this is for me and Uncle Ron?"

"Uncle Ron gets hives when he eats fruit," she said. "I guess you'll have to eat it all."

Kelvin's eyes got bigger. He thought about his little sister and his parents.

"I'm not hungry right now," Kelvin said. "Do you mind if I eat just one strawberry and save the rest to eat later—at home?"

Aunt Nancy smiled. "That's a terrific idea," she said.

Thank you, Jesus! Kelvin prayed. *This fruit isn't just for me—it's for my family, too!*

Jesus said, "When you give a gift to someone in need, don't shout about it." *(Matthew 6:2)*

What would Jesus want you to share with someone? How does Jesus feel when you give to others?

Craig's Party

"This is fun, Dad," said Craig, sitting down with a notepad and pencil. "How many kids can I invite to my birthday party?"

"Start with your closest friends. Then we'll see how many more we have room for. We can't invite the whole world!"

Craig finished his guest list, then started to plan what kind of food he wanted. Suddenly he stopped. "Sammy! I have to add Sammy to my list! He never gets invited to parties. It's hard for him to get around in his wheelchair, but I'll help him."

Craig's father hesitated. Cerebral palsy had left Sammy with weak arms and a severe limp. He couldn't walk far without his wheelchair. "Are you sure you want to invite him?" asked Father.

"I'm sure," said Craig.

When Craig's birthday arrived, Sammy's parents dropped him off. "I'll give him all the help he needs," volunteered Craig. "And we'll bring him home when we're done."

During the party, Craig organized charades, a round of darts, and some relay games. He made sure to include Sammy in everything. Instead of concentrating on himself as the center of attention, Craig helped his friend enjoy the party. Craig's other friends caught on, and everyone had a great time. Sammy glowed with delight—he'd never had such an afternoon!

That night Craig lay in bed thinking back on the day. *It's amazing,* he thought. *By thinking of someone else's happiness, I had my best birthday ever!*

"Be humble, thinking of others as better than yourself."
(Philippians 2:3)

What would Jesus want you to do for someone with special needs?

Bible Story Blast

Get Set Fill a dress-up box with robes, shawls, scarves, towels, and neckties. You'll also need note cards, pencils, paper, and a small basket. You may want to invite another family to join you in this devotion. Prepare Bible-time treats such as grape juice, canned or dried figs, dates, and matzo bread.

Go!

Have everyone *write down* the names of four Bible stories, each on a separate note card.

Place the cards in a basket.

Form teams. (A team may be as small as one person.)

Have each team *draw* a card.

Using the items in the dress-up box, *create* costumes for your Bible story.

Take turns *acting out* your Bible stories with actions, but no words.

Let the other team *guess* the story.

Act out several stories this way, then *put away* the costumes.

Give each team a pile of paper and some pencils.

Pull a story from the basket, then *draw* scenes from the story as the other team guesses.

When you've done all the stories, *set out* the Bible-time treats.

As you enjoy the treats, *talk about* which Bible stories are your favorites and why.

Power Wash

Get Set Set out a clear glass, a pitcher of water, a container of dirt, a teaspoon, and a cross.

Go!

Pour water into the glass.

Explain: This is like God pouring life into us.

Add a spoonful of dirt to the glass of water.

Have everyone **tell** one way sin can spoil our lives, then **add** a teaspoon of dirt.

Read King David's prayer in Psalm 51:7–10.

Can you make this water pure again? Can you make your heart pure?

Hold up the cross.

How does God wash us clean?
Why was Jesus willing to die?

Walk to the kitchen sink. **Turn on** the water and the garbage disposal. Let water flow into the glass until all the dirt is washed out.

Hold up the glass.

How can this happen in our hearts?

Pray silently, confessing any wrongdoing to Jesus. Then **be confident** and **rejoice** that he forgives you!

Sing a praise song together.

Stolen Flowers

"Mommy will love these flowers!" Katie excitedly walked down the row of tulips and snapped off each one, then put them carefully in her wagon.

What a great birthday surprise for Mommy! thought the five-year-old, pulling her treasures home from the neighbor's yard. She parked her wagon inside the garage, then went back into the house to eat lunch.

The next morning, Katie woke early. She couldn't wait to give Mommy her present. But when she walked into the garage, she gasped.

I forgot to water the flowers! she realized. Grabbing a bucket, she filled it at the outside faucet and carefully placed the wilted tulips in the water.

"Perk up!" she begged them. "And please hurry."

Leaving the garage, she glanced over at the neighbor's yard. It looked different than yesterday. Katie's heart skipped a beat. She didn't want to think about what she had done.

When Katie walked into the kitchen, Mother asked, "Do you know what happened to Mrs. Sullivan's tulips? She just phoned. All her flowers are gone."

Hot tears filled Katie's eyes. Her lips quivered.

Mother put her arm around Katie. "Tell me about it, honey."

"I didn't think about who owned the tulips," Katie sobbed. "I only thought about your birthday! I'm so sorry!"

"Let's talk to Jesus about it, Katie," said Mother.

They prayed together. Then Katie smiled and said, "Whenever I ask Jesus to forgive me, I always feel better. "I'll go ask Mrs. Sullivan to forgive me, too. But could you come with me?"

"Mrs. Sullivan loves Jesus, too," said Mother with a smile. "Let's go talk to her right now."

"What joy for those whose record the Lord has cleared of sin."
(Psalm 32:2)

What would Jesus want Katie to say to her neighbor?
What do you think Mrs. Sullivan would say to Katie?

Repaying Evil

Keith heard a knock and ran to open the door. Dahara, a pastor in the Indonesian village where Keith's parents were missionaries, grinned at him. "I have been praying for a deer," Dahara said. "This morning I found one in my trap. Isn't God good?" He held out a piece of meat. "I want to share this with you."

Knowing how poor Dahara's family was, Keith said, "My dad's not here right now, but we'll pay you for the meat."

Dahara shook his head. "No, no. You are missionaries doing God's work, just as I am. Besides, I am going to share the meat with everyone in the village."

Keith was amazed. He remembered last year when Dahara's family moved to this village to start a church. They had only a few cooking utensils and the clothes on their backs. But the villagers refused to share anything with them. They made Dahara pay for everything his family needed.

"You're giving meat to all the villagers?" Keith asked. "Even the ones who didn't share their food with you?"

Dahara smiled. "Even the people who did not share with me," he said. "In this way, I can be like Jesus. I can show them God's love."

Keith looked into Dahara's eyes. "I would have been angry and kept the meat for myself. But you have shown me how to love like Jesus would."

"Conquer evil by doing good." *(Romans 12:21)*

How does Jesus want you to "pay back" evil actions?

Needing Forgiveness

Carolyn opened her bottom dresser drawer, reached behind her sweatshirt, and pulled out a shiny red bracelet. It matched her skirt and top perfectly. But now she didn't dare wear it. If Dana or any of her friends saw it, they would recognize it immediately. Dana was offering a reward to anyone who found her missing bracelet.

I wanted this bracelet so badly, Carolyn thought. *Now I have to hide it. I'm scared someone will find out what I did.*

A heavy lump stuck in her throat as she shoved the bracelet back in the drawer. After she climbed in bed, Mother came in and knelt down beside her. She held Carolyn's hands and prayed. Finishing with a song, she hugged and kissed her daughter.

"Good night, honey. Remember to talk to Jesus after I leave. He's listening for you."

Tears trickled down Carolyn's cheeks. "He doesn't want to talk to me," she whimpered. "And I'm...I'm scared to talk to him."

"Why?" asked Mother.

"I stole Dana's bracelet! Now I'm sorry, but I don't know what to do." She buried her face in the pillow and sobbed.

"Have you told Jesus you're sorry? Have you asked for his forgiveness?"

"I didn't think he'd forgive me."

"Jesus took the punishment for your sins when he died on the cross," explained Mother. "He *wants* to forgive you. Ask him. I'll pray along with you."

Carolyn closed her eyes and talked to Jesus about what she had done. When she finished, she scrambled out of bed and took the bracelet from its hiding place. "I'll take this to Dana tomorrow. I pray that she can forgive me, too."

"If we confess our sins to him, he is faithful and just to forgive us and to cleanse us from every wrong." *(1 John 1:9)*

Do you believe that Jesus <u>wants</u> to forgive you?
Do you need to ask forgiveness of another person?

Hot Pink Bikes

"Don't you love hot pink?" Connie asked her friend Sharon.

The two girls stood in Connie's driveway admiring the new paint job on their old bicycles. Dad's shiny black Buick was parked just beyond them, inside the open garage door.

"Our bikes look beautiful," Sharon agreed. "Are you sure your mom won't care we used her paint?"

"Yes. As long as I don't make a mess, it's fine."

She and Sharon gathered up the newspaper that had protected the cement while they spray painted their bikes.

"Look!" Connie pointed at Sharon, laughing. "You've got tiny pink dots all over your arms!"

"So do you!" giggled Sharon. "We've got hot pink freckles!"

"It's a good thing we wore old clothes." Connie said. "Sometimes spray paint drifts and you don't even notice." The girls wadded up the papers and stuffed them into grocery sacks. "The trash goes inside the garage," Connie said.

Each girl grabbed a sack. As they squeezed past Dad's new Buick, Connie saw bright pink dots all over the back of Dad's shiny black car. All at once she couldn't breathe.

"No!" Connie started to cry. "How could that happen?"

Sharon started crying too. "Spray paint doesn't wash off!"

"Let's ask Jesus what to do," Connie said. The girls hugged each other and began to pray. They were still praying when Dad walked up. Sobbing, Connie told Dad everything.

"We can't do anything to make it better," Connie said. "And it will cost a lot to fix. Please forgive us."

Dad put his arms around both girls. All the fear flowed out of Connie as she snuggled close. "You are a lot like Jesus, Dad," she said. "You pay for my mistakes and you still love me."

"Give all your worries and cares to God, for he cares about what happens to you." *(1 Peter 5:7)*

How was Connie's dad like Jesus? How does it feel when someone forgives you?

Fighting Mad

Derek hid behind the kitchen door and listened to the angry neighbors shout at his mother in their living room.

"Derek gave my son a black eye!"

"And he threw rocks at my Patrick!"

"Ever since your family moved into the neighborhood, we've had nothing but trouble!"

After all the neighborhood mothers left, Derek's mom found him and said, "We have a problem, son. You're fighting a lot. You've never done that before. Want to tell me about it?"

Derek was relieved that his mom didn't yell at him. He blurted out, "Jarrett said if I gave him five dollars he'd be my friend. So I gave him my birthday money."

"And?"

"And Jarrett *isn't* my friend. He makes fun of me and gets the other kids to tease me. I'm really mad!" Derek blinked back angry tears.

"Sometimes we get angry because someone hurts us. We feel like striking out and hurting others."

Derek nodded.

"Think about Jesus' crucifixion. What did Jesus do?"

"He forgave the people who killed him," said Derek.

"Stephen said the same thing, remember? We read about him last night in devotions. He forgave the people who stoned him."

Derek patted his mother's arm. "Don't worry about any more visits from the neighbors, Mom. I'm going to forgive instead of fight. It's what Jesus would want me to do."

"Be...slow to get angry." *(James 1:19)*

How do you act when someone hurts you?
How would Jesus want you to act?

Does God Ever Forget?

Get Set Gather a variety of ten items on a tray. You might include a saltshaker, toothpicks, a bandage, a tea bag, a coffee mug, sunglasses, a vegetable, a fruit, an eraser, or a can opener. Cover the tray. Set out pencils and paper for everyone.

Go!

Uncover the tray and invite everyone to *study* it.

Explain that you'll take the tray away after one minute.

Remove the tray.

Have everyone *write down* all the items they can remember. (Young children can whisper answers to an older person to write down.)

Bring back the tray.

Mark your papers and find out who remembered the most items.

Give that person a round of applause.

Which items were the hardest to remember?
Does God have a problem remembering?
Does God ever forget anything?

Read Isaiah 43:25 and Isaiah 44:21–23.

How does God forgive us?
Are you willing to forgive and forget when you've been wronged?

Talk over and *forgive* any hurtful words or actions that have happened in your family.

Close with a big group hug!

A Family Blessing

Get Set — Fix a special dessert to eat at the end of devotions. Wrap it in foil or gift wrap. Add a fancy ribbon and bow.

Go!

Hold up the wrapped dessert.

Explain: Each person in our family is like a wonderful gift.

Form a circle.

Have one person **stand** in the middle of the circle, **hold** the dessert, and **say:** I am a gift to my family.

Have each person in the circle **respond** by saying: You are a blessing to our family because…"

Bless the person in the middle by reading Numbers 6:24–26.

Repeat for each family member.

Stand in a tight circle and join hands.

Lean back slowly, keeping a firm grip on each other's hands.

Lean forward slowly, still holding hands.

How did we help each other in this leaning circle?
How is that like the way we help each other from day to day?

Open and **share** the dessert.

Decide on a secret signal that means, "I will always support and bless you."

Peacemaker Pete

"What's the hardest job you do during the week?" Pete's Sunday school teacher asked.

Pete thought for a minute. "Being a big brother," he answered. "It's tough work."

"What's so hard about it?"

"Well, my little brother shares my bedroom. He's a big—He never picks up his stuff, leaves dirty clothes laying around. Then I'm supposed to clean it up!"

"Do you two work things out together?"

Pete sighed. "It's hard to work with Joey. For one thing, Joey's stubborn. For another, he won't do anything I say. My parents don't understand how difficult it is to share the bedroom with him."

Pete's teacher smiled and said, "Tell me more."

Pete continued, "Yesterday our parents said we couldn't go swimming until we cleaned our room. So I told my brother, 'You clean your half of the room and I'll clean my half.' His half was a mess."

"Did it work out?" asked his teacher.

"Not at first!" said Peter. "Joey sat down in the middle of the floor and bawled. He complained that he had the hardest job and I had the easiest. Then I remembered how Jesus washed his disciples' feet, so I decided to help my brother even if he didn't deserve it. I made it into a game. I told him, 'You clean *my* half of the room and I'll clean *your* half. Let's see who's the fastest.' Joey jumped up and we both finished at the same time because I clean faster than he does. Then we went swimming."

"Do you realize what you did?" asked his teacher. "You've been a peacemaker! Jesus said, 'Blessed are the peacemakers.'"

"I've heard that verse," said Peter with a grin. "Yeah, I guess that's what I did. I made peace."

Jesus said, "God blesses those who work for peace, for they will be called the children of God." *(Matthew 5:9)*

When have you been a peacemaker? How would Jesus want you to make peace in your home?

Rema's Sister

Margo stopped her swing and glared at Sara. "Rema is my sister."

"No, she isn't. She's six years old, but she's never lived with you. She lives in a different country and she can't even speak English."

For a moment Margo hated Sara. Then she remembered what her mom said: "When people hurt you, don't let it make you bitter."

Margo prayed silently, *Help me forgive Sara.*

"We've been trying to adopt Rema since she was born," Margo explained patiently.

"Then why is she still in that orphanage in Romania?"

Margo thought about Rema's big brown eyes. She knew Sara didn't understand how much she loved her sister.

"For three years we've prayed for her and sent her gifts. Last year we flew over to spend Christmas with her," Margo said.
"They'll never let her go," Sara said, running off.

Margo took a deep breath. "Nothing is impossible with you, Jesus." she prayed. "I know you can bring Rema to live with us. But if you don't, in my heart she is still my sister and I'll always love her. I know you will protect her wherever she lives." She stopped for a moment, then added, "Although I couldn't make Sara understand, I know that you can do that, too. Thank you that she can't make me bitter."

"His faithful love endures forever."
(Psalm 136:1)

WWJD

How does Margo's love for her sister remind you of Jesus?
What opportunities have you had to show Jesus' love to others?

Willing to Lose

Lauren's mom made a special celebration dinner. In two weeks little Kelli would have the kidney transplant that would save her life. While the rest of the family enjoyed ham, mashed potatoes, and all the trimmings, Dad ate nothing but a small piece of chicken and a plate of vegetables. He'd eaten that way for a whole year.

"Can't you eat just one piece of pie, Dad?" Lauren asked. "It's pecan, your favorite. You've already lost a hundred pounds."

Dad smiled at Lauren, then at five-year-old Kelli. "Remember how hard we prayed for Jesus to give me self control so I could give up pie?" he asked. "I love pie, but I love my girls more. I can't give Kelli my kidney if I start gaining weight."

Doctors had diagnosed Kelli with a kidney disease three years earlier. For a long time Lauren feared Kelli would die. She prayed and prayed for the Lord to heal her sister. Then, last December, the doctors discovered that Dad could be a donor. He could give Kelli one of his kidneys and save her life. There was just one problem—he was one hundred pounds too heavy!

Dad asked Lauren to pray that Jesus would help him lose weight. She prayed faithfully and Dad ate only one small meal each day. He never ate a single piece of pie, even though he loved it.

But before he'd lost enough weight, Kelli's condition got worse. The whole family feared that Kelli wouldn't survive until Dad had lost the necessary weight.

Lauren prayed earnestly. "Dear Jesus, help Dad lose fast enough."

Jesus *did* help Dad lose the weight. In just two weeks Kelli would have Dad's kidney and she would be well again.

Lauren pushed her piece of pie away and pressed her cheek against her dad's. "I don't need a piece, either," she said.

Jesus said, "My nourishment comes from doing the will of God."
(John 4:34)

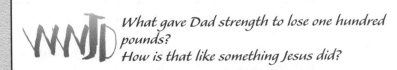

What gave Dad strength to lose one hundred pounds?
How is that like something Jesus did?

Family Awards

Lyle gave his mother a big squeeze. "I'm so excited about our dinner tonight. And since it's our first family dinner since we adopted Lindsay, I'm going to make a special award for everyone."

Mother laughed at Lyle's excitement. "Do whatever you like! But make sure you get the table set while I finish the salad."

As he set out the lace tablecloth and the blue-and-white dishes, Lyle thought of the titles he would put on his awards. His parents had adopted six children, and he was the oldest. There must be a special award for everyone.

Lyle gathered flowers from the backyard and floated them in glass bowls at both ends of the table. He set out the tallest candles he could find and added five smaller votive candles by the flower bowls. Later, in his room, he finished hand lettering the awards for each member of the family.

After a delicious dinner, everyone gathered in the living room. One by one, Lyle called each person forward to receive an award. There were awards for the most creative child, the most cheerful family member, the bubbliest personality, the hardest worker, the most encouraging, the most organized, and special awards for the best father and mother in the world! As each individual stood in the center of the room, other members of the family cheered and applauded.

Lyle's parents also took time to thank each child for the contribution they had made to the family. They finished the evening by praying together and thanking God for each other. Everyone in the Marsh family knew they were blessed to be part of a unique family!

"May the Lord make your love grow and overflow to each other and to everyone else." *(1 Thessalonians 3:12)*

How would Jesus want you to appreciate your family?

The Blue Horse

"My favorite horse!" Chloe rushed over to the blue horse at the fast food restaurant. It was the one she always begged Mom to let her ride. She loved the way it bobbed on its silver springs.

Climbing on, she happily rocked back and forth. Then she glanced over Mom, who was holding her little sister Alexis. Mom looked tired.

"I could ride forever," Chloe told her horse.

Alexis stared at Chloe. It made Chloe feel guilty. Chloe looked away and rocked harder. "Alexis should stop staring at me," she said to her horse. "It's my turn to ride you. Alexis likes to ride. But she's too little to stay on, and Mom's too tired to help her."

Out of the corner of her eye she could see Alexis leaning her head on Mom's chest and watching her. Chloe rocked hard, then slid off the horse.

"Come here, Alexis," she called.

Alexis jumped off Mom's lap and ran to Chloe. Mom gave Chloe a weary smile.

Chloe lifted Alexis onto the horse and held her so she wouldn't fall off.

"Thank you, Chloe," said Alexis. "How come you gived me your horsey?"

"I knew Jesus wanted me to," Chloe replied. Watching her little sister, Chloe discovered that pleasing Jesus gave her greater happiness than riding the blue horse.

Jesus said, "Just as I have loved you, you should love each other." *(John 13:34)*

 *How did Chloe show Jesus' love?*

Family Talent Show

Get Set Have each family member prepare a short performance. It could involve telling a joke, reading a poem or short story, performing a musical piece, or doing a trick. Encourage everyone to wear a costume. Set out items that can be used as awards, such as chocolate kisses, ribbons, or gold stars. You'll also need a large bowl, spoons, and toppings for an ice-cream sundae buffet.

Go!

As master of ceremonies, **explain:** We're here to enjoy each other, have a good time, and celebrate the greatest family on earth!

Read Proverbs 15:30.

What good news can you tell about each other?
What good news can we tell about our family?

Announce each person's act.

Lead in rousing cheers and applause after each performance.

Have everyone **give** awards, high-fives, and hugs to each performer.

Do the Bunny Hop and **lead** everyone to the kitchen.

Build a massive ice-cream sundae in a large bowl.

Read Proverbs 15:15 and **enjoy** your feast.

Truth or Lies?

Get Set Set out paper, pencils, a funny-looking hat, a can opener, two bowls, a can of fruit, and a can of vegetables. Secretly cut off and switch labels on the two cans. Set out two bowls to hold their contents.

Go!

Why do cans have labels? Can we trust the labels?

Open both cans. *Pour* the contents into the bowls.

Do some people wear the label "Christian," but inside they're really not? Is that the same as lying? Explain.
Can people tell if you're Christian by watching you?

Explain: We're going to play a game called "What's the Truth?"

Have everyone *write down* three things about themselves—two things that are true and one that's false.

Take turns *wearing* the "crown of truth" (the funny hat) and *reading* your three statements.

Let others *guess* which are true and honest.

Read Proverbs 16:2. *Why should we tell the truth?*

Read John 14:6. *Who is the Truth?*

Ask volunteers to put on the "crown of truth" and tell about a time when they weren't totally honest. Share what happened.

The Heavenly Referee

Ben threw his baseball glove on the front seat of the van and climbed inside.

"Cry hard, you loser!" yelled a boy from the other team.

"They cheated, Dad!" Ben slammed the door shut.

"That's rough, Ben. You guys played a great game!"

"But we lost the championship."

"You came in second and beat fourteen other teams to do it! That's quite an accomplishment."

"But it isn't fair! Just because the umpire needs new glasses—"

"Son, things aren't always fair here on earth. Remember, God doesn't need glasses. He sees everything and will ultimately carry out justice."

Ben folded his arms across his chest and scowled.

His dad went on. "Those boys on the other team didn't believe they were championship material, or they wouldn't have cheated."

Ben straightened up in his seat. "I hadn't thought about it that way."

"They have to live the rest of their lives knowing that they won the championship by cheating."

"I know I feel pretty horrible when I don't do what Jesus wants me to do," said Ben.

"Someday they'll stand before God and so will you and I." His father smiled. "So tell me, whose shoes would you rather be in?"

Ben sniffed his shoes and grinned. "My smelly ones! You know, I'm glad we didn't cheat, Dad."

"For he has set a day for judging the world with justice..." *(Acts 17:31)*

How does knowing that God will judge everyone fairly in the end help you handle unfair situations now?

The Baseball Card

Nathan pretended to be reading as he listened to Kent talking to T. J. "My Ken Griffey Jr. card is missing!" said Kent. "It's my most valuable card!"

"It must be there somewhere," said T. J. "Look through your cards—you have over a hundred of them."

"It's gone! And I'm going to find out who took it."

After class, Kent came to Nathan and asked, "Do you know where my Ken Griffey Jr. card is? You wanted me to trade it."

Nathan's face turned red. "I didn't take your stupid card," he insisted.

The next day Nathan found Kent during recess. "Let me see your cards, Kent. Maybe I can find the missing one." As Nathan pretended to look through the cards he slipped the stolen card out of his pocket and into the box. Then he turned and showed it to Kent. "Here it is. You just overlooked it."

"I'll bet you put it back in there!" accused Kent, snatching the box away.

During the following weeks, Nathan tried to forget what he'd done, but he couldn't. One night his father asked, "Where are your baseball cards? I haven't seen them lately."

Nathan blushed and hung his head. "I…I'm not collecting them anymore."

Father put his arm around Nathan's shoulder. "What's wrong, son?"

Nathan explained what he'd done, then added, "I put the card back, but I can't forget what I did."

"Let's pray about it," Father suggested.

Nathan bowed his head and prayed, "I'm sorry, Jesus. Forgive me for taking that card. Forgive me for lying. You died for my sins. Help me live for you and be a giver, not a taker."

The next thing Nathan did was call Kent. He confessed that he stole the card, asked Kent's forgiveness, and offered to buy Kent a new package of trading cards.

"Stop stealing. Begin using your hands for honest work, and then give generously to others in need." *(Ephesians 4:28)*

Have you ever tried to cover up a wrong? How does it feel when Jesus forgives you?

Playing Favorites

Rory pressed the channel selector on the TV remote. Nearly every television station was carrying the news of basketball star Jeremiah Keyes's latest bad boy stunt. TV cameras showed some fans marching in support of Jeremiah while other people called for him to be fired.

Rory's older brother Brendon walked into the room, glanced at the TV, and said, "Why don't they just let Keyes play basketball?"

"He's known for playing dirty, Brendon."

"What's important is that he's a great player," argued Brendon. "He had a triple double last night. He's awesome!"

"But what about the way he acts?" asked Rory. "Coach says good character and sportsmanlike conduct are more important than talent. Besides, athletes are role models for other people, especially kids like me."

Brendon snorted. "You're just quoting your coach. You're not old enough to have your own opinion."

"Athletes are supposed to be good sports. They're supposed to play a clean game and not hurt others," insisted Rory.

"But these players are special. There are only a few guys in the whole world who can do what they do," said Brendon.

The TV cameras showed a clip of Keyes yelling at a referee, then jumping into the stands to argue with an angry spectator. Teammates followed, trying to stop him.

Rory couldn't believe his brother was defending Keyes's behavior. "Are you saying great players can do anything they want? Jeremiah Keyes just punched out a fan! Is that good sportsmanship?"

Brendon shrugged. "So he gets a little angry. He's a superstar."

"Coach says God doesn't have favorites. We're all judged by the same standards."

Brendon laughed. "Your coach is a Sunday school teacher. What does he know?"

"He knows the Bible and he knows what Jesus wants us to do," said Rory. "*That's* what's important."

"God has no favorites who can get away with evil." *(Colossians 3:25)*

 *What would Jesus say to Brendon?*

An F for Buzz

"An F in math? I've had it with your teacher!" Buzz's dad picked up the phone. "I'm going to tell your teacher what I think about this."

Buzz broke into a sweat. "Dad…"

Dad stopped and hung up the phone. "What's wrong, son?"

"I deserved an F." Buzz blinked back tears.

"But I checked your homework. It was perfect." Dad paused, studying Buzz. "Unless you didn't turn it in."

Buzz dropped his head. "I didn't."

"You worked hours on it." Dad looked angry. "You said you turned it in. Why did you lie?"

Buzz started to cry. "I'm always forgetting things, Dad. It just slipped my mind. And I was afraid you'd be mad."

Dad took a deep breath. "We're all tempted to lie to protect ourselves sometimes," he said. "Let's ask Jesus to help us do what he wants us to do."

"Okay."

"Jesus," Dad prayed, "please help me treat Buzz lovingly. Help Buzz to remember to turn in his work and give him courage to tell the truth."

"Jesus, please forgive me for lying," Buzz prayed. "I should have been honest, no matter what. Help me always tell the truth."

Dad hugged Buzz. "Thank you, Lord, for a son who wants to serve you."

"The Lord hates those who don't keep their word, but he delights in those who do." *(Proverbs 12:22)*

When have you been tempted to lie to protect yourself?
How do you think Jesus feels when you resist the temptation to lie?

The Answers in Red

Jillian reviewed her notes one last time before the test started.

"Take everything off your desks except a pencil and an eraser," the teacher said. "Keep out a blank sheet of paper to cover your answers so no one can copy you."

Jillian scooped her notes and history book into her desk. She'd memorized facts and dates for hours last night.

"I'm ready for this test," she whispered to Tobin, who was sitting in the desk in front of hers. "I studied all night."

Tobin turned around and hissed, "It's stupid to study." Tobin never studied.

Why do I try to talk to Tobin? wondered Jillian. *I guess I want him to like me because he's popular.*

At the front of Jillian's row, Miss Howell counted out five tests. She handed them to Tobin, the first person in the row. When she turned to pass out the rest, he slipped one paper in his desk, put another one on top of his desk, and passed the rest back.

But Jillian saw what he did. The test Tobin put in his desk had all the answers marked in red. Miss Howell had accidentally passed out her answer key!

The last girl in Jillian's row raised her hand. "We need one more test, Miss Howell," she said. The teacher looked puzzled, but handed a copy to the girl.

Jillian's heart pounded. She knew what Jesus wanted her to do. She also knew that if she caused trouble for Tobin, everyone in class would hate her.

Tobin eased the answer key out of his desk. Jillian nudged him and whispered, "Put it away!"

He glared at her, then glanced at the answer key and wrote on his test.

Jillian raised her hand. She would do the right thing, no matter what.

"Take no part in the worthless deeds of evil and darkness; instead, rebuke and expose them." *(Ephesians 5:11)*

 *When have you risked someone's anger to do what Jesus wanted?*

Rocks and Sand

Get Set You'll need a mixing bowl, instant pudding mix, milk, graham crackers, large marshmallows, a plastic bag that zips, a rolling pin, and a wire whisk. Set out cups and spoons for everyone.

Go!

Read Matthew 7:24–27.

What can we learn from these two men?

Place two or three large marshmallow "rocks" in the bottom of each cup.

How do we build our lives on Jesus?

Place graham crackers in the plastic bag and **crush** them with the rolling pin.

When do we build on sand?

Mix the milk and pudding mix and **beat** the mixture with the wire whisk.

How is the "storm" in the pudding like the storms that happen in our lives?

Pour the pudding over the marshmallow "rock" foundations.

How does our faith in Jesus protect us from those storms?

Sprinkle graham cracker "sand" on top of each cup of pudding.

Before you eat, **pray:** Dear Jesus, we want to build our lives on you. Help us to live for you and obey your teachings. Help us to be honest and faithful in all we do. Amen.

For the Birds!

Get Set   You'll need a large needle, yarn, several slices of bread, cookie cutters, peanut butter, knives, and birdseed. Preheat the oven to 250 degrees.

Go!

Step   outside your house.

What kinds of birds do you see? Which are your favorites?

Read   Matthew 6:25–27.

Why did Jesus tell us to look at the birds?
Why don't birds worry? Why do people worry? What do you worry about?

Explain: We're going to make a treat for our bird friends.

Cut   slices of bread with cookie cutters or scissors.

Bake   5 minutes at 250 degrees.   **Turn** over and

bake   five more minutes.

Spread   with peanut butter.

Press   birdseed into the peanut butter.

Make   a yarn hanger in the top of each cookie.

Hang   the cookies from trees and bushes.

Pray   and ask God to help you trust him to take care of all your needs.

Slam Dunk

"Whoa!" said Michael. "Three weeks ago we had two mice. Now we've got *twenty!* They're almost grown up already. Wish I could grow that fast."

He and Jaewoo pressed their noses against the glass aquarium where Mrs. King kept the mice. She had left the boys in the classroom to finish their math while the rest of the class played outside at recess.

"I wish I jump like mice," said Jaewoo.

"Can they jump high?"

"They superman," said Jaewoo.

"I'm going to check it out," Michael said, lifting the wire lid off the aquarium. He folded his arms and waited. Pretty soon a white spotted mouse leaped at least a foot above the aquarium and landed on the table. "Whoa!" said Michael. "If I could jump like that I could clear a forty-story building!"

Michael grabbed the mouse and put it back. "It felt wiggly," he told Jaewoo.

"They muscle man," said Jaewoo.

Another mouse jumped above the silver aquarium rim. Without thinking Michael slam-dunked it back. "Hey, look! We've got NBA Mousketball!" He laughed.

Jaewoo slam-dunked another mouse back into the aquarium. Then Michael's conscience kicked in. *I'll bet Jesus wouldn't like this too much,* he thought. *I think he would want me to be kind to animals.*

Michael put the lid back on the aquarium. He felt ashamed. He knew he had been a bad influence on the school's only Korean exchange student. Michael felt that Jesus would want him to apologize.

"Jaewoo, I shouldn't have done that. I'm a Christian. I know Jesus wants me to treat people well, and I think he wants me to be kind to animals, too. Besides, we're supposed to be doing our math." They sat right down and started studying.

"Even the animals…know their owner and appreciate his care." *(Isaiah 1:3)*

Why does Jesus want us to take good care of our animals?
How do you care for your pets?

Feeling Sheepish

Adam raced his twin brother Alan to the back door. They dropped their backpacks on the kitchen table, opened the refrigerator, and got out the burritos.

"Don't forget your afternoon chores," said Mother.

"We won't," they promised between bites.

"Did you give the sheep clean water this morning?" she asked.

The boys looked at each other and nodded.

"You measured out their feed and put fresh hay in the bins?"

They nodded again.

When they came to dinner that evening, Mother said, "You boys are spending less and less time taking care of your sheep." She put a plate of spaghetti and a salad at her place. In front of the boys she set bowls of runny oatmeal and glasses of water cloudy with oat bran.

"What's this?" asked Adam. "Why don't we get spaghetti?"

"I checked the sheep shed before dinner," said Mother.

Adam glanced at Alan. *Uh-oh!* thought Adam, remembering the bucket filled with scummy water and the dirty hay strewn over the shed floor.

"I thought you'd enjoy eating the way your sheep are eating."

Adam bit his lip.

"God gave you those sheep to care for, just as he's given me the privilege of caring for you."

"Let's go out to the sheep shed, Alan," said Adam. "I think Jesus wants us to take better care of Eunice and Sam."

"You put us in charge of everything you made." *(Psalm 8:6)*

 *How does Jesus want you to treat the animals in your care?*

Praying for Hobie

Robin heard a knock and opened the door. There stood her friend, Kelsey.

"Mom ran over Hobie," said Kelsey with tears in her eyes.

Robin still grieved for her own cat, who had died of leukemia. She hugged Kelsey and they both started crying. "What happened?" asked Robin.

Kelsey wiped her tears. "When Mom drove the car into our garage this afternoon after school, we heard a horrible meowing. I *knew* we'd hit Hobie! I jumped out of the car and found her. It looked like her back was broken."

"Did you take her to the vet?" asked Robin.

Kelsey nodded. "I prayed all the way to his office. While he examined Hobie, I cried so much, I used up all our tissues."

"I remember praying for my cat, too," Robin said quietly.

"The vet thought Hobie had a punctured lung," explained Kelsey. "When we left her there, I didn't know if I'd see her alive again. But we just got his phone call. He looked at the X rays and he thinks Hobie will be okay. We're going back to pick her up. I'm praying Jesus will keep her alive. I wanted to tell you because I knew you'd understand how I feel."

After Kelsey left, Robin found her mother. "Mom, why is Kelsey's cat alive and mine is dead? We both prayed. Doesn't God love me?"

Robin's mother laid aside her sewing and hugged Robin. "Even when God doesn't say yes to your prayers, he still loves you. Remember when Jesus prayed in the Garden of Gethsemane? He asked to have the suffering removed and—"

"Oh! I understand," said Robin. "God said no to his own Son. He loved Jesus, but he still let Jesus die on the cross. God loves me, too, even when he says no. I can trust him."

Jesus said, "Father…I want your will, not mine." *(Luke 22:42)*

 *What should you remember when God says no?*

A Brave Rescuer

The ice gave way beneath Jeremiah's feet without warning, and he plunged into the icy lake. He struggled to reach the surface. *Help me!* he prayed.

Jeremiah's head surged up through the hole in the ice. He choked, gasping for breath in the freezing water. A few feet away, he could see his black Labrador, Sadie, watching him from the bank where he had told her to stay.

Don't let me die, Jesus!

Jeremiah grasped the edge of the ice and gave a mighty heave to pull himself up onto it. The ice broke away in his hands and he sank below the surface again. *Don't let me drown,* he prayed. When Jeremiah's head came out of the water, he saw Sadie pacing on the bank.

I'm freezing, Jesus, he prayed. *Don't let me die of hypothermia. Show me what to do!*

Sadie! Could Sadie help? Jeremiah had told her to stay. She would never disobey.

"Sadie!" Jeremiah whispered. His teeth chattered. Could she hear him?

Jesus, please tell Sadie what to do, he prayed. He hoped she would run for help, or… It was getting hard to think.

Splash! Sadie jumped in beside him, jarring Jeremiah back to consciousness. She churned all four legs and licked Jeremiah's face.

Sadie turned and rammed the edge of the ice with her powerful chest, then clawed it with her front feet. The ice gave way in front of her. She kept lunging and breaking the ice all the way to shore as Jeremiah swam weakly behind her.

Jeremiah flopped onto the shore, barely conscious. Sadie's barking was the last thing he heard.

He awoke in his father's arms, wrapped in a blanket.

"Jeremiah," his father whispered, "you're going to be all right. Sadie found us and led us back to you."

Thank you, Jesus, Jeremiah whispered, *for using Sadie to answer my prayers.*

"Save me, for I serve you and trust you. You are my God." *(Psalm 86:2)*

 When has Jesus answered your prayers in an unexpected way?

Changing Seasons

Adam stood proudly in the center of the ring at the state fair with Eunice, his grand champion sheep. Adam looked at the purple ribbon and thought back over the last eight months. He barely heard the auctioneer start the bidding.

Adam had bought Eunice for his 4-H Club project when she was a lamb. He fed and watered her, protected her from disease, and studied all about this breed of sheep. He spent hours combing and clipping her. No wonder she won the grand prize. She was the best!

"Sold!" said the auctioneer. A large man walked up and took the tether out of Adam's hand.

Startled, Adam said, "Let go! She's mine!"

"But I just bought her," said the man.

"No!" shouted Adam, winding his arms around his sheep's neck.

Adam's dad hurried over and gently loosened Adam's grip on Eunice. "Son, you knew Eunice would be sold after the fair."

"But…"

Adam's dad led Adam to a seat in the stands. Adam crumpled in his father's arms and sobbed. His dad said softly, "God gave you Eunice for a season, to raise and care for her. Now she will provide wool for many people and you will find another little lamb to raise. Remember, son, people and circumstances come and go…"

"But Jesus never changes," finished Adam. "He is always with me."

Jesus said, "I am with you always." *(Matthew 28:20)*

Why does Jesus want you to remember that he is always with you?

Animal Fair

Get Set You'll need animal crackers and an encyclopedia.

Go!

Read what God said in Job 39:1–27.

Do you think God takes delight in his creatures? Explain.

Read Genesis 1:26–28.

*What is our responsibility to God's creatures?
How can we carry out that responsibility?*

Pass the box of animal crackers and have everyone *take*
one. In an encyclopedia, *find* an interesting fact about the
animal you're holding.

Continue passing the box and finding information about animals until
everyone has had three or four turns.

*How does the variety of the animal world bring glory to God?
How can we show respect for God's creatures?*

Pray, and ask God to help you be a good caretaker of his world.

Enjoy your animal cracker treats!

Head Count

Get Set Pour a package of jelly beans or other candies into a glass jar. Count the candy as you pour it and write the total on a slip of paper.

Go!

Have everyone **guess** the number of jelly beans in the jar.

Check the number you wrote down.

Name the person with the closest guess as the winner.

Share the jelly beans.

Explain: Now I have something else for you to guess.

How many hairs are there on your head?

Form pairs. Let one partner *count* the other's hair for one minute.

How many hairs could you count in a minute?

Read Matthew 10:29–31.

Why does Jesus want us to know that God knows the number of hairs on our head?
What else does God know about you?
How much does God care for you?

Pray and thank God for his loving care.

Man of the House

Andrew ran after his three-year-old brother, who was headed down the street. "Come inside the house," Andrew yelled.

Andrew ran after his brother, picked him up, then opened the door for his mother, who was balancing a toddler and a grocery bag. Depositing the grocery sack and toddler on the floor, Mother flopped into a kitchen chair. Andrew heard her sigh. He felt worried about her. House-cleaning jobs plus family responsibilities left her exhausted each night.

"I can fix macaroni and cheese," he offered.

Mother gave him a tired smile. "Thanks, but you've been helping with the little ones all afternoon. You need some time to play."

"I'm eight years old! I figure I'm the man of the house since Dad left."

Mother hugged him. "Andy, I love you! But tell me, when you helped your dad build the tree house, did you carry the 2 x 4s he bought at the lumberyard?"

"No," said Andrew. "They were too heavy."

"Trying to take your dad's place is a little too heavy for you right now."

"But who will take care of you, Mom?"

"God promised to be a husband to women without husbands and a father to children without fathers. Can you trust Jesus to help us and give us what we need?"

Andrew nodded.

"I still need you to be my strong helper."

"I'll be right here, Mom. It's what Jesus would want me to do."

"Father to the fatherless, defender of widows—this is God." *(Psalm 68:5)*

 *What will you trust Jesus to do for your family today?*

The Empty Rice Jar

Paul held his sister and little brother by the hand as the Chinese secret police handcuffed their parents. Government threats had not stopped Paul's parents from teaching God's Word to others. Now they were being arrested for sharing their faith.

Before the police drove off, they warned all the neighbors not to help the children. Paul could only pray silently, *Jesus, we trust you to be with us.*

Paul's sister tugged at his shirt sleeve, interrupting his thoughts. "I'm hungry," she said. She and her little brother followed Paul to the kitchen, where he searched through the cupboards. He knew that his father had not been paid at work for weeks. All they'd had to eat lately was rice. When Paul lifted down the rice jar, he found just a little rice — enough for one meal.

After Paul cooked the rice, he divided it into three small bowls, and the children prayed over their supper. "Thank you, Jesus, for taking care of us. Take care of our parents, too. Bless this food. Amen."

After eating, they all went to bed, exhausted by the day's trouble.

The next morning the little ones woke Paul early. "We're hungry!" they said.

"The rice is all gone!" he reminded them. "We ate it last night."

They started crying, so he took them to the kitchen and pulled down the rice jar. "See! It's empty!" he said, tipping it so they could look inside. But at the bottom of the jar they saw just enough rice for one more meal.

"Every day God answered our prayers and took care of us," Paul told his parents when they were released from prison ten days later. "There was always enough rice for the next meal!"

"Give all your worries and cares to God, for he cares about what happens to you." *(1 Peter 5:7)*

Do you believe Jesus can take care of you when things look hopeless?

Joe the Worry Wart

Joe didn't like coming into the Sunday school classroom late, but he went in and sat down in an empty seat up front.

The teacher was writing the word *worry* on the blackboard. She turned around and said, "Today I'd like all of you to be really honest. Please raise your hand if you worried sometime during this past week."

Joe, along with most of the class, raised his hand. The teacher looked around the room, then turned to Joe and asked, "How much do you worry?"

Wanting to be honest, Joe said quietly, "I worry all the time."

The teacher looked surprised. "Do you mind telling us what you worry about?"

"I worry about everything," he admitted. "Homework, soccer, riding home on the bus, science tests, tough bullies, not having any friends, getting cancer and dying... But doesn't everybody worry?"

"There probably isn't a person in the world who doesn't worry," agreed the teacher. "But read what Jesus said about worrying. Open your Bibles to the book of Luke, chapter 12."

After they read Jesus' words, Joe blurted out, "Now I'm worried about how much I worry!" The class laughed and agreed with Joe. "How can we stop worrying?" Joe asked.

"Read verse 31," the teacher said. "What are you supposed to care about more than anything else?"

Joe's eyes lit up. "God's Kingdom," he said. "I guess I'm supposed to look at God instead of my problems!"

The teacher agreed. "What if we'd all relax, keep our eyes on Jesus, and let God take care of us instead of worrying about everything?"

Joe whispered to the boy beside him, "Wow—I wish I'd known this sooner. I've wasted a lot of time worrying instead of trusting Jesus."

Jesus said, "So I tell you, don't worry about everyday life." *(Luke 12:22)*

Why is it wrong to worry?
What will you do the next time you're tempted
to worry?

Christi's Coat

Christi stared at the blue-and-yellow ski jacket. It was exactly what she wanted! She slipped it off the hanger and tried it on. A perfect fit!

But what if this coat was too expensive? Christi remembered the three ten-dollar bills in her pocket and her stomach tightened. She wanted this jacket so badly, but her family could only afford thirty dollars.

Feeling a hand on her shoulder, Christi turned. Her mother smiled at her. "Did you already find a jacket you like?"

Christi nodded.

"It looks great! How much is it?"

Christi glanced down at the white tags dangling from the right sleeve. "I haven't looked."

"Well, you won't know until you look."

Christi hugged the jacket and prayed silently, *Dear God, this morning we asked you to help us find a coat. I'll be thankful for any coat you provide, but I really like this one. Please don't let it be too expensive.*

She peeked at the tag. The prices of $89.98 and $59.98 were crossed out, and $29.99 was written at the bottom in red ink. Christi grinned and showed the tag to her mother.

Her mom smiled and hugged her. "Sometimes God not only provides for our needs, but grants our desires as well," said her mother.

"Your Father knows exactly what you need even before you ask him." *(Matthew 6:8)*

What need do you have that Jesus can meet?

Pumpkin Pie and Manna

Maury stared at the slice of pie on his plate. "If I see one more turkey drumstick or one more piece of pumpkin pie, I'll throw up. That's all we've eaten for five days!"

He looked at his mother, who was making turkey soup. "Mom, couldn't we have potato chips and pop sometimes? That's what my friends have for snacks. I'm tired of pie and turkey."

"I know it's hard, but your dad hasn't found a job yet. And since we've lived away from the United States so long, that could take a while."

Maury poked at his pie with a fork. "Sometimes I wish we were still missionaries back in Africa. We wouldn't be eating pumpkin pie over there."

"We don't have any other food right now. I'm grateful that the Rescue Mission shared their leftovers from the holidays with us."

"Don't they have potato chips at the Rescue Mission?"

Maury's mother stirred the soup. "The pie and drumsticks are God's provision for right now. He never promised to give us everything we *want*. He promised to take care of us. Our job is to trust him."

Maury remembered last week's Sunday school lesson. He said, "This is like the people of Israel wandering in the wilderness, isn't it? God gave them manna every day, but they got tired of eating it. They grumbled and complained. They didn't appreciate God's provision."

"What a good insight, Maury!" said his mom, giving him a hug.

"I know Jesus wants us to trust him. I don't want to complain about the way he cares for us," Maury said.

Taking his fork, he drew a smiley face on his slice of pie. "I think I'll see how many different ways one kid can eat pumpkin pie!"

"In everything you do, stay away from complaining and arguing."
(Philippians 2:14)

How would Jesus want you to respond when his care is different than what you expected?

Aware of God's Care

Get Set   You'll need a large bowl, peanut butter, and powdered sugar.

Go!

Gather in the kitchen and have everyone **wash** their hands.

Place equal amounts of peanut butter and powdered sugar in the bowl.

Take turns kneading the mixture until a dough forms.

Add powdered sugar if the dough is too sticky; **add** peanut butter if it's too stiff.

Give everyone a piece of dough.

Model the dough to form something that reminds you of a time when God took care of you.

Show your dough figures and **tell** how God took care of you.

Give everyone a second piece of dough.

Model a figure that represents one way God is caring for you right now.

Read Psalm 55:22.

Pray and thank God for his care.

Eat your dough figures!

The Sword of the Lord

Get Set You'll need newspaper, rubber bands, and used office paper.

Go!

Have everyone **roll** a section of newspaper and **wrap** one end with a rubber band to form a "sword."

Wad up used office paper to make paper balls.

Choose one person to be It. Have It stand several feet back and

throw paper balls at everyone else.

Try to **block** the paper balls with your swords.

Give everyone a chance to be It.

Read Ephesians 6:10–17.

Why do we need this special armor?
Who are we battling?
How was our paper battle like the spiritual battle we fight every day?
What is the only weapon God gives us?
How is God's Word like a sword?

Pray and thank God for his armor. **Ask** him to help you use it wisely.

Chocolate Chip Temptation

Tyler sniffed the air. His mouth watered as he followed the scent to the kitchen where his mom was just pulling a large tray of chocolate chip cookies out of the oven.

"Mmm—my favorite," he said with a grin as he reached for a cookie that was already cooling on the counter.

"Don't you touch that, young man," warned his mom with a teasing tone. "You know that anyone who touches treats before dinner has to live on bread and water for two weeks."

"Aw, Mom," Tyler replied. "One cookie won't hurt my appetite. I'm starved!"

"You'll survive, starving child," Mom assured him. "Look—Dad already has the burgers on the grill. It will just be a few minutes. Why don't you make the lemonade while I set the picnic table?"

"Okay," Tyler mumbled.

Mom piled up a tray with silverware, potato salad, and buns and headed out to the patio. Tyler stared at the cookies. *She'd never miss just one,* he thought as his hand drifted toward the largest cookie on the pile.

No! his conscience shouted just as he was about to touch it. *Mom said to wait. If you took a cookie now, you'd be stealing and disobeying.*

Tyler sighed, turned to the freezer, and got out a can of frozen lemonade mix. Just as he'd finished stirring in the water, Mom breezed back into the kitchen. Piling the cookies onto a fancy glass plate, she asked, "You didn't snitch one of these cookies, did you?"

"No," Tyler replied, "I didn't. But I'll admit that I thought about it pretty hard."

"Well, I'm proud of you," said Mom. "We *think* about lots of things we shouldn't do. Saying no to small temptations helps us learn to resist larger ones. It's nice to know that I can trust you. Now—as soon as you get that lemonade poured, we can eat."

As Tyler filled the glasses with ice and lemonade, he prayed, *Thanks, Jesus, for helping me obey my mom and earn her trust."*

Jesus said, "You know the commandments:…'Do not steal…. Do not cheat. Honor your father and mother.'" *(Mark 10:19)*

 *When have you been tempted to take something your parents said not to?*

Week
37

Write a Wrong

Molly stared at the red F on her spelling paper. She never got Fs on any of her schoolwork! The attached note read, "Parental signature required."

Tears formed in Molly's eyes. How could she face her mother with an F in spelling? Mom called Molly her "champion speller."

When Molly got off the afternoon school bus, she felt sick. She didn't eat dinner and went to bed early. She couldn't show Mother the spelling paper.

The next morning, while her mom cleaned up after breakfast, Molly looked on her mother's desk. Finding a check with her mother's signature, Molly carefully traced it onto the school note. With a sigh of relief she tucked the paper in her backpack and hurried to catch the school bus.

At dinner that night, Mother said, "Today Miss Peterson called to talk about your spelling. She said she received the note with my signature. But I told her I never saw that paper. Want to explain?"

"I just couldn't show you my bad grade."

"Did you study for the test?"

"No, but I'm usually good at spelling." Molly burst into tears. "I talked on the phone instead of studying the spelling list. But I made it worse by trying to cover up my bad grade. I'm sorry! I want to be honest and do what Jesus says."

"God can use sorrow...to help us turn away from sin." *(2 Corinthians 7:10)*

 *What does Jesus care more about—your grades or your character?*

Red Ants!

"It's no fun visiting Grandma and Grandpa," Cindy mumbled to her two-year-old brother, who was toddling beside her. "I can't understand when they talk in German. And I don't like Nebraska. And I *especially* don't like baby-sitting *you.* Everybody thinks you're so cute. You're the smartest, the best, the greatest…I'm tired of hearing it."

They reached the big tree in the corner of the backyard, and Robby lay down in the grass to nap. Cindy noticed that there was an anthill close by.

So what? thought Cindy. *He'll be all right. Besides, I don't want to wake him up.*

Cindy sat in the swing that hung from the tree and wished she were somewhere else.

All at once Robby started to scream. Cindy rushed over to him. Several red ants were crawling up his arms and legs!

Cindy scooped him up and brushed off the ants. "Oh, Robby," she cried, "I'm so sorry! I didn't know they were *red* ants!"

"Owie, owie," sobbed Robby.

"Don't cry, little brother," said Cindy soothingly. "We'll put some lotion on, and the sting will go away."

As she carried Robby into the house, she prayed, *I'm sorry, Jesus. I was angry and let my little brother get hurt. Please forgive me. Help me love him and take care of him. Help me be good to him—like you're good to me.*

"Remember, it is sin to know what you ought to do and then not do it." *(James 4:17)*

When have you been tempted to be mean to someone? What would Jesus want you to do when you feel this way?

Bible Swordsmen

Grant headed home after school with his younger brother. He affectionately ruffled Briley's hair and asked, "How was school today, Briley?"

Briley waved away his older brother's hand. "Jack Walters tried to get me to smoke a cigarette today."

"What? How dare he try that! What did you say?"

"I told him, 'No way! Smoking makes your lungs black, and I don't want black lungs.'"

"Good for you! If Jack ever does it again, you could answer him with verses from the Bible. God's Word has power."

"Really?" Briley's eyes lit up.

"Yes. God's Word is called 'the sword of the Spirit.'"

"A sword! Cool!"

"Every time Jesus was tempted by the devil, Jesus quoted Scripture."

"Well then, what verse should I say?"

"You could say, 'Our bodies were made for the Lord, and the Lord cares about our bodies.' Or say, 'Don't you know your body is the temple of the Holy Spirit, who lives in you?' or 'You do not belong to yourself, for God bought you with a high price. So you must honor God with your body.'"

"Wow! How do you know so many Bible verses, Grant?"

"I memorize them for Bible Club. I want to be good at using the sword of the Spirit."

"Can I go to Bible Club with you?" asked Briley. "I want to be a Bible swordsman like you!"

"Take the sword of the Spirit, which is the word of God." *(Ephesians 6:17)*

 *What do you do when you are tempted?*

Jon's Temptation

"Look at the price on this one." Jon pointed to the Lego box near the bottom of the stack on the store shelf. His heart pounded. It was the set he'd wanted—and didn't get—last Christmas!

Chad's eyes grew wide. "Six dollars!? The rest of the boxes are marked twenty-four dollars!"

"Maybe something's wrong with it," Jon said, pulling out the box and checking it over carefully.

"Maybe some pieces are missing," Chad suggested.

Jon checked both ends. "It's still sealed. Do you think somebody purposely changed the price on it so they could get it cheaper?"

"That's the set you've been wanting forever, isn't it?" asked Chad.

"Yes! Maybe Jesus made the store people mark it wrong so I can afford it," said Jon. He started for the cash register, then stopped. "What if the store made a mistake when they marked the price? What if it really does cost twenty-four dollars?"

"That's their problem," said Chad.

"What if somebody else changed the price?" said Jon. "I'd be stealing. But if the store messed up, they have to give me the lower price."

"That's right," agreed Chad. "Anyway, I doubt if the clerk will notice. She'll just ring it up."

Jon sighed. "I know it's a steal," he said, "but I don't want to actually *steal* it."

Chad rolled his eyes as Jon walked to the counter and asked a clerk to check the price. The clerk took a closer look. The real price was twenty-four dollars. Someone had deliberately altered the price tag.

"I'm impressed with your honesty," she told Jon. "You're different than other kids."

"Doing what Jesus wants feels better than getting a new Lego set," Jon told Chad later. It felt good to do what was right.

"If you cheat even a little, you won't be honest with greater responsibilities." *(Luke 16:10)*

When have you been tempted to cheat?
How did Jon witness for Jesus?

Blown Away

Get Set Gather several lightweight items such as feathers, Ping-Pong balls, facial tissue, paper, and spools of thread.

Go!

Take turns *naming* temptations you face.

For each temptation named, *set up* one of the items above.

Take turns trying to *blow* the items off the table.

Where can we receive strength to resist temptation?

Read Philippians 4:13.

Gather all the items and place a Bible on top of them.

Try to *blow* them off the table once more.

Read James 4:7.

What does it mean to submit ourselves to God?
How can God's Word help us resist temptation?

Take turns *quoting* verses that help you remember what's right and resist doing something wrong.

Pray and ask God to help you be strong and resist temptation.

Week
38

Blind Faith

Get Set You'll need one blindfold for every two people.

Go!

Have a volunteer **put on** the blindfold, then **choose** one person to be the guide.

Have the blindfolded person **take** the guide's arm.

Let the guide **choose** where to lead the blindfolded person.

After they've arrived, have the blindfolded person **guess** where they are.

Have the guide and the blindfolded person **change** roles.

Have the new guide **lead** to a new destination.

Have the blindfolded person **guess** where they are, until everyone has had a chance to guide and to be guided.

Read Isaiah 30:21.

How does it feel to know God is guiding you?
How was this experience like God's guidance? How was it different?

Share ways God has guided you in the past few months.

Pray and ask God to help you watch and listen for his guidance.

Blake's Birthmark

"What are you gawking at?" Blake knew he sounded nasty, but he didn't care. He was tired of Tommy and Sean making fun of him. They had stared at him all during math class.

"I'm looking at that ugly red face of yours." Tommy snickered, catching Sean's eye.

How come I let them hurt my feelings? Blake wondered.

"It is called a strawberry birthmark," Blake said. *Why can't I just ignore them?*

"Yuck!" Sean grabbed his throat. "I'll never eat another strawberry."

"Well, at least I'm not stupid in math," Blake said. He turned away from them. Later, at home, Blake leaned into the circle of his mother's arms and cried.

"You can have the birthmark removed by laser surgery any time you wish," his mom said.

"I know," Blake said, "but I kind of like it…until someone makes fun of it."

Blake glanced at his self portrait hanging on the refrigerator door. He had colored the entire left side of his face bright red.

His mom smiled. "The birthmark sets you off as someone special."

"I think so, too."

"You know, Blake," Mom said, pulling back to look at his face, "even though you've done nothing wrong, kids mistreat you because of your birthmark. That's kind of what happened to Jesus. Even though he did nothing wrong, people mistreated him."

"But Jesus still loved them, didn't he?"

Tears shone in Mom's eyes. "Can you do that, Blake?"

Blake thought for a long time. "It will be hard. I'll have to ask Jesus for help. When kids make fun of me, I'll think about Jesus and try to treat them the way he would."

"May [God] produce in you, through the power of Jesus Christ, all that is pleasing to him." *(Hebrews 13:21)*

How does Blake's birthmark help him be like Jesus? How does Jesus want you to treat people who are different?

Follow the Pattern

Carley bent over the pattern she was cutting. "I hate sewing," she informed her mother. Her scissors swerved inside the pattern's thick black cutting line, but Carley didn't care.

"Sewing is a useful skill," said her mother as she threaded the sewing machine.

"Just my luck to get a mom out of the Middle Ages," Carley grumbled. She was in a hurry to finish.

But when Carley started to sew, she ran into problems. If she sewed where she should, her uneven cutting left big holes. When she stitched on the wavy edge, her hem rose and fell like the ocean in a storm.

Disgusted, she pulled the material from the machine, cut the threads, and threw it on the table. "Stupid dress!"

"The pattern looked fine to me," said her mother.

"Well, I messed up a little when I cut it out," Carley admitted.

Her mother's eyes drifted to a Bible on the kitchen counter. "I think there's another pattern you haven't followed too closely. You're in trouble at school, you've been picking on your little brother…"

"And my life is as messy as that dress," finished Carley. She was quiet for a long time. "I don't think I can fix the dress, but I can start following this pattern again," she said, picking up her Bible.

"I have hidden your word in my heart, that I might not sin against you." *(Psalm 119:11)*

What has Jesus given you as your pattern for living?

Walking in Jesus' Shoes

Sonya and her teenage brother rummaged in the row of dumpsters behind the mall trying to find a box the right size for her science diorama. She felt discouraged. Only one more bin left. *Dear God,* she prayed, *please help me find the box I need.*

Her brother Ed lifted the heavy lid to the last dumpster. "Here's the perfect box, sis!" He reached in and lifted out a big shoe box.

"Thank you, God," she said aloud.

"Look!" said Ed. "This dumpster is full of shoe boxes—and they have shoes in them. Brand-new shoes! I wonder if they're out here by mistake."

Sonya immediately thought of the people who attended the mission where her family sang and shared from the Bible every Saturday night. Few of them had decent shoes.

Ed and Sonya ran inside and found the manager of the shoe store. "Did you know there are brand-new shoes in the dumpster out back?" they asked.

He nodded. "We had to make room on the shelves for our new shoes."

"Could we have the old ones?" asked Sonya. "We have friends at the mission who need shoes."

The manager looked surprised. "Go ahead. Just don't sell them," he warned.

"Oh, we won't," Sonya assured him.

Ed drove their father's station wagon around to the dumpster. They loaded two hundred pairs of shoes into the car.

Sonya clapped her hands. "God is so neat! He gave me what I needed and lots more to share!"

"[God] is able to accomplish infinitely more than we would ever dare to ask or hope." *(Ephesians 3:20)*

 *When has Jesus surprised you with an answer to prayer?*
When has he given you more than you expected?

Week
38

One Step at a Time

Scott watched darkness creep across the hillside and mountains. He shivered in the chill air. Why hadn't he brought his jacket?

This trip to Glacier National Park with his parents was supposed to be fun. But his mother had twisted her ankle on their hike and was now hobbling along with his father's help. A park ranger was slowly guiding them back to the ranger station. Shadows along the path took the shapes of wild animals in Scott's imagination. A shudder of fear ran up his spine.

"I can't see where we're going," Scott complained, unwilling to admit he was scared.

Their guide switched on his flashlight. "I know the way," he assured them. "You don't have to see very far ahead. Just put your foot where I last stepped." Enough light filtered back from the flashlight for Scott to see the guide's feet. Scott concentrated on stepping where the ranger had just walked. And his parents followed in Scott's footsteps.

When their group finally arrived at the ranger station, Scott's mother thanked the guide and limped to the car.

"Well, that was an adventure!" said Dad.

"I wasn't sure we'd make it," Scott admitted. "The light seemed so small in all that darkness. But since the guide knew the way, all we had to do was follow one step at a time. Kinda like following Jesus, huh, Dad?"

"Your word is a lamp for my feet and a light for my path."
(Psalm 119:105)

 *How is God's Word like the guide's flashlight?*

Just Like You

"Where did you get my picture?" asked ten-year-old Tori, looking at her school picture on the refrigerator.

"Matt brought it home from school—you know, because he's in your class," answered five-year-old Ashley. "My Dad says you're a good role model."

"Really?" asked Tori in surprise. She remembered times when she'd slammed doors and cried and fought with her brothers. She didn't want to be a role model. It was too much responsibility.

"Dad says you're nice to your parents," Ashley continued.

Tori thought about the times she'd argued about doing dishes and cleaning her room.

"Matt says you never get in trouble at school and that you get all A's. He says you're the best girl basketball player in Portland."

"But Matt probably thinks he plays better than I do, doesn't he?" Tori asked. She tried not to smile. Matt was a good basketball player. They played on the same fourth-grade team.

Ashley nodded. "But I want to play like you, not Matt."

Tori laughed and hugged her. "I'm proud that you want to be like me, Ashley, but I'd rather you'd try to be like Jesus. Sometimes I make mistakes."

Ashley looked surprised.

"I will," said Ashley. "I want to be just like you."

Tori sighed. It looked like she was stuck with her role model job. But if she worked harder to do what Jesus wanted her to, maybe she could handle it. She knew Jesus would help her.

"Be an example to all believers...in the way you live, in your love, your faith, and your purity." *(1 Timothy 4:12)*

 *How can Jesus help you become a leader and role model?*

Write It Right

Get Set   Give everyone a pencil and a sheet of paper.

Go!

Explain: I'm going to give a set of instructions. Don't look at each other's papers. Just write what I tell you.

On the top half of your paper, *draw* a round, squiggly line that almost makes a circle.

On the bottom half of your paper, *make* two vertical marks about an inch apart.

In the top right corner, *draw* a circle.

Make a wavy line across the middle of the paper.

Near the bottom of your paper, *make* lots of short vertical marks.

Show and *compare* your papers.

Explain: I asked you to draw a tree, a sun, hills, and grass. The round, squiggly line is the top of the tree and the two vertical lines are the trunk. The circle is the sun; the wavy line is hills in the background, and the short, vertical marks are grass.

How close is your picture to the drawing I described? Did I give good directions? Explain.

Read   Psalm 119:1–11.

Where do we find God's directions for our lives?
How are God's directions better than mine?

Tell   each other how you will follow God's directions this week.

Handle with Care!

Get Set   Secretly hard-boil two eggs. Chill them and take them from the refrigerator just before you meet.

Go!

Explain: These eggs represent the people in our lives. We're going to see how many times we can throw and catch them in thirty seconds. (Don't let anyone know the eggs are hard-boiled!)

Quickly   *toss*   the eggs to two different people as you   *count:* one thousand one, one thousand two, etc., up to thirty.

Set   the eggs on the table in front of you.

How did you feel about tossing the eggs like that?
If you were one of the eggs, how do you think you'd be feeling right now?
How is that like the way you sometimes feel at the end of a day?
Are you always as gentle with people as you were with these eggs?
Explain.

Read   Ephesians 4:2, 31–32.

How can we be more careful of people we see every day?

Reveal   that the eggs are hard-boiled.

Would you have played differently if you'd known they were hard-boiled? Explain.
Do some people need to be treated more gently than others?

Pray,   asking God to help you be gentle and kind.

Prayer Partners

"I'm scared," whimpered Charee's six-year-old brother. "Hold my hand, Charee."

Charee reached for Raheem's hand. It felt cold and quivery. She knew the first day of school was hard for him.

"I know you feel scared," she said as they walked to school. "But remember, I'll take you into your new classroom."

"You won't *stay* in there with me," he wailed. "I'll be all alone."

They crossed the street and she held his hand tightly, trying not to laugh. "You won't be all alone! There are twenty other little kids and a teacher in the same room."

"But nobody I *know* is there," he protested.

"Jesus is there with you," Charee said. "Talk to him. He'll go everywhere with you."

"He will?" asked Raheem, sounding more hopeful.

Charee stopped at the school fence. She stooped and looked her little brother in the eye. "Remember when Jesus' disciples were in a boat during a storm?"

Raheem nodded.

"Jesus told them, 'Don't be afraid. I am with you.'" She held his smaller hands in hers. "Jesus doesn't want you to be afraid, Raheem. Give him all your fears. He'll throw them away in God's big trash can. Do you want to pray before we go to your class? I'll pray with you."

Raheem nodded again. He squeezed his eyes shut and began to pray softly, "Stay with me, Jesus. Help me not to be so scared. I give all my fears to you. Will you please throw them in God's trash can? Thank you, Jesus. Amen."

He opened his eyes and smiled at his sister. She smiled back. "Now I feel better, Charee. Thanks for praying with me."

Raheem squared his shoulders and bravely walked through the front door of the school.

"Pray at all times and on every occasion." *(Ephesians 6:18)*

 *Who will you pray with today?*

Fruit Salad

"Mother," asked Jennifer, scooping out watermelon balls, "can we take the fruit salad to Amy's mom instead of to Dorothea?"

"Why, honey?" Jennifer's mother mounded strawberries and blueberries in the hollowed-out watermelon while Jennifer edged it with fresh mint.

"I don't know. I feel like we should give it to Amy's mom."

"But we made it for Dorothea."

Jennifer dropped her eyes and repeated, "I think we should give it to Amy's mom." How could she explain to her mother what she didn't understand herself?

"Okay." Mother carried the watermelon to the car. "We'll take it to Amy's mom."

Opening the car door at Amy's house, Jennifer asked her mother, "Could we give Amy's mom five dollars, too?" She knew it sounded like a strange request.

Jennifer's mom questioned with her eyes but said, "Sure."

When Amy's mom saw the salad, her face lit up. And when they gave her the five dollars, she cried.

"We have a Japanese student staying with us," she told them. "Tonight is a potluck for her. They asked me to bring a salad, but I didn't have the ingredients. And I haven't any money for gas. I asked God to provide. He sent you!"

Thanks, Jesus, Jennifer prayed, *for helping me listen to your voice when I didn't know it was you.*

"And the Lord came and called as before, 'Samuel, Samuel!' And Samuel replied, 'Yes, your servant is listening.'" *(1 Samuel 3:10)*

Have you ever had an idea from Jesus?
Are your ears open?

A Busy Sister

"Benjamin! Watch out!" Jennifer exclaimed. "Aunt Helen, look! He's going to knock over the whole tin of popcorn!"

Jennifer dashed to the coffee table and grabbed the large tin just as her little brother pulled off the lid and stuck his pudgy hand inside.

"Ben, the popcorn will spill if you tip the can," she explained. She placed the popcorn tin on the floor and held it steady. "Ask me to hold it for you if you want some popcorn. We're all going to share this gift from Aunt Helen. Do you understand?"

Benjamin laughed. He grabbed fistfuls of popcorn in both of his chubby hands.

Jennifer looked back at her aunt and smiled. "Ben loves popcorn," she said.

Content with his hands full, Ben toddled off, eating his treat. Jennifer patiently put the lid on top of the tin and put it back on the coffee table.

"Your little brother is a lot of work, isn't he?" asked Aunt Helen.

"Yes," said Jennifer. "But I'm so glad Jesus gave him to us. I want to be a good sister. But it's not very easy sometimes." She glanced back and noticed Ben trying to climb into his high chair, still holding his popcorn tightly in his fists.

"He keeps me pretty busy!" she called over her shoulder, racing to keep her brother from falling over backward.

Helping him turn around and get seated in his high chair, Jennifer grinned and said, "I just wonder if I was this much work when I was little!"

Jesus said, "Anyone who welcomes a little child like this on my behalf is welcoming me." *(Matthew 18:5)*

How does Jesus want you to feel toward little children?

A Thoughtful Gift

"Way to snag that ball, Cam!" yelled the first baseman.

"What a catch!" whooped the shortstop.

Cam stood up and dusted himself off, savoring the cheers of his teammates. He had worried that he wouldn't be accepted on the new team. But all the guys liked him. The coach had recognized Cam's willingness to work right away. He gave Willy's third-base position to Cam during the second week of practice. That bothered Cam. He hadn't intended to take anyone's spot.

Cam waved to the subs howling praise at him from the dugout. He noticed Willy sitting on the bench with his head down. Cam remembered how it felt to sit on the sidelines. It had happened to him in third grade.

The team jumped up and down, cheering for Cam. They were ahead ten to one in the championship game.

Crack! The ball shot toward third base and Cam dived to snatch it before it hit the ground. He felt a slight twinge in his ankle.

If I were Willy, I'd feel awful not to play, especially in this game, thought Cam. *Jesus, help me do what you'd want me to do.*

Cam stood up and held the ball in his glove above his head to show he'd caught it. Then he limped back to third base.

The coach ran over to him. "Are you okay?"

"I twisted my ankle a little," said Cam. It was true. His ankle did hurt—a little. He could stay in the game, but he wanted to give Willy a chance to play.

"Can you play?" Coach asked.

"If I have to, but you don't need me now, Coach," said Cam.

"Willy," Coach barked, "get in here!"

Cam grinned as Willy dashed to third base. *Thank you, Jesus, for showing me how to make Willy feel a little better,* he prayed.

"Don't do your good deeds publicly, to be admired." *(Matthew 6:1)*

 *What quiet good deed would Jesus want you to do for someone today?*

Sick and Tired

Carin looked at the textbooks stacked on her bedside table and sank back on her pillows. She stroked her dog, Hambone, who was lying on the bed beside her.

Carin felt too tired to open her books, much less keep up with her schoolwork. She was tired of being behind in all her classes, tired of trips to the hospital, and tired of being sick.

"My friends at school take life for granted," she told Hambone. "Did I say *friends*? Ha! What friends?" The dog raised his head and looked at her.

"The last time I went back to school Jenny had a new best friend and she didn't even speak to me! It happens all the time. My friends just forget all about me!"

Tears ran down Carin's cheeks. Hambone rested his chin on her leg and looked up at her with big eyes.

"No!" Carin said, wiping her tears. "I promised Jesus I wouldn't have any more pity parties."

Pulling out some paper, Carin wrote to Danny, a boy she'd met in the hospital. She added silly pictures to make him laugh and drew a big heart with "Jesus loves you" printed inside. It made her feel better.

"You know, Hambone," said Carin happily, "I can help Danny because I know how it feels to be sick."

Hambone licked her hand, and they settled down together for a nap.

"When others are troubled, we…give them the same comfort God has given us." *(2 Corinthians 1:4)*

 *How does Jesus want us to treat those who are sick?*

Kings and Queens of Kindnes:

Get Set   You'll need balloons, tape, a bottle of bubbles, and a bubble wand

Go!

Set   a chair in the middle of the room.

Explain: We're going to make a throne for the Kings and Queens of Kindne

Have everyone   *blow*   up a balloon and   *tape*   it to the "throne."

Have a volunteer   *sit*   on the throne.

Blow   a puff of bubbles over the person's head and   *say:*   "I proclaim
you the [King/Queen] of Kindness."

Tell   one kind act you've seen that person do this week.

Pass   the bubbles to another person and have him or her   *blow*   a p
of bubbles and   *tell*   of another act of kindness.

Continue   until everyone has praised that person, then have another
person   *sit*   on the throne.

After everyone has received the royal treatment,   *read*   Matthew 25:34 –

How does it feel to know that Jesus feels this way about our acts of kindness?

Pledge   to become the world's kindest family!

Flame Out!

Get Set　You'll need a wide-mouthed quart jar, several votive candles, and matches.

Go!

List　friends and family who especially need your prayers right now.

Talk　about their needs.

Read　Ephesians 6:13–16.

Name　one "flaming dart" Satan might throw at each person on your list.

For each thing you name, **light** a candle.

Read　Ephesians 6:18.

Pray　for each person, asking God to help them resist temptation and trusting Jesus to help them in their difficult circumstances.

As you pray, **place** the jar over a candle until the flame goes out.

Read　Matthew 18:19–20.

What has Jesus promised us?

Have each person **keep** one of the votive candles as a reminder to continue to pray.

The Skating Party

Patti burst into her older sister's bedroom. "Oh, Alisha! I'm invited to Kathryn's roller-skating party on Saturday. It's going to be so much fun! Kathryn's mother said you could come too."

Alisha untied her ballet shoes. She loved to roller skate, but she wasn't sure she wanted to spend a whole afternoon with younger kids. *Should I go to this party, Jesus? Is there a reason you want me there?* she prayed.

"Please come with us," Patti begged. "There'll be caramel corn and hot dogs for everyone. You'll have fun."

"All right, Patti," Alisha agreed. "Tell Kathryn I'll be there."

At the rink on Saturday, Alisha skated with her little sister and some younger girls who couldn't skate very well. Then, skating around the far end, she glanced over and saw Kathryn sitting on a bench, crying.

Alisha knew that something was wrong. She prayed, *Dear Jesus, show me how I can help.*

She skated to the bench and asked, "Why are you crying, Kathryn?"

"Grandmother came for my party, but she fell and hit her head. My mom and dad just took her to the hospital."

"I'll pray with you for your grandmother," offered Alisha. "Jesus can help her, even when we aren't there." As they prayed together, Alisha knew why Jesus wanted her at the skating party.

"When God's children are in need, be the one to help them out."
(Romans 12:13)

How did Alisha serve Jesus?
Are you willing to serve as she did?

Car Pool Accident

Adam heard Mrs. Loomis scream. Her minivan swerved and screeched to a stop in some gravel at the side of the road. Adam slammed into the back of the front seat. His head hurt.

"I almost hit that old man!" said Mrs. Loomis. Adam could see her shaking. She started to cry. Her five-year-old son, Bobby, was crying, too.

"He walked right out in front of my car! I can't believe I didn't hit him," she said in a shaky voice. She turned to Adam and Bobby. "Are you okay?"

Adam touched his forehead. "I have a bump," he told her, "but I'm okay. I had my seat belt on."

"I'm okay," whimpered Bobby.

"Are you hurt?" Adam asked Mrs. Loomis. "Did you hit the steering wheel?"

She nodded. "I'm pretty shook up."

Mrs. Loomis put her hand on the gearshift to back the car onto the pavement, but she couldn't get the car in reverse because she was shaking so hard. Other cars drove past, but no one stopped to help.

"Are you all right?" Adam asked.

"I don't know if I can drive," she said.

"Can I pray for you?" asked Adam. "My mom and I do that when we're upset."

Mrs. Loomis nodded. Adam bowed his head and prayed, "Dear Jesus, please calm Mrs. Loomis. Help her be able to drive us home safely." Adam remembered how his mom always thanked and praised the Lord, so he added, "Jesus, we praise you for protecting us. Thank you for keeping us from hitting that old man."

Mrs. Loomis opened her eyes and took a deep breath. She had stopped crying and she didn't appear to be shaking.

"Thank you for praying, Adam," she said quietly. She put the car in reverse and backed onto the road. Five minutes later Adam arrived safely at home.

"Don't worry about anything; instead, pray about everything."
(Philippians 4:6)

How did Jesus use Adam?
When have you prayed to calm someone?

A Grumpy Neighbor

Karl searched for his floppy-eared rabbit along the fence that separated his yard from the neighbor's. Across the fence a grumpy old man stopped weeding carrots long enough to smirk at Karl and his sister.

Karl thought he had smiled. "Jodi," Karl whispered, "I think Mr. Tripp smiled at us!"

"You're kidding," said Jodi.

"No, he did! Maybe he's learning about Jesus and he's nice now. Let's wave if he looks over again. Do you think he'll help us find Fluffy?"

Jodi rolled her eyes. "Sure…like he returns all our balls that go over the fence."

"We didn't hit any of them over there on purpose," said Karl.

While Karl searched for Fluffy under the bushes, he kept watching the neighbor. He wanted to be ready to smile back as soon as Mr. Tripp glanced up.

The next time Mr. Tripp looked over the low fence, he scowled at Karl. But Karl grinned and waved.

"Mind your own business," grumbled the old man.

Karl wanted to cry. Mr. Tripp didn't like them. He would never help them find Fluffy.

Jodi pointed at a hole in the fence. "Oh, no! Fluffy got into Mr. Tripp's yard."

"Jodi, we have to pray! If Mr. Tripp catches Fluffy, he'll eat him!" Crying, Karl fell to his knees by the hole in the fence.

Dear Jesus, he prayed, *if you don't help Fluffy, he'll be gone forever. Nothing ever comes back from Mr. Tripp's yard.*

Soft fur brushed against Karl's knee. A white bunny with floppy ears squeezed back through the hole in the fence. Karl and Jodi grabbed him and hugged him excitedly.

"If Jesus can save Fluffy," said Karl, "he can save Mr. Tripp. I'm going to start praying for him today. Jesus might even make him nice by the time we all get to heaven."

"The earnest prayer of a righteous person has great power." *(James 5:16)*

What unhappy person would Jesus want you to pray for?

Praying Grandma

Molly looked at the old marble clock on the mantel. In five minutes Grandma would stop whatever she was doing and go to her bedroom alone to pray.

Molly breathed in the scent of homemade bread and settled into the overstuffed chair. On the other side of the woodstove, her two youngest cousins giggled and played with the dollhouse Grandpa had made.

"Do you want to play dolls with us?" her cousins asked.

Molly shook her head. She loved this time of day—Grandma's prayer time. She loved listening for her own name. She'd be third in the line of cousins. Grandma had prayed for Molly every day since she first learned Molly's mother was pregnant nine years ago.

The clock bonged one…two…three. Molly heard Grandma take the last pan of cookies out of the oven and set them on top of the stove. Then Grandma appeared, blew a kiss to Molly, and entered her bedroom.

Molly slipped from her chair and peeked through the crack by the door. Grandma knelt beside her bed with her worn Bible in front of her. "Lord, you are so good," she began. "Thank you for all the blessings.…"

Softly, Molly opened the door, tiptoed to Grandma, and knelt beside her. Grandma took Molly's hand and together they lifted their voices to the Lord.

"Future generations will also serve him." *(Psalm 22:30)*

Who prays for you every day?
What family member would Jesus want you to pray for every day?

Left Behind

Dustin scanned the parking lot, looking for Dad's car. Dad had been there a minute ago. He had been talking to the coach while Dustin and Angela played on the swings after their older brother Bill's baseball game. Now Dad's car was gone. He must have left and taken Bill home.

"Do you think Dad forgot us?" asked Angela.

"Don't be afraid," Dustin said. "I can find the way home." Taking Angela's hand, he started walking down the busy road, past the library and the taco store. He hadn't been to Sunset school very often. Now he wondered if he should turn left or right at the stoplight.

"Mom will be mad at Dad," Angela said. Her little hand trembled in Dustin's. "Mom would never forget us."

"Let's pray while we walk," said Dustin.

Angela closed her eyes as Dustin led her down the sidewalk. "Dear Jesus, please tell Mommy that Daddy forgot us," said Angela.

After she finished, Dustin walked and prayed with his eyes open. "Jesus, please protect us. Bring someone to help us. Amen." He paused for a second, then added, "And help us not to be angry at Dad."

Angela opened her eyes. "Dad might have thought we were getting a ride with someone else," she said.

They turned down a hill, onto a road with no sidewalks. Mom wouldn't want them walking on this road, that was for sure.

"Dustin, look! There's Mom."

Mom's blue minivan stopped beside them. She jumped out and hugged them. Dustin could tell she'd been scared, too.

"We asked Jesus to let you know we got left behind," said Dustin, getting into the car. "Jesus answered our prayers, and here you are!"

"Stop putting your trust in mere humans. They are as frail as breath." *(Isaiah 2:22)*

How does Jesus want you to treat someone who lets you down?
Why can you be sure Jesus will never fail you?

Bag o' Blessings

Get Set   You'll need paper lunch bags, apples, markers, scissors, curling ribbon, and a hole punch.

Go!

Brainstorm   two or three people you'd like to bless this week. They might be people you've been praying for or just someone the Lord brings to mind.

To *prepare* a Bag o' Blessings for each person, *share* the following jobs:
  Write Psalm 17:7–8 on one side of each bag.
  On the other side of each bag, write: "We prayed for you today."
  Wash and polish the apples.
  Cut and curl three or four colors of curling ribbon.

Have everyone *autograph* the bags.

Place an apple in each bag.

Fold down the tops of the bags and *punch* a hole in each one.

Tie several ribbons through the holes.

Place the completed bags in the center of the table and *pray* for each person who will receive one.

Leave the bags where they'll be discovered.

A Surprise Inside

Get Set Ask an adult to help your prepare this devotion. You'll need refrigerator biscuits, two or three kinds of jelly, mustard, a rolling pin, oil, and a small pan for deep frying. Also set out paper towels and a cereal bowl with a small amount of sugar.

Go!

Explain: We're going to make jelly doughnuts with surprises inside.

Have an adult **heat** a small amount of oil in a pan for deep frying. (Be sure to have an adult in charge.)

Have everyone **flatten** a biscuit with a rolling pin.

Place a dab of your favorite jelly in the middle of a biscuit.

Prepare one biscuit with mustard filling. (Yuck!)

Fold the biscuits in half and **pinch** the edges securely.

When all the biscuits are filled, have an adult **fry** them to a golden brown on both sides.

Drain the biscuits on paper towels.

When they've cooled a bit, **roll** them lightly in sugar.

Read James 2:1–9.

Can you tell what's in the biscuits by looking at the outside?
How are people like that?
Does Jesus care whether a person is rich or poor? Explain.

Pray that Jesus will help you see people as he does.

Enjoy your jelly doughnuts!

Who Needs You?

Dominic steadied himself on a ledge and reached down to help Craig up the rocky slope.

"Thanks, Dom," said Craig, wiping his face on his Camp Yakamuk shirt. "Now I see why the counselor made us hike in pairs. I was dumb to think I could make it alone."

"Well, you kept me from falling back there," said Dominic. He looked ahead at Reggie, their counselor, who was carrying Kyle on his back. "Just imagine if we were trying to carry Kyle. I don't know why our counselor wanted to bring him along on a hike, knowing Kyle can't walk."

"I know—Reggie must be tired from carrying him. He probably had to do it because Kyle is the camp director's son," said Craig, adjusting his backpack.

At a fork in the trail, Kyle directed the boys off the main path. "That's the trail we want."

"The surprise we're supposed to find had better be worth this hike," grumbled Dominic.

At the top of the hill, the boys trudged through underbrush until they reached an outcropping of rock. "Go through there," Kyle said, pointing to a narrow opening between the rocks.

Dominic squeezed through the open space. Cool air and blackness greeted him. Then the counselor switched on his flashlight. All the boys stared in amazement at a cave furnished with bearskin rugs.

"Wow!" said Dominic.

"We couldn't have found this place without Kyle," the counselor explained.

"My family calls it the Hermit's Cave," said Kyle. "It hasn't been used for years. I convinced Dad to let us camp here tonight."

"Cool!" said Craig.

As the boys gathered firewood, Dominic said to Craig, "You know, I was wrong about Kyle. His part in our hike was important."

"All of you together are Christ's body, and each one of you is a…necessary part of it." *(1 Corinthians 12:27)*

 *Why does Jesus want his followers to depend on each other?*

Hit Man

Trent sat on the school bus watching the younger boys bounce in their seats and blow spit wads at each other.

"Hey, you guys. Sit down and shut up!" yelled Trent.

"*You* shut up. Just because you're a sixth-grader doesn't make you our boss!" one boy shouted back.

Trent grabbed his notebook and whacked the boy on the head. The boy howled. "Mr. Bus Driver, Trent hit me!"

"If you'd stay in your seat, I wouldn't have to," retorted Trent.

That night the bus driver phoned Trent's parents.

Trent's father said, "The bus driver told me you've been causing trouble on the school bus. Is it true that you've hit younger kids over the head with your notebook?"

"They were jumping out of their seats when they weren't supposed to. I was just trying to keep order!"

"That's not your job, son. It's the bus driver's."

"But he wasn't doing it!"

"I know it's frustrating, but you don't have the authority or the ability to stop those boys. There *are* several things you can do. We talked about them this week in family devotions."

Trent thought about their dicussions of how Jesus wants us to live. "I can pray for those boys...I can be a good example...and I can tell them about Jesus!"

"Don't let anyone think less of you because you are young. Be an example to all believers." *(1 Timothy 4:12)*

 *What would Jesus say to Trent?*

Donica's Germs

Maria squeezed in line between her two friends, Jill and Leah. "Thanks for saving me a place," she said.

Jill jumped back suddenly, almost knocking Maria off her feet. "Yuck!" Jill yelled. "Donica touched me! I've got her germs!" Jill rubbed her hands on Maria's sleeve. Maria pretended to wipe the "germs" on Leah. But when Maria caught sight of Donica's face, she felt ashamed.

Donica's family had moved to Maria's small town in November after everyone else in school had already made friends. Every day the third-grade girls passed on Donica's "germs." Every day Donica ate lunch by herself and stood alone on the playground.

That Sunday at church, Maria felt God was telling her to quit making fun of Donica. *I love Donica as much as I love you,* God told her. *Are your classmates more important to you than I am?*

Maria felt fearful. In her mind she could already hear her friends shouting, "Yuck! Donica and Maria have germs. Stay away!" But Maria knew she couldn't keep on being mean to Donica, no matter what the other kids did.

Monday morning as Maria and her friends stood around the drinking fountain, someone called, "Here comes germy Donica. Stand back!"

With her heart pounding, Maria spoke up. "I don't think God wants us to do this anymore. There's nothing wrong with Donica. Why can't we all be friends?" Maria's surprised friends just stood and stared at her. So did Donica. After an uncomfortable silence, the conversation turned to other things.

All that day Maria resisted teasing Donica. Soon Donica became Maria's special friend. And before two weeks had passed, everyone else accepted Donica too!

"Dear friends, since God loved us…we surely ought to love each other." *(1 John 4:11)*

 *What does Jesus want you to do when your friends make fun of others?*
Who needs your kindness and love today?

The Feud

The day after Thanksgiving, Liza was feeling anything but thankful.

"Mom! I'm sick of having a little brother! Mitch won't leave me alone when I have friends over. And he's always coming into my room and messing with my things when I'm not there." Glaring at her brother, she warned, "If you touch my things once more, I'll break down your Lego city and throw it all over the backyard!"

That night Liza overheard her parents discuss the fact that she and Mitch were always fighting. Liza felt guilty. *I don't mean to be mad at Mitch all the time,* she thought, *but I just can't help it.*

The next day Liza's parents called a family meeting.

"How can we put an end to this fighting?" asked Father. "We're tired of you two not getting along. You fight about everything. I think you've both been pretty selfish."

Liza silently looked away. Mitch shrugged his shoulders.

"If the fighting doesn't stop," Father said, "we won't buy a single Christmas present for either of you. All you'd do is fight about them."

Liza's mouth dropped open. No Christmas presents! Did her parents really mean it? She avoided her brother the rest of the weekend.

In the car driving to school on Monday, Liza started to yell at Mitch about touching her book bag. Remembering what her parents said, she quickly shut her mouth.

Mother glanced over at her and smiled. "I'm proud of you, Liza. I know you stopped yourself from reacting to your brother."

Liza held her head up proudly. "I'm trying to be good. I hope Mitch tries too." Suddenly Liza realized what she was doing and she burst into tears.

"I'm trying to be good just so I can have some presents! Pray that Jesus will help me really care about Mitch and not just about what's on my Christmas list!"

"Don't just pretend to be good!" *(1 Peter 2:1)*

Have you ever done what was right just to get something?
What would Jesus want you to do to make peace in your home?

Marshall the Magnificent

Marshall threw his hand triumphantly in the air and yelled, "I won! I'm the best!" He strutted around while the other boys on his track team pounded his back and gave him high fives.

"Kneel before Marshall the Magnificent!" he commanded as he held up the blue ribbon with "Riverside School Field Day—1st Place" printed in gold letters.

His father walked over and squeezed Marshall's shoulder. "Congratulations, son. I'm proud that you won. But is this how Jesus would handle winning a race?"

Irritated, Marshall turned away.

The next day at lunch, all Marshall talked about was the race. "I'm good enough for the Olympics!" he bragged. Other students groaned. A few changed tables.

At recess Marshall said, "I ran so fast, I probably broke the world record yesterday."

"You can't even break Melanie's record," Kelli taunted.

"I'll challenge her to a race," said Marshall. "Watch her eat my dust!"

Many students crowded around after school as Marshall and Melanie crouched in a starting position. "Ready, set, go!"

Everyone cheered as the two raced the length of the playground and back. Melanie outran Marshall by yards.

Marshall's face flushed. His dad was right. Jesus wouldn't have boasted and bragged. It was about time he did what Jesus would do. He walked over to Melanie and shook her hand. "Good race, Melanie. Congratulations!"

"Pride ends in humiliation, while humility brings honor."
(Proverbs 29:23)

Who deserves praise for what we accomplish?
How would Jesus want you to act when you win?

Conflict Busters

Get Set You'll need a balloon for each person.

Go!

Give each person a balloon.

Have each person *tell* one way conflicts arise at your house, then *blow* a puff of air into his or her balloon.

Continue naming what causes conflicts and puffing into the balloons until the balloons are nearly full.

Tell what kinds of attitudes make conflicts worse, then *tie off* your balloons.

Read Proverbs 3:34; 6:20; 15:1; 15:4; 16:7; 16:24; **and** 17:1.

What kinds of attitudes are pleasing to God?
How can we encourage each other to have those attitudes?

Name one way you'll avoid conflicts this week, then *drop* your balloon to the floor.

Pray, and ask Jesus to help you develop attitudes that are pleasing to him.

Stomp the balloons until they're all popped!

Pour on the Salt!

Get Set Wash a potato and bake it in a microwave oven on full power for six minutes or until it's soft. Let it cool and cut it in several pieces. Set out two large, clear glasses, two uncooked eggs, a box of salt, a tablespoon measure, and a saltshaker.

Go!

Give everyone a bite of the baked potato.

How does it taste?

Sprinkle on some salt and *give* everyone a second bite.

What does salt do for the potato?

Read Matthew 5:13.

How is the salt on the potato like what Christians are to do for the world?

Explain: Let's look at another amazing thing that salt can do.

Pour water into the glasses until they're about two-thirds full.

Measure two tablespoons of salt into one of the glasses.

Stir until all the salt has dissolved. Carefully place an egg in each glass.

What happens to the egg in the salt water?
How can we Christians "lift" the people around us?

Pray, asking God's help to make the world a better place.

The Extra Hamburger

John grabbed his coat and baseball cap and ran to catch up with his father.

"Oh, Dad!" he exclaimed, jumping in the car, "I'm starving! Thanks for taking me out to eat."

At the drive-up window they ordered two large hamburgers and two orders of fries to go.

"Let's take our hamburgers to the park and eat there," John suggested.

When his father handed him the paper bag with their food, John hurriedly opened it.

"I just want to smell it," he explained. "Mmmm." Looking inside the sack, John's mouth watered. But instead of two wrapped hamburgers, he saw three!

"Hey! I think they gave us too many hamburgers—one, two…three! Somebody put in an extra hamburger, Dad!"

"Good deal! We could sure use an extra one," said his father as they drove up the street. "One hamburger won't fill me up. One burger probably won't fill you up either."

John frowned. "Dad! You can't be serious! You know we shouldn't keep this extra burger—that would be like stealing! We didn't pay for it. This is not our hamburger."

John's father silently turned the car around and headed back to the restaurant. "You're right, John," he said. "Jesus wants us to be honest and fair in everything we do. I'm proud of your attitude and your willingness to be truthful and do what's right."

When they gave the extra hamburger to the restaurant owner, the man thanked them for being honest. To their surprise, he handed it back and told them to enjoy it, which they did!

"Your throne is founded on two strong pillars—righteousness and justice. Unfailing love and truth walk before you." *(Psalm 89:14)*

*What would Jesus say to John's father?
Have you ever been tempted to keep something
that wasn't yours?*

A Better Idea

Erika dropped into the bus seat next to Shannon. "Are you coming to my birthday party?" she asked.

"If my mom says it's okay," Shannon replied.

"Great! It's going to be a blast. I just got a new Ouija board! I hear they're great for parties."

"No way. I don't want anything to do with that."

"Why not? It's just for fun," Erika protested.

"That's not my idea of fun."

"Nobody really believes in it."

Lord, Shannon prayed, *please help me explain this to Erika. And help me give her a better idea for her party.*

Suddenly a flock of birds swooped by and landed on a power line beside the road. An idea clicked in Shannon's mind.

"See that power line?" Shannon asked, pointing out the window. Erika nodded.

"If there were a storm and the power line blew down, would you touch it?"

"Of course not."

"Why not?"

"There might still be current running through it and I could get electrocuted!"

"What if it were just a little wire?"

"No way! Not worth the risk."

"It's the same with a Ouija board," Shannon explained. "The Bible warns us to leave those things alone."

"Oh." Erika was quiet for a moment. "But what about my party?"

"How about having a glamour party instead?" Shannon suggested. "My mom just gave me some of her old makeup. We could do each other's hair and fix our nails. And I could bring the jewelry-making kit I got for my birthday."

"What a cool idea!" Shannon exclaimed. "This'll be lots more fun than what I had planned." Shannon smiled and whispered a prayer of thanks.

"Fix your thoughts on what is true and honorable and right. Think about things that are pure and lovely and admirable. Think about things that are excellent and worthy of praise." *(Philippians 4:8)*

When has Jesus helped you guide a friend away from trouble?

Surprise Party

Sharene set her suitcase down and knocked on Vicki's front door. Vicki answered the door, but the house was dark inside. "Where's your mom?" asked Sharene. "You told my mother she'd be here all weekend."

"She will be," Vicki assured her. "Mom has to work late so we're going over to Mrs. Bennett's for dinner."

This sounded a little strange to Sharene. "Mrs. Bennett? As in Gregg Bennett's mother?"

Vicki's eyes sparkled. "Neat, huh?"

Sharene frowned. "You're twelve and he's sixteen. You're a Christian, he's not. Why do you want to hang around with him?"

"You'd like him if you got to know him," said Vicki. "Anyway, let's not make this a big deal. It's only dinner."

The sound of rap music greeted them when Gregg opened the door of his house. "Welcome to the party," he said, ushering them into the living room. A group of teenagers sprawled on the couches and floor, sipping sodas and eating pizza.

Sharene was angry. "This is *dinner* with Gregg's *family*? He lied to you, Vicki," she said, taking her friend's arm. "Let's get out of here."

"Well, he didn't exactly lie…" said Vicki. "Look, as long as we're here, let's get something to eat."

"No way! I'm leaving."

"But Gregg has this really cute friend he wants you to meet. You'll like him."

Sharene's anger turned to pain as she finally understood the truth. Choking on tears, she said, "You knew about this party! Vicki, what's happened to you? You used to love Jesus and want to follow him. Now you've lied to me. I'm not staying. I'll call my mom to come get me."

On the ride home, Sharene prayed silently, *Dear Jesus, please help Vicki to choose you…and friends who love you.*

"Bad company corrupts good character." *(1 Corinthians 15:33)*

Why does Jesus want us to choose friends who love him?

Bethany's Decision

"We will work on a special project in music class this week," the teacher announced. "You'll be listening to examples of Halloween music. Then our class will make up our own Halloween song."

Bethany cringed. She knew what some of the music sounded like. A tape had been playing at the beginning of class. *It's full of witches and evil things*, thought Bethany. *I don't want to fill my mind with it. But what should I do?* She said a quick prayer asking Jesus to guide her.

The teacher looked around the classroom and added, "If anyone doesn't want to do this project, there's another assignment you can do. Just pick it up in the back of the room and go work in the library."

Bethany struggled with her decision. *If I don't do this class project, others may make fun of me*, she thought. *I don't want to be laughed at for not participating.* Finally she stood and walked to the back of the room. *Be with me, Jesus*, she prayed silently. Another boy got up and followed her. They picked up the assignment by the door and went to the library.

Later some students asked her, "Why didn't you stay and do our music project?"

"Because I felt Jesus didn't want me to," answered Bethany. "I'd rather fill my mind with *good* things."

"Follow what is right and good." *(1 Timothy 6:11)*

What important decision can Jesus help you with today?

Mud Slide

Brian watched Jared mix sand from the sandbox with water from a mud puddle. He laughed. Some little kid would be surprised when he used the slide.

Jared smoothed his mixture onto the slide's metal surface. Then he wiped his hands on his pants and picked up his basketball. "Let's shoot hoops. We'll watch the slide from the basketball court."

Ten minutes later, a man in a suit strolled into the park with a little girl dressed in a pink ruffled dress. The man said, "Honey, we have five minutes until the ceremony. Do you want to swing?"

"No," she answered. "I want to slide."

Jared grinned broadly. "This will be sweet!"

Brian wasn't so sure. "Maybe we should tell the dad that there's junk on the slide."

Jared scowled. "What! And spoil the fun? Hey—you wouldn't ruin this, would you?"

"We wouldn't have to say who did it."

"If you so much as clear your throat," Jared warned, "I'll beat your face in!"

Brian watched the little girl climb the steps of the slide. *Why should I say anything?* he thought. *I don't even know those people.*

Jared stood next to him, looming a full head taller than Brian. Jared's hands were big and powerful. Brian's heart pounded as the little girl sat down at the top of the slide.

Brian knew what Jesus wanted him to do, even though it might cost him a black eye or a bloody nose. Without looking at Jared, he darted toward the playground equipment. "Wait!" he called. "Don't go down that slide!"

Brian hoped Jared wouldn't carry out his threat. But no matter what happened, Brian had made his decision. He was going to live for Jesus and do what was right.

"My child, if sinners entice you, turn your back on them!"
(Proverbs 1:10)

Has someone ever tried to get you to hurt others? If you were Brian, what would you have done?

Dizzy Directions

Get Set Set a special treat somewhere in your house or yard a good distance from where you'll meet for devotions. You'll also need a blindfold.

Go!

Take everyone to the location where you've placed the treat, then **return** to where you usually meet for devotions.

Explain: We're going to try to return and claim these treats, but in order to do it, we'll have to make the right decisions.

Blindfold a volunteer and **spin** him or her around several times.

Have the blindfolded person **decide** which direction to go, then lead everyone twelve steps in that direction.

Blindfold a second person, **spin** him or her, then have the blindfolded person **lead** you twelve more steps.

Continue taking turns being blindfolded and leading until you eventually end up at the treat.

Read Hebrews 10:35–11:1.

What did we have to look forward to at the end of our little adventure?
What has God promised to those who live for him?
How does God help us find the right way in our lives?
What does your faith make you sure of?

Pray: Thank you, Jesus, for the promise of heaven. Keep our faith strong and help us make right choices as we live for you. Amen.

Can't Catch Me!

Get Set   Set out pencils, paper, and a baseball cap.

Go!

Have everyone *write* their name on a slip of paper and *place* it in the cap.

Have each person *draw* a name from the cap. Keep the names secret!

Explain: This is "Secret Act of Kindness" week. Your job is to do a secret act of kindness each day for the person whose name you drew. And you must never get caught! If anyone gets caught, we'll meet, draw names, and start over again.

Read   Matthew 6:1–4.

Why does Jesus want us to be quiet about the good things we do? How do you feel about people who brag about the kind things they do? What kind of reward can we look forward to someday?

Brainstorm   secret acts of kindness you could do for each other.

Have everyone *stand* and *repeat* this pledge: I promise to be God's secret agent, to do an act of kindness each day, and never to get caught.

Secret Agent

Andrew felt so upset that even Mom's chili didn't look very appetizing. His father said, "You're the biggest chili eater in the family. Why aren't you gobbling it down? Is something wrong?"

Andrew sighed. "Mike's dad lost his job last week. Mike and I were going to be bunk mates at church camp, but now they won't have enough money to send him. Registration money for camp is due this Sunday."

"Hmm," said Andrew's dad. "Let's stop and pray for the Grants right now." He bowed his head. "Dear Lord, thank you that you care for us all. Please help Mr. Grant find another job. Take care of all their family's needs. And show us how we can help. In Jesus' name, amen."

When Andrew looked up, a thought struck him. "I've saved fifty dollars toward new Rollerblades. I could give that to Mike for camp!"

Dad patted Andrew's shoulder. "I'm proud of you for being willing to share your hard-earned money. Tell you what—your mom and I will pay the rest of Mike's camp fee." He glanced at Andrew's mom, who nodded and smiled.

Andrew jumped up from the table. "Great! I'll take him the money now."

Dad laid his hand on Andrew's arm. "Wait a minute. Why don't we give the money through the church—like a scholarship?"

"You mean, don't tell them who gave it?" Andrew felt disappointed.

His dad nodded and said, "Think about it. Who gets the thanks if we hand Mike's family a check?"

"We do, I guess," said Andrew slowly.

"Who gets the thanks if we give the money secretly?"

Andrew's face lit up. "God does!"

Dad nodded again. "The Grants will be able to receive it freely from God's hand without feeling they owe us anything."

"Yeah!" said Andrew. "It will be a secret between God and our family. Hey! It's fun being God's secret agents."

"When you give...give your gifts in secret." *(Matthew 6:3, 4)*

 *Could someone in God's family use your help this week?*

Alone at Gymnastics

Six-year-old Kira sat on a vinyl mat in the dimly lit gym waiting for her dad. All the other kids had already been picked up by their parents. Kira was left alone. Had Dad forgotten her?

"Jesus, please send someone to help me," she prayed quietly.

She could see her gymnastics teacher working in the office at the side of the gym. The teacher didn't notice her.

Kira folded her hands in the lap of her pink leotard, sat up straight, and tried to be brave.

The door opened and several big boys came in, laughing loudly and wrestling each other on their way through the gym. Kira decided it was time to leave. She slipped outside and stood by the bushes at the front of the building.

Which way is home? she wondered. She felt worried as several strangers walked by. The sky began to darken and Kira grew more and more fearful.

Suddenly a familiar car pulled over and stopped in front of the gym. It was Agnes, Kira's eighty-year-old neighbor.

Agnes smiled and waved. "I thought I saw a pretty pink lady," she said cheerfully.

Tears ran down Kira's cheeks. "I don't know how to get home," she whimpered.

"I do," said Agnes. "I was on my way to the store and Jesus sent me to help you."

Kira held out her hand. She felt safe.

"You are my hiding place; you protect me from trouble." *(Psalm 32:7)*

 *When has Jesus sent someone to help you in a time of trouble?*

Ice Cream for Jimmy

Debbie's three-year-old brother lay in his hospital bed holding his throat. "Does it hurt?" Debbie asked Jimmy. He nodded.

"Do you want some ice cream?" Debbie asked. "The doctor said you can have as much as you want. That's the good part about getting your tonsils out."

Jimmy shook his head. Holding his arms, he made a rocking motion.

"Are you asking me for something?"

Jimmy nodded and repeated the rocking motion.

"I'm sorry, Jimmy." She leaned close, wanting to help. "I can't understand what you want."

Jimmy put his hand on his throat again and tried to whisper. No sound came out. He pouted and pounded on the bed in frustration.

"It hurts to talk, doesn't it?" Debbie asked. She felt so bad for her little brother.

Jimmy grabbed Debbie's hand and whispered, "I…want…my…baby."

Good grief! thought Debbie, understanding at last. *Jimmy thinks that anyone who goes to the hospital gets a baby!* Six months earlier their mom had gone to the same hospital and come home with their baby sister.

Debbie wanted to giggle, but she didn't want to hurt Jimmy's feelings.

"Jimmy," she said solemnly, "Mama came to the hospital to have our baby sister. But that doesn't mean you get a baby too."

Jimmy frowned and shook his head.

Debbie brushed Jimmy's hair back from his forehead. "I know you're disappointed," she said, "but I'll feed you strawberry ice cream with your special mouse spoon. You'll love that."

Jimmy turned away and wouldn't look at her. *Please show me how to comfort him,* she prayed. "Jimmy," she said, "you're too young to take care of a baby now. But when you get big, you can be a daddy. That will be fun."

Jimmy smiled and Debbie knew he felt better. She kissed the top of his head and loaded his mouse spoon with ice cream.

"Are your hearts tender and sympathetic?" *(Philippians 2:1)*

 *How can you show understanding for someone who's upset?*

Jesus Sent Me

How humiliating, thought Kira, *to stroll down the sidewalk of a busy street wearing a striped leotard! Why did this have to happen to me?* This was the second time Dad had forgotten to pick Kira up from gymnastics practice.

"At least I know the way home this time," she mumbled.
She had been only six years old the last time. Agnes, her elderly neighbor, had found her waiting by the gym, scared to death. Agnes took her home and Kira had adored her ever since.

But Kira hadn't seen Agnes much lately. She never came outside any more. Whenever Kira passed her house, Agnes simply stood at the window and waved. Mom said she had Alzheimer's disease. If she left her house, she'd get lost.

Two more blocks—I'll be glad to get home, thought Kira. Turning the corner, she saw Agnes standing on the sidewalk, looking lost and afraid. Kira knew Agnes must have wandered from home.

Agnes turned to her with a confused look. "I don't know where to go," she told Kira.

"I do," said Kira, smiling and holding out her hand to lead Agnes home. "Jesus sent me to help you."

Dear Jesus, Kira prayed, *thank you for letting Dad forget me. Thank you for letting me help Agnes.*

"Do not withhold good…when it's in your power to help." *(Proverbs 3:27)*

What would Jesus want you to do to help an older person?

Shane's Prayer Map

Ten-year-old Shane tacked a colorful map of the world on his bedroom wall. Randy, his five-year-old brother, asked, "Why do you want a map above your bed?"

"It's my prayer map," Shane explained, "to help me pray for people around the world. This is my week to pray for China."

"Who are you gonna pray for? Do you know somebody in China?" Randy asked.

Shane shook his head. "No. But we learned in Sunday school that things are hard for Christians in China. If they tell anyone else about Jesus they may lose their jobs. Sometimes they go to jail and then there's no one to take care of their families."

"I didn't know that," Randy responded quietly. "That's sad."

"It's hard for Christians in other countries too."

"Where?"

"Lots of places." Shane pointed out several countries on his map.

"Could I pray with you?" Randy asked.

"Sure."

"I don't know how to pray for someone I don't even know."

"God knows."

Shane's face brightened. "Right!"

Together the brothers prayed for Christians in China. They prayed that God would protect them and give them courage to keep on telling others about Jesus.

After they prayed, Shane said, "Thanks for praying with me, Randy. We can't see what God did, but I *know* he did something special."

Randy smiled. "Maybe we'll find out in heaven."

Shane nodded. "I'm sure we will."

"Share the sorrow of those being mistreated, as though you feel their pain in your own bodies." *(Hebrews 13:3)*

What can you do for people who are suffering because they believe in Jesus?

Drive-By Prayer

Get Set   Arrange with a parent to go for a drive for this devotion. Plan to go at a time of day when traffic is light.

Go!

Read   Matthew 9:35–38.

*How did Jesus feel about the people he saw every day?
How does Jesus want us to feel about the people in our town?*

Drive   up and down the streets of your town.

Ask   Jesus to help you see through his eyes.

Pray   for anyone who looks unhappy.

Pull over   when you pass a church and pray for those who worship there.

Sit   in the parking lot of a busy store and pray for the people who come and go.

Stop   by schools and pray for the children and teachers.

Return   to your home.

Decide   on one thing your family can do to reach out to someone you saw as you drove.

Pray   that Jesus will bless your efforts as you reach out in his name.

Only the Best

Get Set Gather a variety of dishes and utensils from the kitchen and china cupboard. Be sure to include something made of gold or silver, something made of wood, a mixing bowl, a fancy dish, and a piece of fine china. Also collect any dishes or utensils that have special meaning to you.

Go!

Hold up the dishes and utensils one by one.

Talk about how each is used and how much it might cost.

Explain why certain dishes have special meaning to you.

Encourage anyone who has a favorite dish that's not on the table to

go get it and *tell* why it's special.

Which of these items on the table is most like you? Explain.

Read 2 Timothy 2:19–22.

How can we keep ourselves "clean" for God's work?
What kinds of special jobs might God have for our family? for each of us?
What does God want his people to be like?

Let each person *hold* a favorite dish and *say,* "God has a special, holy purpose for me."

Close with prayer, asking God to help you be faithful and obedient so he can use you for his special purposes.

"It's Not Fair!"

"It's not fair!" Kimberly complained. "You never let me go bike riding with Julie. Her parents let her go anywhere she wants. I *never* get to."

"I'm sorry you feel that way," said Mother, "but I care about where you are. And I don't agree with the way Julie's parents let her ride all over town. What if something happened to her in a strange neighborhood?"

"I live in a prison!" yelled Kimberly, storming out of the room.

Later that day, Kimberly answered the phone. "Hello?"

"Hello! This is Julie's mother. Will you please tell Julie to come home now?"

"Julie's not here," answered Kimberly. "She stopped by earlier. But Mom wouldn't let me ride with her, so she left. We haven't seen her since."

"I'm worried," said Julie's mother. "She promised to be home by dark. Could you help us look for her?"

"Okay," said Kimberly. She hung up the phone and ran to tell her mother. "Julie's not home and her mother's worried. I told her we'd help look for Julie. Let's drive to Riverside Park. Julie rides there every day."

They grabbed their flashlights, jumped into the car, and headed for the park where they searched for Julie. When they approached the drainage culvert, Kimberly heard a noise. Peering into the culvert, she saw a bicycle—it was Julie's. Further down, she spotted Julie, curled in a heap and crying. She'd fallen into the slippery culvert and couldn't climb out.

After they took Julie and her bike home, Kimberly told her mother, "I thought you were mean. But you're really being the mom God wants you to be. I'm going to pray that Jesus will give me a better attitude about obeying you."

"Children, obey your parents because you belong to the Lord, for this is the right thing to do. 'Honor your father and mother.'" *(Ephesians 6:1)*

When have you been unhappy with your parents' decisions?
What attitude does Jesus want you to have toward your parents?

Betrayed Trust

"We think you're old enough to watch your brother and sister," Dad told Tevin. "We'll be back in an hour."

Tevin felt proud and grown-up as he watched his parents drive out of sight. *They trust me!* he thought. *I'm in charge!*

"Pillow fight!" he yelled, even though Mom had a strict rule against it. Courtney and Zach grabbed small pillows from the couch and pummeled each other, giggling wildly. Tevin snatched a pillow and swung it at Courtney. *Wham!*

Courtney's face paled. She stumbled toward the brick fireplace and fell against it. Tevin rushed over to help her.

Courtney started crying. "My tooth hurts!" She touched her mouth. "My lip is bleeding!" she cried.

"Let me see." Tevin peered into her mouth. "Oh, no," he said, "your front tooth is chipped." Courtney wailed louder.

Zach started to cry. "Mom and Dad will be mad."

Tevin sank to the floor with his head in his hands. "They trusted me," he said. "The dentist can fix your tooth. I'll tell Mom and Dad it was my fault." He felt sick.

"They'll ground you forever," Courtney said, sniffling.

"I deserve it."

Zach patted his big brother's head. "Jesus forgives you. So will Mom and Dad."

"Think I can win their trust back?" asked Tevin.

"Yes," said Zach.

"I won't blow it again," Tevin vowed.

"A wise child accepts a parent's discipline." *(Proverbs 13:1)*

How can Tevin earn back his parents' trust? How would Jesus want you to show yourself trustworthy?

Broken Hearts

"Mom," said Alissa, following her mother into the master bedroom, "I need something for show-and-tell tomorrow."

"How about your glow-in-the-dark watch?" asked Mother as she laid clean clothes in her dresser drawer.

"I've already shown it," said Alissa. Catching a glint of gold at the back of the drawer, she said, "Wait. What's that?"

Her mother smiled and pulled out a plastic bag containing a small gold heart necklace. She showed Alissa how it separated into two pieces, then fit back together. "My name is engraved on one half and your dad's is on the other," she said.

"It's beautiful! Can I take it to show-and-tell?"

"No. It's very precious to me. Your father gave it to me when he was in the war. I wore it every day and prayed for his safe return."

All evening Alissa thought about the gold heart. She knew Jesus wouldn't want her to disobey her mother, but the heart necklace would be awesome for show-and-tell.

The next morning she crept into her mother's bedroom, took the heart, and placed it in the zipper pocket of her backpack. *I'll return it before Mom misses it,* she thought.

On the way to school, Alissa pulled out the heart necklace and showed it to several friends. Right before show-and-tell time, she reached into her backpack, but the heart necklace wasn't there! All she found was a hole in the zipper pocket. Alissa wanted to cry.

During the next few days Alissa looked everywhere for the necklace. She had trouble sleeping at night. She couldn't even pray. Sooner or later she knew her mother would notice the heart necklace was gone. Finally Alissa told her mother what had happened.

"Please forgive me. I'm sorry I took the heart," Alissa sobbed. "Because I didn't obey, you've lost something precious that can never be replaced."

"Children, obey your parents." *(Ephesians 6:1)*

Why does Jesus want you to obey your parents? When is it hardest for you to obey?

A Stubborn Pony

Ben stomped toward the grandstand ahead of his dad, angry that he couldn't have another bag of popcorn. Coming around the stables, he nearly ran into a buggy. Its young driver was trying to make her pony back up.

Ben's father grabbed him by the arm and pulled him out of the pony's way.

"Midnight! Back up!" the girl ordered. "Quit being so stubborn!" She pulled on the reins, trying to get her pony to move. He wouldn't budge.

"Can I help?" asked Ben's father. The girl nodded. Dad reached his hand out slowly, took the pony's harness, and led him to the arena entrance.

"Thank you," said the girl. "Midnight needs to learn to trust me and do what I say. I'm afraid we won't win any awards today."

Ben and his dad found a seat in the bleachers and watched the lineup of horse-drawn buggies. Of all twenty entries, only Midnight insisted on going his own way. As a result, he came in last.

Ben prayed silently, *I've been stubborn and rebellious like Midnight. Forgive me, Jesus. Help me obey my father.* He turned to his dad and said quietly, "I've been acting like Midnight. Please forgive me."

"Do what is right and good in the Lord's sight, so all will go well with you." *(Deuteronomy 6:18)*

When do you tend to be stubborn?
What would Jesus want you to do?

Week
44

Wrong Choices

Dawn looked over the display of lip gloss and nail polish. The tubes were so small—it wouldn't be hard to slip them into her pocket. She hesitated, knowing it would be wrong.

"These are easy to take," Lyla whispered. "No one will notice." She quickly slipped several tubes of lip gloss into her purse.

On their way to the front door, a security guard stopped them. "Come with me, girls," he said, ushering them into an office.

"Let's see what you have in your bags and your pockets," the guard ordered.

"I didn't take anything," said Dawn quietly as she emptied her purse and pockets. Lyla gave up three pairs of earrings, some nail polish, and the lip gloss.

The security guard told Dawn, "I'll have to call your parents, too. Because you were with a shoplifter, you can be punished for the same crime. You didn't stop her."

Dawn felt like crying. Her parents had forbidden her to go anywhere with Lyla. They knew Lyla had often been in trouble with the police. Now Dawn's parents would find out she'd disobeyed them.

Why did I ever agree to meet Lyla in the mall? wondered Dawn. *And why didn't I stop her from stealing?*

When Dawn's parents arrived, the look of disappointment in their eyes added to her misery. She stared at the floor as the store manager said, "We're going to release you to your parents. But if you ever enter this store again, you'll be arrested."

On the way home, Dawn told her parents, "I pray that Jesus and you will forgive me. You were right about Lyla. She thinks it's exciting to shoplift. And I almost followed her bad example. From now on, I'll obey you."

"Only a fool despises a parent's discipline; whoever learns from correction is wise." *(Proverbs 15:5)*

Why does Jesus want you to obey your parents? When is it hardest for you to obey?

Do I Have to Obey?

Get Set You'll need a board game. You might want to choose a brand-new board game that no one's played before.

Go!

Set up the board game.

Explain: Today we're going to play a game without any rules. Play any way you want.

Stop the game after about five minutes.

What was it like to play without rules?
What rules does our family live by?
In what ways are rules good for us?

Read Deuteronomy 28:1–14.

How do God's rules protect us and make our lives better?
What does God promise if we are obedient to him?
How has God blessed our lives already?

Pray: Dear Jesus, thank you for helping us live our lives for you. Thank you for all the good things you bring into our lives every day. Help us keep on obeying you. Amen.

Play the game again, this time by the rules!

Overflowing Love to All

Get Set Place a cup in a large mixing bowl. You'll need ingredients for trail mix, such as peanuts, M&Ms, raisins, coconut, chocolate chips, and chopped dried fruit.

Go!

Have each person **choose** and **hold** one of the ingredients for trail mix.

Explain: Each new day is like an empty cup.

Read Psalm 92:1–4.

What is the first thing God wants us to put in our cup each day?

Have everyone **pour** a little of their ingredient into the cup.

Read 1 Peter 1:22. *What does God want us to do with his love?*

Pour more of each ingredient into the cup.

Explain: Sometimes people put mean and unkind things into our day.

Read Luke 6:35. *How does Jesus want us to react when people are mean?*

Add more of each ingredient to the cup.

Read 1 Thessalonians 3:12–13.

How can we let God's love overflow into the lives of people around us?

Empty all the ingredients into the cup and bowl.

Pray and ask God to help you overflow with his love today.

Stir the trail mix and help yourselves!

Christine's Dilemma

Christine hung up the phone and whirled in a circle, laughing and cheering. "Ha! Seth sneaked out of the house and his parents found out about it. Now he's grounded for a whole month! I love it!"

"Seth may deserve his punishment, but aren't you sorry that he made some wrong choices?" asked her mom.

Christine defended herself. "I don't remember the Bible saying we should feel sorry when others make wrong choices."

"What about Proverbs 24:17? It says, 'Do not rejoice when your enemies fall into trouble.'"

"Yes, but Seth is different," Christine insisted. "He's always making fun of me at school—and of other Christian kids. He always acts like he's so cool. I'm glad he's in trouble."

Christine's mother sighed. "Have you ever heard of hating the sin but loving the sinner?"

"No."

"Do you think Jesus loves Seth?"

"I guess so."

"Do you think Jesus loves the things Seth does?"

"No."

"Could you love Seth without loving the things he does?" Mother challenged.

"I suppose so."

"Do me a favor. Go read Luke 15:7, then come back and tell me what Jesus says."

Christine looked up the verse in the Bible on the lamp table.

"It says that there's great rejoicing in heaven when a sinner repents. I guess I should be praying for Seth instead of gloating because he got in trouble."

"Good plan!" said Mother with a smile.

"Heaven will be happier over one lost sinner who returns to God than over ninety-nine others who are righteous and haven't strayed away!"
(Luke 15:7)

Have you ever felt good when someone else got in trouble?
What would Jesus say about that?

Who's the Bully?

"You give that ball back!" Becky chased Calvin around the church parking lot and grabbed his shirt.

Calvin scowled and pulled away. "What's the matter with you?"

"You stole the ball from my little brother!" Becky yanked the basketball away from Calvin. She felt like beating him up. And she could do it.

"I did not steal it. I just used it for a while."

"Without his permission?" She stuck her face in Calvin's. She couldn't stand him. "Picking on little kids—is that what Jesus would do?"

Calvin's face turned red. "Are you going to beat me up?"

Becky could tell he was scared of her and it made her feel good. "I might," she said, moving closer. She enjoyed making Calvin squirm.

Calvin's next words shocked Becky.

"Is *that* what Jesus would do?" he asked. "I already gave you the ball."

Whew! she thought. *He's right, even if he didn't "give" the ball back. Jesus wants me to stick up for my brother, but I crossed the line into revenge when I threatened Calvin.*

Becky sighed and cleared her throat. It was hard to admit she was wrong. "You're right, Calvin." she said. "I'm sorry."

Jesus said, "And why worry about a speck in your friend's eye when you have a log in your own?" *(Matthew 7:3)*

Who was the bully in this story?
What does Jesus say about getting?

Do Bears Swim?

"You're planning something," said Amy, following her big sister Tara outside.

"Who, me?" Tara pasted a shocked look on her face and opened the gate to Sally's yard. "Hi, Sally, get a new teddy bear?" She smiled sweetly.

Amy knew her sister hated it that Sally's family could afford a big pool and they couldn't. It bothered Amy, too.

Sally grinned at them as she played beside her pool with her big white teddy bear.

"Do you want to hold my bear?" asked Sally, offering it to Amy. Tara grabbed it.

"Be careful. Aunt Jodie sent it from Illinois for my birthday. I love it."

"It looks expensive," said Tara.

The bear was made of beautiful white fur and sported denim coveralls and leather shoes with heart socks. Amy fought back a twinge of jealousy.

"Can it swim?" Tara asked. Sally frowned.

"Let's see if it will float," said Tara.

"No!" Sally planted a fist on each hip.

Tara winked at Amy. "You got any popsicles, Sally?" she asked.

"Sure," said Sally. She ran inside to get popsicles.

Amy knew she should stop Tara. But she just stood and watched as Tara dropped the fluffy white bear into Sally's pool.

The bear sank slowly to the bottom and stayed there.

The next hour turned out to be the worst one of Amy's life, but she knew she deserved it. She didn't blame Sally for screeching and pushing her in the pool. She didn't blame Sally's parents for telling on her and Tara. She didn't even blame Dad for grounding them for a month.

Amy didn't feel better till she got out her birthday money to help pay for Sally's bear. It was the first thing she'd done to please Jesus all day.

"Do not covet." *(Exodus 20:17)*

 *How can Jesus help you when you feel jealous?*

Foreign Brother

The year was 1912. Horses and buggies lined up with a few motorcars outside the little white church building.

Estelle looked at the empty pew in front of hers. She turned and whispered to Elana, "Why isn't Noah's family here?"

"Doc Greene was over at their house last night to take care of Noah's father," Elana whispered, shaking her head. "My mother said Noah's family would get sick if they kept letting immigrants live with them."

"What do you mean?" Estelle asked.

"People who come from other countries bring all sorts of diseases with them." Elana shuddered.

By the time church was over, everyone had heard the whispered rumor that Noah's father was dying from a strange, foreign disease.

The next Sunday Noah and his mother came to church, bringing a new boy with them. "This is Ivan," Noah announced proudly. "His family just arrived from Russia. They're staying with us until they find a home of their own."

All the children backed away from the two boys. Noah looked puzzled and hurt. Later he found Estelle and Elana. "Ivan doesn't know much English but he does understand 'Hello'. What's wrong? Why is everyone so unfriendly?"

"We don't want to get a terrible disease from him like your father did," said Estelle. Noah's mouth dropped open. "What?"

"Isn't your father…you know…dying?"

"Of course not! He just broke his leg. Where did you get the idea he was dying?"

Estelle looked at Elana, whose face turned red.

Noah said, "Even though Ivan is from another country and doesn't speak English, he's asked Jesus into his heart. That makes him our brother in Christ. Someday we'll all live in heaven together."

Estelle smiled and held out her hand to Ivan. "Hello, Brother Ivan. Welcome to Jesus' family in America."

"I saw a vast crowd…from every nation and tribe and people and language, standing in front of the throne and before the Lamb." *(Revelation 7:9)*

 *How does Jesus want you to treat people of different nationalities?*

A Sticky Problem

Allison held back tears as she yanked open the front door of their house. "Mom? Where are you?"

"In the kitchen," called her mother.

Allison rushed into the kitchen, dropped her backpack on the counter, and threw herself into her mother's arms.

"What's wrong, sweetheart?" asked Mother, stroking her long dark hair. Mother's hand stopped abruptly. "What's in your hair?"

"Carli put glue in my hair and sprinkled it with glitter," Allison sobbed. "She says we're enemies. Now you'll have to cut my hair!"

Mother kissed Allison's forehead. "It'll wash out."

A few minutes later, Allison bent over the sink as her mother carefully washed out the glitter and glue. "Why are you and Carli enemies?" asked Mother.

"I haven't done anything to her. She's mean to all the kids."

"Maybe she needs a friend," suggested Mother, wrapping Allison's hair in a towel.

"Everybody in our class stays away from her," said Allison. She thought a moment. "But Jesus would be her friend…maybe I can too. Maybe I can even invite her to Sunday school."

Mother smiled. "Sounds as if you'd be doing the whole class a favor."

It wasn't very long before Carli accepted Allison's invitation and went to Sunday school. Soon after that Carli asked Jesus into her heart.

"Don't let evil get the best of you, but conquer evil by doing good." *(Romans 12:21)*

Do you have an enemy who needs your love?
How could you show love to that person?

Week
45

Kindness Scramble

Get Set You'll need scissors, paper, and pencils or markers.

Go!

Write down something mean that you heard this week. It may have been said to you or to someone else.

Share the mean things you've written.

Why do people say mean things?

Read Jesus' words in Luke 6:27–36.

How does Jesus want us to respond when people are mean to us? Are you usually able to do that? Why or why not? How can Jesus help us return good for evil?

Explain: We're going to change these mean words into kind words.

Cut apart the sentences you've written.

Combine all your cut-apart words in the center of the table.

Work together to *arrange* the words into kind, caring statements. (If you need to, cut apart letters of some words.)

Make as many caring statements as you can.

Pray and ask Jesus to help you return good for evil.

The Truth...or Imitation?

Get Set   You'll need a piece of rope and a roll of masking tape. Cut two pieces of masking tape about two feet long. Use the tape to mark start and finish lines on the floor about six feet apart.

Go!

Explain: Today we're going to start with a game of tug-of-war. I'll name the teams.

Point   to the smallest person in the family and   *say:*   You're team one.

Gather   everyone else by you and   *say:*   We're team two.

Stand   between the two masking tape lines.

Hand   one end of the rope to the smallest person in your family.

Have everyone   *sit*   down.

What's wrong with our game?
When have you experienced something unfair?

Read   Psalm 34:15–22.

How can God help us when things are unfair?
Is it all right if things don't always come out fair on earth? Why or why not?
When were people unfair to Jesus?

Pray: Thank you, Jesus, that you were willing to take our punishment even though you never sinned. Help us to be fair and honest in everything we do. Help us to trust you when people are unfair to us. Amen.

Darren's Lie

Darren and James panted as they leaned against the tree that served as the finish line for their races.

"I won!" said Darren, knowing it was a lie.

"No way. *I* won!" James insisted.

"*I* tagged the tree first." Darren almost believed his own lie. He couldn't admit he saw James touch the tree a split second ahead of him. He had never come this close to beating James before.

"Cheater!" James's face reddened.

"Take that back!" Darren threw James to the ground. The two friends struggled on the lawn.

"I hate you!" James yelled as he bolted for home.

Guilt settled over Darren like a fog. He tried to pray, but he felt like God wouldn't listen. So he confessed everything to his mom.

"Well," his mom said, "what would Jesus do?"

"Jesus would never mess up." Darren said softly. "So how can I know what he would do?"

"Jesus never sinned," said Darren's mom as she put her arm around him. "But he knew we would. He left instructions for us to follow when we do. Jesus said that when you try to pray, if you think of someone who has something against you, you need to first go and apologize."

Darren nodded his head. "I need to go find James and tell him I'm sorry."

Jesus said, "Go and be reconciled to that person. Then come and offer your sacrifice to God." *(Matthew 5:24)*

 *Is there something you need to make right with a friend?*

The Unfair Coach

Ten-year-old Brad climbed into the minivan and slammed the door. "Coach's son, Ryan, made the all-star team, but I didn't." He fought back tears.

"I don't understand," Dad said. "You're the best outfielder in the league."

Brad worked to get his voice under control. "I guess Coach Tom told the other coaches I have an attitude problem."

"What?" Dad's knuckles turned white on the steering wheel. "When did he say that?"

"When the coaches met to choose the all-star team."

Dad looked confused. "You don't have a bad attitude."

Brad didn't understand either. He always listened to Coach and treated the other players well.

A look of understanding crossed Dad's face. "But no team can have more than three kids on all-stars."

"Right."

"Coach probably felt like he had to choose the two twelve-year-olds for the team. That leaves one. Since you play better than Ryan, the other coaches would have voted for you. So he figured out a way to keep you off." Dad hit the steering wheel hard. "He lied about your attitude. I expected better of him."

"Remember how you told me that God made him my authority?" asked Brad.

"Yes."

"How could he lie about me?"

Dad sighed. "Not all people in authority make right choices. That's one reason the Bible tells us to pray for them—so they'll be fair."

"I don't feel like praying for him. I'll have to ask Jesus to help me."

"Good for you," said Dad. "I guess that means you're on God's all-star team!"

Brad smiled a little. "That's a good team to be on."

"Pray this way for kings and all others who are in authority, so that we can live in peace and quietness." *(1 Timothy 2:2)*

 *What would Jesus say to the coach? to Brad?*

Water Balloons

Joel crouched behind the hedge and rolled a water balloon around in his hands. *Would Jesus want me to do this?* he wondered. But he pushed the thought out of his mind.

Joel and his friends, Dylan and Carlos, had been hiding behind the hedge for the last half hour, throwing water balloons at passing cars. Joel's job was to keep his eyes glued to the road in front of Tom's house and watch for cars.

"Here comes a truck," Joel said in a low voice.

Tom and Carlos grabbed balloons from the plastic bucket, then waited as the blue pickup drove into view.

"Watch this!" said Tom. When the truck drew even with them, he jumped up, launched a purple balloon over the bush, then dropped to the ground. Through the bush, Joel watched the balloon splat on the driver's window.

"Bull's-eye!" hissed Tom.

The startled driver shook his fist in their direction and hollered. All three boys hid behind the bushes and laughed.

"This one's mine!" Joel said, spotting a black sports car coming toward them. He popped up and hurled his balloon, then ducked down to watch. "Yes!" he whispered as it soared toward the car. "Bull's—" Joel stopped, shocked. The balloon sailed through the driver's open window and exploded against his face.

The car screeched to a halt. Joel's heart pounded like a drum.

"Run!" yelled Tom. He and Carlos disappeared around the corner.

The driver sprang out of his car and started toward Joel's hiding place.

Joel wanted to run, but he knew he needed to face the consequences of what he'd done. Stepping through a space between the hedges, he squared his shoulders and prayed silently for Jesus to help him tell the truth and face the consequences.

"Be strong and very courageous." *(Joshua 1:7)*

What would Jesus say to Joel?
When have you bravely told the truth?

God's Man

Coach Larson put his arm around Jamil's shoulders. "Three minutes left and we're down by five. We've got to stop their man Parker. It's up to you, Jamil. He's defending you. When you go up for a shot, give him an elbow in the face."

Jamil stared at his coach. A knot formed in his stomach. The coach was asking him to hurt another player!

Coach Larson slapped him on the back. "All right! Go for it! I can taste that win already."

Jamil didn't move. "I can't do it, Coach," he said in a low voice.

"We're talking about winning the game, Jamil. Only first place counts. Second is nothing." The coach gripped Jamil's arm. "Do you know who ran against Abraham Lincoln for president or who lost the World Series in 1990? Nobody does. Only winners are remembered."

Jamil shook his head. "It's not right, Coach. I won't try to hurt him."

The coach turned and shouted, "Brett! Sub for Jamil!"

Jamil sat out the rest of the game, but he held his head high. He may have been benched, but he had acted like a man—God's man.

"For our conscience is clear and we want to live honorably in everything we do." *(Hebrews 13:18)*

What makes you a success in Jesus' eyes?

Piñata Peeker

Rosita jumped up and down, anxious for her turn to whack the brightly colored piñata. Miguel swung wildly at the papier-mâché donkey. Rosita laughed. Miguel had boasted he would break the piñata and grab all the candy before she could get any.

Miguel struck out again, but the teacher grabbed his arm. "Sorry, Miguel. Your turn is over."

Miguel stomped his foot, ripped the blindfold from his eyes, and threw down the stick.

Ignoring him, the teacher tied the blindfold over Rosita's eyes, knotting it securely. "Can you see, Rosita?"

"No," said Rosita. But she knew that was a lie. She *could* see under the cloth—just enough to know exactly where to hit the piñata. She couldn't wait to see the look on Miguel's face.

The teacher spun Rosita around and around, then handed her the stick. Rosita pretended to stagger a little as she positioned herself near the piñata. The other kids yelled at her to take a swing.

Rosita raised the stick. *You're not playing fair,* said a voice in her head.

She dropped the stick to her side. "The blindfold isn't quite right," she said to the teacher. "I can see a little."

"Well, let's fix it and spin you again," said the teacher as she adjusted the blindfold. "There. How's that?"

"I can't see a thing!" said Rosita. This time she was telling the truth.

Rosita smiled. She was still determined to knock down the piñata. But she would do it fair and square. And she might even give Miguel some of her candy.

"We pray to God that you will not do anything wrong."
(2 Corinthians 13:7)

 *When is it hard for you to play fair?*

All about Jesus

Get Set   You'll need pencils, paper, and two pairs of salt and pepper shakers.

Go!

Form   two teams.

Assign   one team the books of Matthew and John.

Assign   the other team the books of Mark and Luke.

Have each team   *make up*   seven true or false questions about Jesus based on the stories in their books.

Beside each question,   *write*   the Scripture reference that contains the answer.

When both teams are ready,   *take turns*   asking each other the questions you've written.

To answer "true,"   *raise*   the salt shaker.

To answer "false,"   *raise*   the pepper shaker.

Have the people on the team with the most correct answers   *give*   the other team members a back rub.

If you tie,   *give*   back rubs all around!

Draw a Psalm

Get Set Set out paper and a variety of art materials, such as water-color paints, finger paints, markers, colored pencils, and crayons. You'll also need a timer and a CD or tape of worship music.

Go!

Read Psalm 121.

Let everyone *choose* one or two verses of the psalm to illustrate.

Decide how many minutes you will allow for drawing.

Set a timer for two minutes less than that amount of time, so you'll know when time is almost up.

Play worship music as you draw.

When time is up, *share* your drawings.

Tell why you drew what you did.

Arrange your drawings in the right order and *display* them on your refrigerator or in a hall.

Talk about times when God has protected you from harm.

Read Psalm 121 again.

Close with a circle of prayer, thanking God for his love and protection.

Thankful Teresa

Teresa dangled her feet in the lake and soaked in the warm sun at Camp Crestline. *I need to trust you more, Jesus,* she prayed quietly as she sat on the dock. *I thought camping would be a disaster. Thank you for this wonderful experience of learning to know you better and finding out how much I can do.*

"The girls have all helped me," Teresa told the camp director on the last day. "I've found my way around buildings and forest trails better than I imagined I could. Best of all, I've discovered God loves me and has a wonderful plan for my life."

"You've inspired all of us with your determination and good attitude," said the director. "Tonight at our final campfire, I'm going to ask campers to share what they are thankful for. I hope you'll share, too."

That evening, Teresa sat by the roaring bonfire and listened to each camper share her thoughts about the week.

"I thank God for all the friends I've made here."

"I'm thankful for this fun place and the quiet woods."

"I'm glad God made horses to ride and mountains to climb."

Finally Teresa nervously took her turn. "I'm thankful I was born blind," she said.

Everyone sat in stunned silence. How could anyone be thankful for blindness?

"Why do you feel that way, Teresa?" asked the director.

"Well, this week I realized how much God really loves me. I've asked Jesus to be my Savior. I'm thankful my eyes have never seen anything because now the very first thing I will ever see is Jesus."

"No matter what happens, always be thankful, for this is God's will for you who belong to Christ Jesus." *(1 Thessalonians 5:18)*

 *Can you be thankful for something that's difficult for you?*

A Time of Trouble

Dan hurriedly filled the outdoor barbeque grill with charcoal briquets. Company would arrive soon for dinner. Wanting to get the fire started quickly, he poured on extra lighter fluid. Then he got out the box of matches and struck a match.

The moment Dan lowered the burning match to the grill, the fluid on the briquets exploded into a ball of fire.

A blaze of red hot flames leaped out of the grill and struck Dan in the face. He closed his eyes and backed away screaming.

As unbearable heat seared his skin, Dan began praying, *O Jesus, help me! Don't let me go blind. Help my parents know what to do!*

Dan's screams of pain brought his mother and grandmother running. His grandmother pulled off her apron and threw it over Dan's burning hair to smother the flames.

Dan's father came running, picked him up, and carried him to the car. On their way to the nearby emergency room, they prayed together that Jesus would heal Dan's face.

In just a matter of weeks Dan's face was healed. Even the doctors were astounded at how quickly Dan completely recovered.

But Dan knows why he got well so quickly. Every time he tells his story, he explains how he and his family prayed for help, and he gives all the credit for his recovery to Jesus.

"Trust me in your times of trouble, and I will rescue you, and you will give me glory." *(Psalm 50:15)*

Do you remember to call on Jesus first when trouble comes?
Why does Jesus want you to trust him during times of trouble?

The Swiss Incident

"Why didn't I buy extra stamps the last time we were here?" Jay's father grumbled. A wild wind whipped through Jay's hair as he and his dad walked across the street to the old Swiss postal building. It was the last day of their visit to Switzerland and they had a lot to do. Jay's father groaned when he saw the long line of people waiting inside.

Then Jay remembered what he'd read in his Bible that morning. "Thank you, Jesus," he whispered.

His father looked at him and asked, "What did you say, son?"

"I said, 'Thank you, Jesus.'"

"Why are you thanking Jesus?" asked his father.

"I'm thankful we're standing in line," answered Jay. "Aren't we supposed to be thankful no matter what happens?"

"Well, yes," said his father hesitantly. "But I'm having trouble thanking God for this."

Whenever a customer left the building, a blast of wind blew in. Jay watched people hang on to their hats and coats as they walked up the street. A whirlwind of leaves and dirt flew past the post office window. Slates from another roof clattered against the building.

After the postmaster finally stamped their letter, Jay and his father went out to the car. Broken branches and debris littered the road. They drove down the hill, wondering at the wreckage they saw. Halfway down the hillside an uprooted tree lay across half the road. An overturned tractor and wagon of hay littered the otherwise tidy Swiss field.

"Dad, aren't you thankful?" exclaimed Jay. "If we hadn't been delayed at the post office, we would have been on this road during that terrible windstorm! Thank you, Jesus, for that long line of people!"

"You will always give thanks for everything to God the Father in the name of our Lord Jesus Christ." *(Ephesians 5:20)*

What attitude does Jesus want you to have when things don't go the way you want?

The Worst Christmas?

Brandi ripped the gold foil paper from her last Christmas present. Maybe this was finally something she'd asked for. She stared at the box— a rock polisher?! She'd asked for a fashion doll, a makeup case, and earrings.

Throwing the box aside, Brandi stomped off to her room. *What a lousy Christmas this has been,* she thought. *Who wants clothes, a dumb puzzle, and a rock polisher?*

Mother opened the door to Brandi's bedroom. "It's time for breakfast. And remember, you haven't thanked everyone for their gifts."

"Didn't anyone listen to me?" stormed Brandi. "I didn't get one thing I asked for!"

"Brandi, we all chose your gifts with love. Even though you're disappointed, you can be grateful that people love you enough to give you something."

"If they really loved me, they would have given me what I wanted."

"If you don't want your presents, we can give them to someone who will appreciate them."

"Fine. Do that! This is my worst Christmas ever!" Brandi cried into her pillow. But then she began to think about all the wonderful things she *did* have: parents and a brother who loved her, lots of friends, a warm home, and plenty of food. Feeling ashamed, she wiped her tears and went to find her mother. Breakfast was over and the Christmas clutter was gone. There was no sign of Brandi's presents.

She found her mother in the dining room rewrapping Brandi's gifts. "What are you doing?" asked Brandi.

"There's still time to make someone's Christmas happy," said Mother.

"No, there's still time for *me* to make someone's Christmas happy," said Brandi. "I'm sorry for my bad attitude, Mom. Thanks for the clothes."

Mother smiled and handed her the brightly wrapped presents. "Merry Christmas! A grateful heart will help you enjoy your gifts, even if they're not quite what you wanted."

"No matter what happens, always be thankful, for this is God's will for you who belong to Christ Jesus." *(1 Thessalonians 5:18)*

What's your attitude when a gift is not what you hoped for?

A Special Birthday

"Jesus can help us make Mom's birthday special," Cassie told her two older sisters. "It doesn't cost money to show love."

"We can't afford presents," Michelle said, frowning.

"We could clean the house and fix dinner," said Cassie. "She'd love that."

Jenny agreed, and Michelle's frown became a smile. "You're right."

The girls flew to work. Cassie scrubbed the bathroom while Michelle vacuumed and dusted. Jenny fixed her special macaroni and cheese dinner. They worked together to bake and decorate a cake. Cassie spread a pale blue sheet over the table and set out two candles in holders she found in a drawer.

Michelle sighed. "I wish we could afford flowers."

"Maybe we can," said Cassie. She hurried across the street to the neighbors'.

"Mrs. Fix, may I have one flower from your garden?" asked Cassie. "It's for my mom's birthday." Mrs. Fix gave her a red tulip.

Next Cassie asked Mrs. Ross for a daffodil and Mr. Ellis for one sprig from his flowering plum tree. Every neighbor on the block gave Cassie a flower.

When Mother walked in after work, she found a beautiful cake and bouquet sitting on the table in the glow of candlelight. Three happy faces beamed at her.

"We may not have money," Cassie told her mom, "but Jesus has given us lots of love in our home."

"There is treasure in the house of the godly." *(Proverbs 15:6)*

How would Jesus want you to please your mother today?
What do you appreciate about your family?

God's Care Collage

Get Set You'll need a scrapbook, photocopies or duplicates of family photographs, scissors, a glue stick, and clear Contact paper.

Go!

Cut out people, faces, and important items from photographs.

Work together to *place* the cutouts on the cover of a scrapbook.

Hand letter or use a computer to *print* labels, titles, and favorite family expressions. *Add* the words to the cutouts you've already placed.

Use a glue stick to hold everything in place.

Cut a piece of clear Contact paper large enough to cover your collage. Work together to *peel* the backing off the Contact paper and *smooth* it over the collage.

Have everyone who worked on the collage *autograph* the first page of the scrapbook.

Collect items that are important to you and *place* them in the scrapbook. You might include postcards, newspaper clippings, ticket stubs, photographs, brochures, and handwritten notes.

Read Psalm 103:1–18.

Discuss how God has blessed and guided you in the activities and events that are represented in your scrapbook.

Pray, thanking God for his goodness and care.

Flop Cake

Get Set Set out ingredients for baking a chocolate cake: flour, sugar, eggs, water, oil, baking soda, cocoa, vanilla, and salt. You'll also need vinegar, a mixing bowl, and two nine-inch baking pans. Preheat the oven to 350 degrees. Grease and flour *one* baking pan.

Go!

Explain: We're going to bake a cake just using our own ideas about how much of each ingredient to use. We should be able to come up with a pretty good cake.

Have family members **take turns** deciding how much of each ingredient to use. Don't allow advice from other family members!

Mix the batter, **pour** it into the greased pan, and **put** it into the oven.

Read Psalm 25:4–10. *How is the Bible like a recipe for our lives?*

Work together to **mix** and **bake** a second cake according to this recipe:

> In an *ungreased* cake pan, mix 1 cup sugar, ¼ cup cocoa, 1½ cups flour, 1 teaspoon baking soda, ½ teaspoon salt. Then stir in ⅓ cup oil, 1 tablespoon vinegar, 1 teaspoon vanilla, and 1 cup water. Stir until the batter is smooth. Bake for 30 minutes at 350 degrees.

What's surprising about this recipe?
When have you been surprised by the way God leads us?
Why is it always important to follow God's directions?

Later, **sample** and **compare** the two cakes.

Give thanks to God for his guidance.

Popularity Trap

Melissa giggled at Tiffany's joke as the two girls stood in the door of the lunchroom. *I'm so lucky that someone as popular as Tiffany wants to be my friend,* Melissa thought.

Just then Melissa saw Ruthie coming down the hall. Ruthie had only been in this country a few weeks and had made very few friends. She wore strange clothes and spoke with an accent that was hard to understand. *Tiffany might brush me off if she finds out I'm friends with Ruthie,* Melissa thought. So when Ruthie said hi, Melissa ignored her and turned the other way.

Tiffany's mouth dropped open. "Melissa!" she said. "I didn't think you were that kind of person. Why did you ignore Ruthie? I think you made her cry!" Tiffany shook her head in disbelief and ran to catch up with Ruthie.

Melissa felt miserable. She knew her attitude had been all wrong. *Tiffany didn't get to be popular by ignoring people,* she thought. *She's already made friends with Ruthie and I didn't even know it. Now they both think I'm stuck-up. How will I ever tell either of them about Jesus? I'm such a jerk!*

As soon as school ended, Melissa hurried home and told her mom how ashamed she was of her behavior. They bowed together and Melissa prayed, "Jesus, please forgive me for thinking more about being popular than about loving people. Help me be friends with Ruthie and Tiffany again. I promise that from now on I'll only think about being loving and kind. I'll never worry about being popular again."

Melissa kept her promise. Six years later, the students at Melissa's high school chose her as their homecoming queen. They chose her because she cared about people and was a friend to everyone.

"How can you claim that you have faith in…Jesus Christ if you favor some people more than others?" *(James 2:1)*

How do you treat people who don't have many friends?

Super Glue Seat

Joseph had a bad feeling as he watched Hank unscrew the lid of the glue bottle and pour glue on a chair in front of them. *I shouldn't let Hank do this,* he thought.

"Distract Bill so he won't see the glue on his seat," whispered Hank. "Punch him in the arm so he'll hurry and sit down. C'mon—let's meet him at the door."

When Bill arrived, Hank started teasing right away. "Hey, Bill, what did you bring for lunch? I'm hungry. Let me look in your lunch sack."

"Eat your own lunch," Bill said, gripping his sack.

The two bullies punched Bill's arms and pulled on his book bag. Bill rushed to his seat, quickly sat down, and stuffed his lunch inside the desk.

Hank smirked at Joseph. "We did it!" he whispered. "Wait and see what happens."

All during class, Joseph worried. *What will happen when Bill stands up?* he wondered.

The bell rang for recess and Bill was the first one to get up. *R-R-R-RIP!*

Hank howled with glee and pointed to the rip in Bill's pants. The room erupted with laughter.

Joseph remained silent. It felt terrible to embarrass Bill like that. *I shouldn't have gone along with Hank,* he thought. He knew what Jesus would want him to do. Taking off his sweat shirt, Joseph tied it around Bill's waist to cover the back of his pants.

Bill looked grateful. "Thanks," he mumbled.

Joseph went with Bill to the office. "I'll stay here with you while you wait for your mom to bring some other pants," he volunteered. "I'm sorry I didn't stop Hank. Please forgive me. I'll help buy some other pants for you. I'll never do this again!"

"Fools make fun of guilt, but the godly acknowledge it and seek reconciliation." *(Proverbs 14:9)*

   *Do you think practical jokes are pleasing to Jesus? Why or why not?*

White Powder

Posters of rock groups covered the walls of Kirk and Stu's bedroom. Heavy rock music blared in Bill's ears. He couldn't believe he was actually spending the night at the twins' house. He had tried to be their friend for three years, but they'd always ignored him. Until now.

Bill stared at the small plastic bag filled with white powder that Kirk was dangling in his face. Bill would do anything to be Kirk's friend.

"Chicken!" Kirk taunted. Stu snickered.

Bill's heart pounded. If he refused, they wouldn't be his friends. "I don't know…" Bill said. His palms felt damp.

Kirk snorted in disgust. "He's got no guts," he said to Stu. Kirk opened his dresser drawer and shoved the bag under a pile of socks.

"No, wait!" Bill was shocked to hear the words come out of his mouth. He nervously wiped his hands on his pants.

Kirk cleared a space on his dresser where he sprinkled a little pile of the white powder. Bill felt dizzy. *What if I overdose?* he wondered. *Will I die?*

Bill bent over the powder like he'd seen guys on television do. *Jesus wouldn't do this*, thought Bill, and he backed away from the dresser.

"What a loser," said Kirk.

I want them to like me, Bill thought. Quickly he leaned over the white powder and sniffed.

Kirk and Stu started laughing so hard they couldn't stand up. Bill stared at them, confused. "Hey, stupid," said Kirk. "That's not drugs—it's powdered sugar."

"I don't need friends like you," Bill said, fighting tears. The twins only laughed.

Bill stumbled from the room to find a phone and call his mom. *Jesus, forgive me*, he prayed. *I'll never care more about friends than you again.*

"My child, if sinners entice you, turn your back on them!" *(Proverbs 1:10)*

What does Jesus want you to do when you're tempted?

A Change

Kara and Maggie had been best friends all during grade school. But when Kara went to church camp the summer before sixth grade, her life changed.

"I've decided to live for Jesus," Kara explained to Maggie. "Now I realize that a lot of stuff on TV is really bad. And most of the songs on the radio put thoughts in my mind that I don't really want there."

"You're no fun to be around anymore," said Maggie. "You don't want to listen to music or watch TV with me like we used to. We couldn't even agree on a video to rent last night."

"I know I've changed," Kara said, "but it's for the better. Accepting Jesus as my Savior is the best thing I've ever done."

"Oh, please," said Maggie, "don't start preaching at me."

"I'm not preaching," Kara replied. "I'm just explaining how happy I am now that I'm a Christian. And I want everything I do to please God."

"I guess we can't be friends then," Maggie said as she walked away.

That night Kara and her mother talked things over. "You and Maggie have been friends for a long time," Mother said. "This must be hard for you."

"It is," Kara replied.

"There were lots of people who wouldn't be friends with Jesus when he was on earth," Mother said.

Kara brightened. "I never thought of that. And I made lots of new friends at camp. I know they'll be friends forever."

"Who knows? Someday you may be able to help Maggie find Jesus."

"Wouldn't that be cool?" Kara said. "I'll pray for her every day."

"Let us cleanse ourselves from everything that can defile our body or spirit." *(2 Corinthians 7:1)*

What do you think Jesus would say to Kara? Is there any way Jesus would want your life to change?

Forgiven

Bill tried hard to keep from crying as he waited for his mom on the curb in front of Kirk's house. He could see into Kirk's bedroom window where Kirk and Stu were laughing and throwing pillows. Bill was glad it was dark so they couldn't see him.

Bill's mom pulled up and Bill jumped into the car. "What's wrong?" she asked as they drove off.

Feeling ashamed, Bill covered his face with his hands. "I'm so stupid," Bill said. "They brought out some white stuff. They said it was some kind of drug…and I tried it."

Bill heard his mom gasp. He quickly added, "But it turned out to be powdered sugar."

"What if it had been drugs?" she asked.

Closing his eyes, Bill shuddered. "I'll never do it again," he promised. "I already asked Jesus to forgive me." He saw how frightened his mother looked.

"I'm sorry I hurt you," Bill whispered. "I'm sorry I hurt Jesus. Can Jesus ever forgive me?" Guilt weighed Bill down like a rock.

"Honey, Jesus *always* forgives," Mom said as she pulled into their driveway. "Jesus forgave you the instant you asked him to."

"Then why do I feel so awful?" he asked.

"Because you aren't accepting God's forgiveness," Mom explained. "You're feeling guilty because you're still thinking about what you did instead of remembering what Jesus did for you on the cross."

"You mean I'm not really guilty anymore?"

"No. You need to believe what the Bible says: if we confess our sins, God is faithful and will forgive us."

"I *do* believe God forgives me," Bill said. "And I'm thankful Jesus protected me when I did something stupid."

"We're both thankful," said Mom.

"He forgives all my sins." *(Psalm 103:3)*

Have you ever done something you thought Jesus couldn't forgive?
Will you accept Jesus' forgiveness now?

Hit-the-Spot Slingshot

Get Set   You'll need a piece of soft leather, oil cloth, or soft vinyl for each person. You'll also need leather shoelaces, an ice pick, and a bag of large marshmallows.

Go!

Read   1 Samuel 17:1–50.

How did David stand up for what was right?
What did David take into battle?
How did God help David?

Explain: We're going to make our own slingshots as reminders of David's great victory.

Cut   the leather into 4-inch squares.

Use the ice pick to   **poke**   a hole near each corner of the square.

Cut   a leather shoelace in half.

Slip   one piece of shoelace through two holes, then tie it to form a loop.

Slip   the other shoelace through the other two holes and tie it to form another loop.

Go   to an open area.

Place   a marshmallow on the leather square and   **grasp**   the two loops.

Swing   the slingshot,   **release**   one of the loops, and   **watch**   the marshmallow fly!

Practice   hitting a safe target, such as the side of a house with no windows.

Thank   God for helping David.   **Ask**   God to help you to stand up for what's right.

Flowers and Trees

Get Set   You'll need a fresh flower or a plant blooming in a pot.

Go!

Read   Psalm 145:1–13.

What can we learn from older Christians in our family and church?
How are older people usually treated?
How would Jesus want us to treat older people?

Take   the flower and go **stand** by a large, old tree.

How is this tree different from this flower?
How does the tree compare to an older Christian?
How do we compare to the flower?

Read   Proverbs 15:28–33.

Let each person **tell** about one older person who has served as an encourager and role model.

How can we return encouragement to older people?

Choose   an older relative or church friend to honor this week.

Plan   to invite him or her for a treat next weekend (see Saturday's devotion).

Joy Ride

Todd stood in the farmyard, gazing at his grandpa's old Chevy truck. He loved it when Grandpa let him drive around the farm. Opening the door, he climbed onto the worn leather seat. Old Bill, Grandpa's favorite dog, jumped in beside him.

"Sorry, boy. No ride today. Grandpa's busy with the vet," said Todd. Then he spotted Grandpa's keys dangling from the ignition. "Well, it won't hurt to drive to the end of our dirt road."

Todd started the engine and eased the truck through the farmyard gate. His grandpa's words echoed in his mind as he bounced down the long dirt lane: "Driving is a necessary skill on a farm, but you're not old enough to drive on the road."

Todd had been driving with Grandpa for two years. *I can handle this,* he thought, shifting into third gear.

Ignoring his uneasy conscience, Todd pressed down on the accelerator. Old Bill stuck his head out the window. Todd grinned. "How do you like my driving, Old Bill?"

At the end of the lane, Todd said, "There's no place to turn around. I'll have to drive to the McConnells' place and turn around there."

Todd pulled onto the paved road and drove toward the neighboring farm. Rounding a sharp curve, Todd spotted a cow in the road.

Oh, no! I'm going to hit her! thought Todd, jamming on the brakes. The truck swerved across the road, slid on the gravel, and swerved into a ditch.

Shaken and bruised, Todd climbed out of the truck. Old Bill followed. Staring at the crumpled door and fender, Todd knew he'd have to tell Grandpa. "Now look what I've done!" he told Old Bill. "I should have obeyed Grandpa."

"Children are known by the way they act, whether their conduct is pure and right." *(Proverbs 20:11)*

Why does Jesus want us to obey those in authority over us?
What can you learn from older adults?

Grandpa's College Money

"Why didn't you go to college?" Mindy asked. She sat in Grandpa's lap while he drove the tractor.

"When I turned eighteen back in 1929," Grandpa began, "my family raised chickens and canned vegetables just to have enough to eat.

"So after I graduated from high school, I took a logging job. I climbed up to the tops of fir trees. I sawed most of the way through the tree trunks, then tied ropes to them so the workers could pull the tops off."

Mindy tried to imagine Grandpa's yellow hard hat and rainbow suspenders on a young boy climbing to the tops of fir trees. She couldn't. Hadn't Grandpa always been old?

"It was such a dangerous job that the company paid me extra," Grandpa continued, "and in one summer I saved enough for college."

"Why didn't you go?" Mindy asked.

"Just before college started, my father died and Mother didn't have money to bury him. Then the bank threatened to take away our farm. So I gave Mother my college money and I went to work in the steel mill."

Mindy patted Grandpa's shoulder. "You gave up your dreams for your family."

Grandpa smiled. "I've had everything I need—a place to live, plenty to eat, Grandma, and your dad." Grandpa tickled Mindy and she giggled. "And you!"

"You're like Jesus, Grandpa," said Mindy. "You care more about others than yourself."

"Be satisfied with what you have." *(Hebrews 13:5)*

How did Grandpa show his love?
How does Jesus want you to feel about money?

A Unique Gift

Kaylyn picked up the present wrapped in gold paper. It was the only birthday present left to unwrap. Had anyone given her the one thing she really wanted? *Please let this be it,* she prayed.

Kaylyn felt a little ungrateful. Her parents had given her a T-shirt and jeans plus a huge stuffed elephant. She didn't need anything else. *Help me not to cry if I don't get it,* she prayed. She had a special reason for wanting this present.

Grandma Iris smiled at Kaylyn. Hunched in the blue velvet chair, Grandma's feet barely touched the floor.

"Don't you look pretty opening your presents!" she said to Kaylyn in her quavering voice. Kaylyn knew that watching her open presents was exciting for Grandma. She lived in the apartment Dad had built onto their house for her. Kaylyn knew she must be lonely, but she never complained.

Kaylyn squealed with delight as she ripped off the paper. "Thank you!" she said, running to hug Mom. Then she showed the present to Grandma.

"What's a cappuccino maker?" Grandma asked, reading the box.

"It makes special coffee," Kaylyn told her. Kaylyn knew how much Grandma loved coffee.

Grandma looked horrified. "Do *you* drink coffee?"

Kaylyn laughed. "No. I'm not old enough."

"Then why do you need a coffee machine?" Grandma asked.

Kaylyn smiled mysteriously. "You'll see."

The next day after school, Kaylyn hurried to the kitchen and made a cappuccino with her new coffeemaker. She poured it into an antique flowered teacup and carried it to Grandma's apartment. For the next hour Kaylyn and Grandma chatted while Grandma drank her special coffee. From then on, at the same time every day, Kaylyn and Grandma enjoyed their "cappuccino time." Kaylyn had wanted the cappuccino maker so she could show Jesus' love to her grandmother.

"He will not forget…how you have shown your love to him by caring for other Christians." *(Hebrews 6:10)*

How did Kaylyn show Jesus' love?
What do you do to show Jesus' love?

Bringing God

Caleb and the other boys paused in the doorway of the Oaklawn Senior Residence. Their fourth-grade Sunday school class had come to sing to the elderly people living there.

"I wonder what they're like," whispered Caleb.

"I hope no one will kiss me," said Zach, wiping his face. The boys laughed.

A nurse led the boys into a large room where about twenty older people sat on couches, chairs, and wheelchairs. The nurse told the residents, "These boys are from Oakdale Church down the street. They're here to sing for you."

"That lady over there is asleep," whispered Daniel to Zach. "Your croaky voice is sure to wake her up!"

An elderly man smiled at them. Caleb noticed that one side of his mouth drooped a little.

The boys sang their favorite praise songs and one hymn they had learned especially for this occasion. Afterward Caleb and two other boys walked over to the man who had smiled. "Hi!" said Caleb. "My name is Caleb and these are my friends, Zach and Daniel."

The old man's hands and face began to shake. Caleb gently touched his shoulder. "We're from Oakdale Church." He thought a moment and added, "We want you to know God loves you. He hasn't forgotten you."

The man's eyes filled with tears. His lips moved, but the boys couldn't understand what he was trying to say. Caleb leaned closer.

"Thank...you...for bringing God...here," said the whispery, trembling voice.

The boys smiled and hugged him. Then it was time to go.

In the parking lot Zach said, "He liked us!"

"He thanked us for bringing God," said Caleb, awed that such a thing was possible. He turned to his teacher and asked, "Can we go back again next week?"

"So don't get tired of doing what is good.... Do good to everyone."
(Galatians 6:9, 10)

Is there an older person Jesus would want you to visit? Where could you "bring God"?

417

Micah's Burden

"Here's your room, Grandma."

Micah didn't know how many times today he had taken Grandma by the hand and led her back to the bedroom. Grandma sat down on a chair in the room that used to belong to Micah. She silently folded her hands in her lap. She had moved in with Micah's family a week earlier. A month ago red striped wallpaper had covered the walls. Now pink flowers had replaced the stripes and Micah slept in his brother's room.

"I don't want to be a...burden," said Grandma.

Micah buttoned the top of Grandma's warm sweater. He thought about how Grandma used to be able to bake ginger cookies.

Jesus, what should I say? I want to comfort her, he prayed silently.

Micah sat down on the bed. "Do you remember when my dad was a baby? You fed him and washed his diapers. He was a lot of work, wasn't he?"

"Well, yes." Grandma looked at Micah. A tear glistened on her cheek.

"He was a burden," said Micah. "But you didn't mind because you loved him. Well, now it's our turn. We're taking care of you. But we don't mind because we love you."

Tears filled Grandma's eyes as she reached for Micah's hand. He smiled. He knew he had comforted her.

"He comforts us in all our troubles so that we can comfort others." *(2 Corinthians 1:4)*

Who would Jesus want you to comfort today? How do you treat older people?

Guest of Honor

Get Set Invite a grandparent or older person from church to visit your house as an honored guest. Prepare a special old-fashioned treat such as warm apple crisp with ice cream.

Go!

Read Proverbs 16:31 and 20:29.

How can we treat older people in our family and in our church with honor?
Why is it important to do that?

Prepare the treat you've planned.

Pick up your honored guest.

As you enjoy your treat together, *focus* your conversation on these issues:

> *What was church like when you were growing up?*
> *When did you give your heart to Jesus?*
> *What kind of chores did you do as a child?*

Tell about a funny experience that happened when you were little.

Tell about a time when God answered your prayers.

Pray together. Thank God for your guest and his or her life of faith.

As you *take* your guest home, *thank* him or her for spending time with you.

A Giving Christmas

Get Set Gather paper lunch bags, curling ribbon, and a hole punch. Set out a popcorn popper, a roasting pan, cinnamon, sugar, butter, salt, and a large glass measuring cup. You'll also need markers or Christmas stickers or rubber stamps and stamp pads.

Go!

Pop three quarts (twelve cups) of popcorn and place it in a roasting pan.

Melt ½ cup butter in a glass measuring cup in a microwave oven set on low.

Add ¼ cup sugar, ½ teaspoon cinnamon, and ¼ teaspoon salt to the melted butter and **mix** thoroughly.

Pour the mixture onto the popcorn and **stir** well.

Bake the cinnamon popcorn in the oven for fifteen minutes at 300 degrees.

Read John 3:16–17.

What did God give at Christmas?
At Christmas, do you think more about giving or getting?

Read Acts 20:35.

What would Jesus want your attitude to be at Christmas?

Choose three or four people to surprise with a gift of cinnamon popcorn. decorate a bag for each person and add popcorn to the bag.

Punch a hole in the top of the bag and **tie** curling ribbon through the hole.

Deliver your gifts. *How does it feel to be a giver?*

Week
50

Paul's Blessing

Paul knew his mother felt worried. It was almost the end of the month and the house payment was still overdue from last month. Bills were piling up and needing to be paid.

Paul's father was a self-employed artist. Paying for food and for basic costs of heat and electricity was difficult even when the galleries paid on time. But now several art galleries hadn't paid Paul's dad for the paintings they had sold months before.

Paul was only seven years old. He prayed about what he could do to help. After supper, he found some yellow paper, colored pencils, and scissors. He cut out three rectangles and drew fancy lines in different colors around the edges to make them look like little coupons.

In the middle of one paper he wrote, "Good for praying together when you're discouraged." On another he wrote, "Good for one free kiss." He drew two fat lips underneath the words. On the third paper he wrote, "Good for one free cooking time with Paul."

Paul went in his parents' bedroom, turned down the bedspread, and placed the three coupons in the middle of his mother's pillow. He prayed that Jesus would use the little coupons to encourage his mother.

"Commit everything you do to the Lord. Trust him, and he will help you." *(Psalm 37:5)*

How would Jesus want you to bless a family member today?

A Christmas Mystery

"I know Mom and Dad feel bad. We don't have many presents under our tree this year," six-year-old Joshua whispered to his older sister on their way home from the Christmas Eve service. Joshua and Aimee agreed not to complain about not having many presents.

But when they pulled into their driveway, Joshua saw a large cardboard box by the front door. He jumped out of the car and reached the box first. "Dad, look!" he said, lifting the flaps. "It's filled with boxes…and they're all wrapped!"

"Who's it for?" asked Aimee, trying to peek inside.

"Wait and see!" said Joshua.

Dad unlocked the door and pulled the heavy box inside. "Let Joshua take out the first box," said Dad.

Joshua lifted out a large package wrapped in Christmas paper. "It feels soft, like a stuffed animal," he said. "And the tag says 'For Joshua.'"

"Look, Aimee," said Mom. "There's a package with your name."

They found eight beautifully wrapped gifts—two apiece. Every gift had one of their names on it.

"Who did this?" asked Joshua. "They must know us."

"Maybe we'll find out where they came from when we open the gifts," said Aimee.

What fun everyone had opening the surprise packages—a furry polar bear, a dump truck, a set of 48 markers, and a big sketch book for the kids. Mom unwrapped a scarf and a vest. Dad received a pen and a wool sweater.

"This is the biggest surprise we've ever had!" said Joshua. "I hope someday we can do something like this for another family!"

The McGregor family never did find out who brought the Christmas box. But this "secret giving" inspired them to give many gifts in secret during the following years.

Jesus said, "Give your gifts in secret, and your Father, who knows all secrets, will reward you." *(Matthew 6:4)*

When have you ever helped anyone secretly? Who would Jesus want you to bless with some "secret" giving?

Valerie's Shoe Boxes

Valerie heard about the Christmas shoe boxes sent to needy children around the world through a Christian ministry. She found an empty box under her bed and ran to show Father.

"Here's one box," she said excitedly. "When can we go shopping to fill it?"

"After lunch," said Father. "Find an extra box for me, too."

Valerie searched the closets and found four more shoe boxes. She made a list of what she wanted to put inside each one. "I've always wanted to give a Christmas gift to children far away. Now I can!" she told Father.

At the store they bought pencils, crayons, and pads of paper. "I'm sure all kids like to draw," she said. "They'll need a few small cars, dolls, and rubber balls." She bought combs and toothbrushes, along with toothpaste and bars of soap.

Valerie and her father filled the five shoe boxes with the gifts they'd bought, then wrapped them with Christmas paper. On Monday Valerie took one box to school. She shared the idea of sending gifts to needy children. "Fill up a shoe box!" she challenged her friends. "Bring it to my house. We'll mail the shoe boxes to South Carolina where they'll be sent overseas."

The idea caught on like wildfire. Students hurried home after school and worked on their shoe boxes. Wrapped boxes poured into Valerie's garage.

On Saturday, Valerie counted the boxes to be shipped. "There are 423 boxes!" she said, jumping up and down for joy. Before mailing them, Valerie and everyone who helped pack them joined hands and prayed over the boxes, asking God to bless each child who would receive one.

Jesus said, "When you did it to one of the least of these my brothers and sisters, you were doing it to me!" *(Matthew 25:40)*

 *How could you bless someone you've never met?*

Sami's Blind Grandpa

"Did you cry when you lost your sight, Grandpa?"

"Yes, at first...when I realized I'd never be able to read my Bible again."

Sami and her grandfather sat side by side in the porch swing, surrounded by the sweet smell of wild honeysuckle. Crows scolded each other from the top of an oak tree.

Sami looked into her grandfather's eyes. A month ago they would have twinkled back at her. Now he saw only dark shadows. A disease called diabetes had taken away his sight in only a few days' time.

Sami felt sad for her Grandpa. She brushed away a fly on his cheek and whispered, "I'm sorry about your eyes." Scooting closer, she laid her head on his shoulder.

Grandpa put his arm around her. "Don't feel sorry for me. God gave me seventy years of good vision. And I have the sweetest granddaughter in the state of Florida. God gave you to me as a special blessing."

"I never realized that," said Sami. She closed her eyes and took her grandpa's hand in both of hers.

"Grandpa, if I'm a special blessing, how can I help you?" she asked.

"By sitting here with me."

"I know! I'll read your Bible to you." Sami felt happy. She could serve Grandpa. "And I'll bring you a glass of lemonade."

Grandpa smiled. "I'd like that."

"Be careful to do good deeds all the time." *(Titus 3:8)*

 *How are you being a special blessing to your family?*

A Gift for Jesus

Chemmi watched his mother wrap the lid of an empty shoe box in red-and-green Christmas paper.

"Who's that for?" he asked.

"It's going to be a Christmas gift for Jesus," said his mother, taping one end.

Chemmi stared at his mother. "Jesus is in heaven. How could you give him a present?"

"The Bible says if we give to others in Jesus' name, it's the same as giving to him."

Chemmi liked the idea. After all, Christmas was Jesus' birthday. "Can I give Jesus a present, too?" he asked.

"Sure. You can go shopping with me."

Chemmi smiled. He ran to get his birthday money. "What will we buy?" he asked.

"This box will go to a little boy in Haiti who is so poor he doesn't even own a comb or a toothbrush." Chemmi's eyes widened. His mother continued, "Missionaries in Haiti will hand out the shoe boxes and tell the children about Jesus and how he died for them."

Chemmi and his mother went shopping that afternoon. They bought soap, a comb, a toothbrush and toothpaste, a shirt and socks, a box of crayons and a pad of paper. Chemmi bought some marbles and a bag of hard candy. He smiled as he imagined the little boy's face when he opened the box.

On their way to the checkout stand, Chemmi paused. He fingered the crisp five-dollar bill that was left in his pocket.

"Mom, I want to use the rest of my money to buy something for Jesus," he said. After searching the toy aisles a long time, he finally found what he was looking for—a small baby doll wrapped in blue flannel.

Chemmi told his mother, "Maybe this will help the missionary tell the children about baby Jesus, the best gift of all."

"For God so loved the world that he gave his only Son." *(John 3:16)*

When have you given Jesus a gift?
What could you give today?

Shoe Box Blessing

Get Set Gather a shoe box, wrapping paper, tape, a holiday card, and a photo of your family.

Go!

Explain: We're going to make a gift box to share with someone who doesn't have all the things we take for granted.

Decide if you will take your gift box to a food pantry, a homeless shelter, or a missionary organization, and if you will make the box for a boy or a girl.

Wrap the shoe box in wrapping paper. Wrap the lid separately.

Go shopping for items from this list: small toy, soap, washcloth, toothbrush, toothpaste, comb, shampoo, pencils, sharpeners, writing pads, erasers, crayons, markers, stickers, wrapped hard candy, Bible storybooks.

Pack the box.

Have everyone *sign* a holiday card. *Include* a picture of your family in the card.

Place the card in the box.

Mark the box with the age and gender of the child you've prepared it for.

Deliver the box to the place you've planned.

Pray for God to bless the child who will receive it.

Family Gallery

Get Set   Gather baby pictures of all your family members. Include as many generations as possible.

Go!

Challenge the youngest member of the family to identify all the baby pictures.

Which person still looks the most like his or her baby picture?

Sort the pictures by the babies who look most alike.

What characteristic of parents or grandparents tends to repeat in the children?
What talents and gifts appear in more than one generation?

Read Psalm 71:17–18.

What "faith characteristics" have been passed to each generation?
What stories of faith can you remember from family members who have gone to be with Jesus?
What stories of faith could your family tell from the last few years?

Look around your house for heirlooms or "treasures" that remind you of God's love and care.

What could you tell your children or grandchildren about them?

Pray, thanking God for faithful Christians who have passed God's love to each generation of your family. Ask God's blessing as you continue to build your heritage of faith.

Kentucky Prayer

Gladys led her horse Jasper along the footpath circling the sugar cane field. Knee-high grass, still wet with dew, brushed her bare feet and legs. Jasper nosed toward the cane, and she pulled on his reins.

"Eat the grass, not the cane," she told him.

"God, do you really exist?" Gladys asked aloud. It wasn't exactly a prayer—it was just a question. Gladys had never heard anyone pray. She didn't know any Christians. A neighbor recently told her that missionaries had started holding Sunday services in the schoolhouse. The school was five miles down the dirt road from her house. But she didn't go to school. Mother needed her help at home.

"God, can you see me walking beside the sugar cane in Kentucky?" she asked. "Do you know I have eight brothers and sisters? Do you care about us? Are you there?"

She tied Jasper to a fallen log and broke off a piece of sugar cane as thick as her thumb. She bit off a piece, chewed on it to get the sweetness, then spit it out. Jasper nibbled on the purple wildflowers.

"Well, Jasper, God's not talking today. I don't think he exists. Do you?"

"I love you, Gladys," a voice said. "I have chosen you to belong to me. I came to earth and died for your sins."

Gladys dropped her sugar cane and jumped up. She looked around to see who had spoken to her. But there was no one around. She began to tremble.

"I think Jesus talked to me," she whispered to Jasper.

"What do I do now?" she called up to the sky.

No one answered. But she knew that Jesus had spoken to her. And she knew he would show her how to be a Christian.

"For the truth about God is known...instinctively." *(Romans 1:19)*

 *How does Jesus speak to you?*

Fire!

Charlie backed up against the weathered boards of the one-room schoolhouse, listening to the girls at recess.

"Little Charlie Poutoo," they chanted as they jumped rope, "cannot hook his own shoe." Laughter rippled across the playground.

Charlie's face burned with shame. They had teased him ever since one of them saw his older sister buttoning his shoe. He couldn't stand it any longer.

When no one was looking, Charlie crawled into the dark space under the school. He didn't care if he found snakes or spiders. He hated the teasing more.

Charlie lay in the dirt and sobbed quietly. He felt he couldn't do anything right.

The schoolmaster rang the bell calling the students back to class. Charlie waited until everyone went inside, then he took off running as fast as he could down the dirt road.

Just before rounding the bend in the road, Charlie took one last look at the school. He couldn't believe his eyes. Flames were shooting from the chimney!

He didn't want to go back, but he knew Jesus wanted him to.

"Fire!" Charlie shouted, bursting through the front door.

After the fire was out, everyone thanked Charlie for saving their lives. Then they apologized to him. He could tell they respected him. Obeying Jesus had solved Charlie's problem.

"Why am I so discouraged? Why so sad? I will put my hope in God!" *(Psalm 42:11)*

What does Jesus want you to do when you feel discouraged and sad?

The New Christian

Gladys burst through the front door, grinning and excited. Her dad stopped with a biscuit halfway to his mouth and studied her face. Molasses dripped off the biscuit and onto his plate.

"Well, don't you look like the cat that ate a pear pie?" he said with a laugh, licking molasses off his fingers.

Gladys worked to get her breathing under control so she could speak. "I'm a Christian!" she exclaimed.

The smile left her dad's face. Her mother sat down. "Now, that's silly," her mother said. "We don't know any Christians."

"God spoke to me!" Gladys told them.

Dad leaned his head back and laughed. "You must have heard a mule bray," he said.

Gladys wavered. Could it have been a mule? Did she just want to hear God so much that she imagined his voice?

"No!" she insisted. "I heard God. I prayed and told him I wanted to be a Christian."

"You prayed?" her mother asked. "Why, I don't know anyone who prays except the preacher. And he doesn't bother coming around but once a year."

"Don't you *ever* pray?" Gladys asked.

"Only nine times in my life," her mother answered. "When I had my babies."

"I think Gladys needs extra chores to keep her busy so she doesn't think mules are God," Dad said.

Mother nodded grimly. Gladys didn't mind. She *knew* God existed and she would do anything to be a Christian. Maybe someday her family would believe in him, too.

Gladys prayed for her family for several years. The whole family, except for her dad, became Christians. Gladys and five of her sisters married preachers. Later, only weeks before he died, Gladys's father accepted Jesus, too.

"God gave his approval to people in days of old because of their faith." *(Hebrews 11:2)*

 *Who in your family does Jesus want you to pray for?*

Dancing for Joy!

Ella hurriedly finished her chores in the barn. After she checked the horses' water, she dashed out the barn door and headed for the back field.

She laughed as she skipped down the dirt path, swinging her arms and squinting in the bright South Dakota sunshine.

"I love summer. I love sun. I love the Lord and everyone!" she sang in a singsongy voice to a tune that she made up as she went along. Bucky her collie loped beside her, wagging his tail.

When she reached the cornfield, she and Bucky sat down underneath a tree. Her heart felt full of God's love. She didn't understand why she was so sure God loved her. She just knew it deep inside.

Ella tried to come out to the cornfield each day to be alone with God. Wanting to express her love and thanks to him, she made up her own songs of praise.

"I lift my hands to you and sing. I love you, Lord, my heavenly king."

Today she felt joy bubbling up inside her. She couldn't just sit and sing. She had to dance! She twirled and danced in the sunlight while she sang. "Accept this dance as praise to you. I'll serve you, Lord, in all I do."

"Praise God in his heavenly dwelling…. Praise him with…dancing…. Let everything that lives sing praises to the Lord!" *(Psalm 150:1, 4, 6)*

What are some ways that you praise the Lord? Do you take time alone with Jesus each day?

Who's Laughing Now?

Rob Olson stared at the long straight pin in his hand as his teacher limped to the blackboard. Rob's palms went sweaty and his mouth was dry.

"Remember, his *right* leg is the fake one," whispered Lars.

Mr. Johnson had lost his leg fighting in World War I. Rob really liked his teacher, but this morning Lars had dared him to stick the pin into Mr. Johnson's cork leg.

Mr. Johnson turned his back to the class and began writing on the blackboard. Even though Rob knew Jesus wouldn't want him to, he slipped from his seat and sneaked up behind the teacher. He hoped he could get back to his seat without being caught. A few students snickered as Rod jabbed the long pin into the teacher's leg and turned to go back to his desk.

"Ouch!" yelled Mr. Johnson. He dropped the chalk, grabbed his leg, and whirled around. Glaring at Rob, he pulled out the pin. Rob hurried to his desk, his face burning. He wondered what had gone wrong.

"Rob Olson, come up here." None of the other students made a sound.

"Tell me," said his teacher, "who looks more foolish—a man with a pin stuck to his pants or an eleven-year-old boy who still doesn't know his right from his left?" The class erupted in laughter.

Totally humiliated, Rob's face reddened with shame. Because he had been so nervous, he'd stuck the pin into Mr. Johnson's left leg instead of his right one!

After class Rob apologized to his teacher.

Lars waited for him outside the school. "You're a dumb-dumb, Olson."

"I was dumb to do something wrong just because you dared me," said Rob. "Next time I'll have the courage to do the right thing."

"My child, if sinners entice you, turn your back on them!"
(Proverbs 1:10)

How does Jesus want us to choose our friends?
What is a temptation for you today?

Celebrate Your Inheritance!

Get Set   Set out an assortment of pots, pans, lids, and wooden spoons. You'll also need wide tape, paper plates, crepe paper or ribbon, and dried beans.

Go!

Read   James 1:12 **and** Matthew 25:34.

What inheritance does the Bible promise those who serve Jesus? Why is that reason to celebrate?

On paper plates, *write* the names of older relatives and church friends who have passed the good news of Jesus from generation to generation.

Read   Psalm 150.

Make   noisemakers to celebrate your inheritance.

Fold   and tape the edges of the paper plates you've written on, or

tape   two plates together, leaving a small opening.

Pour   dried beans into the opening, then *tape* it shut.

Attach   crepe paper streamers or ribbons.

Play   a favorite worship tape or CD.

Sing   along and *keep time* with your noisemaker.

Use   pans, lids, and spoons as drums and cymbals to make a joyful noise!

Week
52

Shake Up a Storm!

Get Set Set out a blender. You'll need vanilla ice cream or frozen yogurt, frozen strawberries, and milk.

Go!

Read 2 Corinthians 11:22–27.

Tell stories of the hardships and storms the apostle Paul experienced.

What are some stormy times our grandparents and older relatives experienced?
What stormy times has God helped us through?

Whip up a storm in the blender as you make strawberry milk shakes.

Scoop ice cream into a blender; *add* frozen strawberries and a little milk, then *blend.*

How does God show his care when we're in the middle of a stormy time?
What important lessons do we learn in stormy times?

Pour and *enjoy* the milk shakes.

Read James 1:12.

What does God promise us when the stormy times are over?
How do stormy times help us grow in faith?

The Family Grocery

Max dusted an empty shelf in his family's grocery store and watched his dad wait on Mrs. Perkins. The smallest of her six children tugged at her coat as she piled a few potatoes and a small sack of flour on the counter.

Then she lifted her chin. "I'll need to put these on credit," she said.

"Certainly, Mrs. Perkins," said Max's dad. He lifted an enormous ledger from beneath the counter, flipped through some pages, then wrote down her bill.

"I'll pay you soon as Charlie gets work," she said, nervously fidgeting with her purse.

Dad smiled. "I know you will," he said.

A bell tinkled, and Mr. Snell entered the store as Mrs. Perkins left. Five minutes later, Mr. Snell left with a few groceries and his name written in the ledger. Max's dad hadn't put any money in the cash register.

Max burned with anger. "They'll never pay," he told his dad. "We're going to lose the store because you give everything away."

Dad sighed and put his arm around Max. "You're right, son," he said. "But they all have to eat. There's a depression. No one has work. What do you think Jesus would want us to do?"

Max hung his head. "He would want us to share." Max leaned against his father. "I'm scared," he said. "What if we lose the store? Where will we live? What will we eat?"

"God will take care of us."

"I guess I need to learn to trust him," said Max.

Within weeks the bank took their house and store. The family lived in a tent, eating nothing but potatoes, for many months. But God protected them, and Max never regretted sharing with their neighbors.

"Suppose you see a brother or sister who needs food…but then you don't give that person any food…. What good does that do?" *(James 2:15, 16)*

 *How does Jesus want you to treat someone in need?*

Salmon Creek

Max rolled up the legs of his overalls and waded into Salmon Creek to help his little sister, Pearl, wash up. Mom peeled potatoes by the tent they now called home.

Pearl hunched her shoulders while Max scrubbed her neck. "I wish I could soak in a warm tub," she said.

"The brook cleans us fine," said Max. "We shouldn't complain."

"Don't you miss living in our house?" asked Pearl.

"The tent keeps us dry." Max tried not to think about how much he missed electric lights and the smell of bread baking. It was the Depression, and their family had lost everything.

"I'm tired of eating nothing but potatoes."

"Shhh!" Max whispered. "Don't let Mom hear you. She feels bad already. We need to thank Jesus that Dad can do odd jobs and earn money to buy potatoes. Lots of folks have nothing to eat."

"Couldn't we ask Jesus for some meat?" asked Pearl.

Would that be complaining? Max wondered. "I think it would be okay," he said. They bowed their heads and prayed together.

Max felt something bump against his leg. He plunged into the water and flung his arms around a huge salmon. Snatching it up, Max hung on tightly and splashed to shore.

Pearl squealed with delight.

"Thank you, Jesus!" Max yelled, hugging the huge fish. "We'll surprise Dad with a feast tonight!"

Jesus said, "This is how you should pray:…Give us our food day by day." *(Luke 11:2, 3)*

 *When has Jesus surprised you with a special blessing?*

Bread, Not Candy

Shane poked Ron and nodded toward the blond boy sitting in a pew three rows up. "Did you see that? He just stole a wad of bills from the offering plate!" Shane whispered.

"I saw! I can't believe it!" Ron whispered back.

Shane looked around. Everyone had their eyes closed while singing the final song. "I don't think anyone else saw him take it," he told Ron.

"He goes to our school," Ron whispered. "He doesn't have a dad. His mom is looking for work." When the service ended, the blond boy hurried out the door.

Shane grabbed Ron's arm. "We'd better follow him and get the church's money back."

The blond boy headed down the street and straight for the grocery store. Shane and Ron followed.

"He's probably going to buy candy," Shane said. "Let's go and catch him when he comes out."

The boys stationed themselves beside the door and waited. Pretty soon the boy came out carrying a brown grocery bag. Shane and Ron stepped in front of him.

"I'll take that!" Shane said, grabbing the sack. "You stole money for this from the offering plate at church!"

The boy jerked away from Shane and the bag ripped. Milk and bread spilled from the sack. Eggs broke onto the pavement. The boy began to cry.

Shane was shocked. "Why did you buy bread instead of candy?" he asked.

"I didn't mean to steal," said the boy. "I thought people at church collected money for people in need. My mom and I need it for food, so I took it."

"I'm sorry," Shane said. "You're right. Christians are supposed to help people in need. Let's go find my parents. We will help your family until your mom finds a job."

"Faith that doesn't show itself by good deeds is no faith at all—it is dead and useless." *(James 2:17)*

 *Is there someone in need Jesus would want you to help?*

flash flood

Jordan looked up sleepily into his grandmother's face.

"Jordan," she whispered, "come with me."

Jordan crawled out from under the warm quilt and followed Grandma to the kitchen. "Is something wrong?" he asked.

"I think so." Grandma looked concerned. "I can't sleep. I think Jesus woke me up to pray for your Aunt Blanche. Would you pray with me?" Aunt Blanche attended college a short distance away.

Outside the window, Jordan heard the sound of distant thunder. A flicker of lightening lit the sky. "What should I pray for?" he asked.

Grandma knelt on a braided rug by a kitchen chair. "Let's close our eyes and ask Jesus to put the words in our minds and mouths," she said.

Jordan knelt by his chair. He could tell this was serious.

For the next three hours, Jordan and Grandma prayed for Aunt Blanche while the storm grew worse. Rain pelted the roof and thunder rumbled continuously. Lightning lit up the room. Jordan had never seen anything like it.

Finally the storm quieted. "I think we can stop praying," Grandma told him.

The next day, the police drove up to their house. Aunt Blanche was with them.

"Yesterday I spent the night with friends who live at the bottom of a gorge," she told Jordan and Grandma. "A flash flood hit the house. I crawled out a window seconds before the whole house collapsed. Since I can't swim, I grabbed a tree limb rushing past and held on, praying. I must have lost consciousness. When I woke up this morning, I was still hanging on the tree. But I was alive! All my friends died."

"We prayed for you!" said Jordan. "And Jesus saved your life."

"Thank you," she said, hugging him.

"You have continued to do great miracles…all around the world."
(Jeremiah 32:20)

What miracles did Jesus perform in this story?
Do you believe Jesus still does miracles today?

Old-Fashioned Revival

Gerald grabbed the oak water bucket in the kitchen and slammed out the back door. *I have to get away from everyone,* he thought. *Filling the bucket with well water is a good excuse.*

Earlier, he and Mother, along with his eight brothers and sisters, had walked five miles to a tent revival. When the traveling preacher gave the altar call, Mother went forward. All the kids followed—even Gerald.

After Mother prayed, her face glowed. "I feel like a whole new person," she said.

His older sister, Lena, cried tears of joy. She told him, "I feel Jesus' arms hugging me."

Gerald cried, too. He asked Jesus' forgiveness for the things he'd done wrong. But he didn't feel anything.

Dropping his bucket in the well, Gerald cried out, "Why don't you love *me*, Jesus?" He heard the door open and glanced back to see Lena. Ignoring her, he pulled up the overflowing bucket.

"What's wrong, Gerald?" she asked softly.

Tears welled up in Gerald's eyes. "Jesus doesn't want me. I haven't felt a thing. I'm not any different."

"You may not *feel* any different, but you are. You're forgiven and you belong to Jesus. Just believe it."

Gerald smiled. He would believe it.

"If you confess with your mouth that Jesus is Lord and believe in your heart that God raised him from the dead, you will be saved." *(Romans 10:9)*

Have you asked Jesus to be your Lord and Savior?
Will you trust Jesus' love...even if you don't *feel* it?

A Look Back

Get Set   You'll need a calendar or date book on which your family has kept dates and appointments for the past year.

Go!

Look   back at your calendar month by month.

Give   each month a title.

What good things happened?
When did you try to do what Jesus would do? What difference did asking that question make in your life?

Read   Lamentations 3:22–26.

How did God help you through difficult things?
What answers to prayer did you experience this year?
What prayers will you carry over to next year?
What's an important lesson you learned this year?
What was the year's happiest moment?

Tell   how each family member has grown in his or her walk with Jesus.

Hold   the calendar in your hands as you pray. Thank God for his love and care. Pray for concerns that you're carrying into the new year. Ask God to help you continue to ask *"What would Jesus do?"* each day.

Be like Jesus!